Going Back to the Future

A Leadership Journey for Educators

Robert Palestini

ROWMAN & LITTLEFIELD EDUCATION
A division of
ROWMAN & LITTLEFIELD PUBLISHERS, INC.
Lanham • New York • Toronto • Plymouth, UK

Published by Rowman & Littlefield Education
A division of Rowman & Littlefield Publishers, Inc.
A wholly owned subsidiary of The Rowman & Littlefield Publishing Group, Inc.
4501 Forbes Boulevard, Suite 200, Lanham, Maryland 20706
www.rowmaneducation.com

Estover Road, Plymouth PL6 7PY, United Kingdom

British Library Cataloguing in Publication Information Available

Library of Congress Cataloging-in-Publication Data

Palestini, Robert H., 1944– author.
  Going back to the future : a leadership journey for educators / Robert Palestini.
    p. cm
  Includes bibliographical references.
  ISBN 978-1-60709-586-6 (cloth : alk. paper)—ISBN 978-1-60709-587-3 (pbk. : alk.
paper)—ISBN 978-1-60709-588-0 (electronic)
  1. Educational leadership. 2. Leadership—Case studies. I. Title.
  LB2806.P34 2011
  371.2—dc22   2010051252

♾™ The paper used in this publication meets the minimum requirements of
American National Standard for Information Sciences—Permanence of Paper for
Printed Library Materials, ANSI/NISO Z39.48-1992. Printed in the United States
of America

Contents

Contents

Introduction

We have recently witnessed what political and economic pundits have called the worst global economic crisis since the Great Depression. However, in my view at least, there seems to be some light at the end of the tunnel because President Barack Obama and his economic advisors are on record as using the lessons learned from the Great Depression to address the current situation. In fact, Ben Bernanke, director of the Federal Reserve, did his doctoral dissertation on the Great Depression.

Early indications are that the approach of applying lessons learned from the past to our contemporary situation will be successful, reinforcing the age-old adage that those ignorant of history are destined to repeat it. Perhaps, it would be a worthwhile for educational and other leaders to emulate the president and look to the past in formulating their leadership approach for the new millennium.

At the turn of the last century, the editors of *Life Magazine* identified the one hundred leaders who they believed had had the most impact on our global society during the second millennium. Using this list as a backdrop, I have chosen eleven of the twentieth-century individuals on the list to explore what it was about their respective leadership behavior that allowed them to have such a significant and lasting impact on our society.

In this book, I examine the leadership behavior of the following individuals, listed here in alphabetical order: Jane Addams, Walt Disney, Thomas Edison, Henry Ford, Mahatma Gandhi, Adolph Hitler, Pope John Paul II, Martin Luther King Jr., Vladimir Lenin, Mao Zedong, and John D. Rockefeller. To a lesser degree, I profile Mother Teresa and Ronald Reagan, but they are submersed in the chapters dealing with Mahatma Gandhi and Pope John Paul II, respectively. Finally, I conclude by profiling the leadership behavior of Jesus Christ.

I argue that these leaders' superlative impact on global society was primarily due to their ability to place situational leadership theory into effective practice. In analyzing their leadership styles, I use Lee Bolman and Terrence Deal's model of situational leadership theory, which posits four frames of leadership behavior: (1) structural, (2) human resource, (3) symbolic, and (4) political. I supplement Bolman and Deal's model with a fifth frame, which I call the moral frame. I posit further that effective and impactful leaders combine and balance their use of these frames, rather than dwelling almost exclusively on one frame to the virtual exclusion of the others.

One might ask why I profile someone as infamous and deplorable as Adolph Hitler. I do so to make a point, the point being that in order for a leader to be a truly great one, he or she must operate not only out of the structural, human resource, symbolic, and political frames of leadership, but also out of the *moral* frame. I will use Hitler as an example of someone who was quite adept at utilizing four of these leadership frames while almost completely ignoring the fifth.

When we examine the leadership behavior of the eleven leaders profiled in this study, we will most certainly find that the most effective of them operated out of all five leadership frames, the lesson learned being that if one wishes to become a future leader, one can learn to do so by reflectively looking to the great leaders of the past.

Basically, then, this is a book about leadership. The conventional wisdom is that leaders are born, not made. I disagree! My experience and (more importantly) scholarly research indicate that leadership skills can be learned. Granted, some leaders will be superior to others because of genetics, but the basic leadership skills are learned behaviors and can be cultivated, enhanced, and honed.

The first chapter of this book speaks to the so-called *science* of leadership, while the second chapter deals with the *art* of administration and leadership. One needs to lead with both mind (science) and heart (art) to be truly effective. The next eleven chapters are about the leadership behavior of eleven successful leaders from history and are predicated on the belief that leadership skills can be learned. Thus the title, *Going Back to the Future: A Leadership Journey for Educators*.

The effective building blocks of quality leadership are the skills of communication, motivation, organizational development, management, and creativity. Mastering the theory and practice in these areas of study will produce high-quality leadership ability and, in turn, will produce successful leaders; doing so with heart will result in not only highly successful leadership, but also what author Chris Lowney calls *heroic leadership* (Lowney, 2003).

There is another broadly held assumption about effective leadership and administration that I would dispute, namely that nice guys (and gals) finish last. To be a successful administrator, the belief goes, one needs to be firm, direct, and even autocratic. Once again, scholarly research, as well as my own experience, indicates that no one singular leadership style is consistently effective in all situations and at all times. Empirical and experiential studies indicate that effective leaders vary their styles depending on the situation. This *situational* approach is the underlying theme of this book. In the concluding chapter, we find that truly effective leaders use both their minds and their hearts in the leadership process, and in doing so, nice guys and gals do oftentimes finish *first*.

Some thirty-five years ago, when I was coaching high school basketball, I attended a coaching clinic where the main clinicians were Dean Smith, then coach of North Carolina University, and Bobby Knight, then coach of Indiana University. Both coaches were successful then, and almost four decades later they remain respected and, in one case at least, revered.

In the morning session, Bobby Knight explained how *fear* was the most effective motivator in sports. If you want athletes to listen to you and you want to be successful as a coach, you need to instill fear in your players, Knight stated. In the afternoon session, Dean Smith explained how *love* is the most effective motivator in sports. If you want to win and be successful, you must engender love in your athletes.

You can understand my sense of confusion by the end of the clinic. Here were two of the most successful men in sports giving contradictory advice. As a young and impressionable coach, I was puzzled by these apparently mixed messages. Over the intervening years, I have often thought about that clinic and tried to make sense of what I had heard. After these many years, I have drawn two conclusions from this incident, both of which have had a significant impact on my philosophy of leadership and on this book.

The first conclusion has to do with the *situational* nature of leadership. Bobby Knight and Dean Smith impressed upon me the truism that there is no one singular leadership style that is effective at all times and in all situations. The second conclusion is that, despite reaping short-term success, the better style for ensuring continued success is one that inspires love, trust, and respect. Just as athletes become robotic and frightened of making mistakes when fear is the only motivator, so do employees who are too closely supervised by an autocratic manager. Initiative, creativity, and self-sufficiency are all stymied by the leader who instills fear in his or her subordinates. Thus I arrived at my conclusion that effective school administration and leadership (my field of interest), and leadership in general, begins with love, trust, and respect.

In addition to an emphasis on the nature of leadership, this book focuses on putting theory into practice. We cannot underestimate the value and importance of theory. Without theory, we have no valid way of analyzing and correcting failed practice. Without a theoretical base, we oftentimes lead by trial and error, or by the proverbial seat of our pants. On the other hand, knowledge of theory without the ability to put it into reflective practice is of no value and is not characteristic of effective leadership. We suggest that leaders and aspiring leaders adopt one of the leadership theories described in this book and put it into reflective practice modeled after the leadership behavior of some of the historical figures highlighted here.

This book uses the case study approach in order to facilitate putting theory into effective practice. Each chapter contains an extensive study of one of the most successful leaders in world history. We will analyze each case and see how these leaders were able to put leadership theory into effective practice. I believe that the lessons learned will prove invaluable to leaders as well as aspiring leaders, whether they be parents, teachers, school principals, or CEOs.

This book also takes an organizational development approach to producing effective leadership. Picture yourself standing in the middle of a dense forest. Suppose you were asked to describe the characteristics of the forest. What types of trees are growing in the forest? How many acres of trees are there? Where are the trees thriving? Where are they not? Faced with this proposition, most people would not know where to start. They would not be able to see the forest for the trees.

Newly appointed executives and administrators often have this feeling of confusion when faced with the prospect of having to assume a leadership role in a complex organization like a school, school system, or company. Where does one start? An effective place to start would be to systematically examine the components that make up the organization. Such a system of organizational diagnosis and prescription will lead to a comprehensive and integrated analysis of the organization's strengths and weaknesses and point the way toward possible improvements.

Using the leadership behaviors found among the successful men and women profiled in this book as a model, the final chapter suggests such a sequential and systematic approach. In the appendix, there is a comprehensive survey instrument, called the Heart Smart Survey, that assesses the health of an organization. Utilizing this instrument effectively can produce dramatic and useful results.

This leads me to what I presumptuously refer to as my Seven Principles of Effective Leadership. Effective leaders:

- need to be able to adapt their *leadership style* to the situation.

- must be keenly aware of the organizational *structure and culture* of the institution.
- must be able to engender a sense of *trust and respect* in their followers.
- need to continuously improve their organizations and therefore must be *agents for change.*
- need to be *well organized* and *creative* and have a clearly articulated *vision.*
- must be able to *communicate* effectively.
- must know how to *motivate* their followers and be able to *manage the conflicts* that arise.

In my view, which is supported by a prodigious amount of empirical research, if an administrator can master the knowledge and skills encompassed in these seven principles, and do it with heart, he or she will be a highly successful leader.

Chapter 1

Contemporary Leadership Theory

The effective functioning of social systems from the local PTA to the United States of America is assumed to be dependent on the quality of their leadership.

—Victor H. Vroom

Leadership is offered as a solution for most of the problems of organizations everywhere. Schools will work, we are told, if principals provide strong instructional leadership. Around the world, administrators and managers say that their organizations would thrive if only senior management provided strategy, vision, and real leadership. Though the call for leadership is universal, there is much less clarity about what the term means.

Historically, researchers in this field have searched for the one best leadership style that would be most effective. Current thought is that there is no one best style. Rather, a combination of styles depending on the situation the leader finds himself or herself in has been found to be more appropriate. To understand the evolution of leadership theory, we will take an historical approach and trace the progress of leadership theory, beginning with the trait perspective of leadership and moving to the more current contingency theories of leadership.

TRAIT THEORY

Trait theory suggests that we can evaluate leadership and propose ways of leading effectively by considering whether an individual possesses certain personality traits, social traits, and physical characteristics. Popular in the 1940s and 1950s, trait theory attempted to predict which individuals successfully became leaders and then whether they were effective. Leaders differ from nonleaders in their drive, desire to lead, honesty and integrity, self-confidence, cognitive ability, and knowledge of the business that they are in. Even the traits judged necessary for top-, middle-, and low-level management differed among leaders of different countries; for example, U.S. and British leaders valued resourcefulness; the Japanese, intuition; and the Dutch, imagination, but for lower and middle managers only (Kirkpatrick and Locke, 1991, 49).

The obvious question is, can you think of any individuals who are effective leaders but who lack one or more of these characteristics? Chances are that you can. Skills and the ability to implement a vision are necessary to transform traits into leadership behavior. Individual capability, which is a function of background predispositions, preferences, and cognitive complexity, as well as technical, human relations, and conceptual skills, also contribute.

The trait approach has more historical than practical interest for managers and administrators, even though recent research has once again tied leadership effectiveness to leader traits. One study of senior management jobs suggests that effective leadership requires a broad knowledge of and solid relations within the industry and the company, an excellent reputation, a strong track record, a keen mind, strong interpersonal skills, high integrity, high energy, and a strong drive to lead (Gordon, 1993, 330). In addition, some view the transformational perspective described later in this chapter as a natural evolution of the earlier trait perspective.

THE BEHAVIORAL PERSPECTIVE

The limitations in the ability of traits to predict effective leadership caused researchers during the 1950s to view a person's behavior rather than that individual's personal traits as a way of increasing leadership effectiveness. This view also paved the way for later situational theories.

The types of leadership behaviors investigated typically fell into two categories: production oriented and employee oriented. Production-oriented leadership, also called concern for production, initiating structure, or task-focused leadership, involves acting primarily to get the job done. An administrator who tells his or her department chair to do "everything you need to do to get the curriculum developed in time for the start of school, no matter what the personal consequences" demonstrates production-oriented leadership. So does an administrator who uses an autocratic style or fails to involve workers in any aspect of decision making.

Employee-oriented leadership, also called concern for people or consideration, focuses on supporting the individual workers in their activities and involving the workers in decision making. A principal who demonstrates great concern for his or her teachers' satisfaction with their duties and commitment to their work has an employee-oriented leadership style (Stogdill and Coons, 1957).

Studies in leadership at Ohio State University, which classified individuals' styles as initiating structure or consideration, examined the link between style and grievance rate, performance, and turnover. Initiating structure reflects the degree to which the leader structures his or her own role and subordinates' roles toward accomplishing the group's goal through scheduling work, assigning employees to tasks, and maintaining standards of performance. Consideration refers to the degree to which the leader emphasizes individuals' needs through two-way communication, respect for subordinates' ideas, mutual trust between leader and subordinates, and consideration of subordinates' feelings. Although leaders can choose the style to fit the outcomes they desire, in fact, to achieve desirable outcomes on all three dimensions of performance, grievance rate, and turnover, this research suggested that managers should strive to demonstrate *both* initiating structure and consideration (Fleishman, Harris, and Buret, 1955; Fleishman and Harris, 1959).

A series of leadership studies at the University of Michigan, which looked at managers with an employee orientation or a production orientation, yielded similar results. In these studies, which related differences in high-productivity and low-productivity work groups to differences in supervisors, highly productive supervisors spent more time planning departmental work and supervising their employees; they spent less time working alongside and performing the same tasks as subordinates, accorded their subordinates more freedom in specific task performance, and tended to be employee oriented (Fleishman, Harris, and Buret, 1955, 45).

A thirty-year longitudinal research study in Japan examined performance and maintenance leadership behaviors. Performance here refers specifically to forming and reaching group goals through fast work speed; outcomes of high quality, accuracy, and quantity; and observation of rules. Maintenance behaviors preserve the group's social stability by dealing with subordinates' feelings, reducing stress, providing comfort, and showing appreciation. The Japanese, according to this and other studies, prefer leadership high on *both* dimensions over performance-dominated behavior, except when work is done in short-term project groups, when subordinates are prone to anxiety, or when effective performance calls for very low effort (Bass, 1990, 332).

MANAGERIAL ROLES THEORY

A study of chief executive officers by Henry Mintzberg suggested a different way of looking at leadership. He observed that managerial work encompasses ten roles: three that focus on interpersonal contact—(1) figurehead, (2) leader, and (3) liaison; three that involve mainly information processing—(4) monitor, (5) disseminator, and (6) spokesman; and four related to decision making—(7) entrepreneur, (8) disturbance handler, (9) resource allocator, and (10) negotiator. Note that almost all roles would include activities that could be construed as leadership—influencing others toward a particular goal.

In addition, most of these roles can apply to nonmanagerial positions as well as managerial ones. The role approach resembles the behavioral and trait perspectives because all three call for specific types of behavior independent of the situation; however, the role approach is more compatible with the situation approach and has been shown to be more valid than either the behavioral or trait perspective (Mintzberg, 1979).

Though not all managers will perform every role, some diversity of role performance must occur. Managers can diagnose their own and others' role performance and then offer strategies for altering it. The choice roles will depend to some extent on the manager's specific job description and the situation in question. For example, managing individual performance and instructing subordinates are less important for middle managers than for first-line supervisors, and less important for executives than for either lower level of manager.

EARLY SITUATIONAL THEORIES

Contingency or situational models differ from the earlier trait and behavioral models in asserting that no single way of leading works in all situations. Rather, appropriate behavior depends on the circumstances at a given time. Effective managers diagnose the situation, identify the leadership style that will be most effective, and then determine whether they can implement the required style. Early situational research suggested that subordinate, supervisor, and task considerations affect the appropriate leadership style in a given situation. The precise aspects of each dimension that influence the most effective leadership style vary.

THEORY X AND THEORY Y

One of the older situational theories, McGregor's Theory X and Theory Y formulation, calls for a leadership style based on individuals' assumptions about other individuals, together with characteristics of the individual, the task, the organization, and the environment. Although managers may have many styles, theories X and Y have received the greatest attention.

Theory X managers assume that people are lazy, extrinsically motivated, and incapable of self-discipline or self-control, and that they want security and no responsibility in their jobs. Theory Y managers assume that people do not inherently dislike work, are intrinsically motivated, exert self-control, and seek responsibility. A Theory X manager, because of his or her limited view of the world, has only one leadership style available, that is, an autocratic style. A Theory Y manager has a wide range of styles in his or her repertoire (McGregor, 1961; Schein, 1974, 3).

How can an administrator use McGregor's theory for ensuring leadership effectiveness? What prescription would McGregor offer for improving the situation? If an administrator had Theory X assumptions, McGregor would suggest that the administrator change them and would facilitate this change by sending the administrator to a management development program. If a manager had Theory Y assumptions, McGregor would advise a diagnosis of the situation to ensure that the selected style matched the administrator's assumptions and action tendencies, as well as the internal and external influences on the situation.

FREDERICK FIEDLER'S THEORY

While McGregor's theory provided a transition from behavioral to situational theories, Frederick Fiedler developed and tested the first leadership theory explicitly called a contingency or situational model. He argued that changing an individual's leadership style is quite difficult, but that organizations should put individuals in situations that fit with their style. Fiedler's theory suggests that managers can choose between two styles: task oriented and relationship oriented. Then the nature of leader-member relations, task structure, and position power of the leader influences whether a task-oriented or a relationship-oriented leadership style is more likely to be effective.

Leader-member relations refer to the extent to which the group trusts and respects the leader and will follow the leader's directions. Task structure describes the degree to which the task is clearly defined or structured, as opposed to being ambiguous or unstructured. Position power means the extent to which the leader has official power, that is, the potential or actual ability to influence others in a desired direction owing to the position he or she holds in the organization (Fiedler and Chemers, 1984).

The style recommended as most effective for each combination of these three situational factors is based on the degree of control or influence the leader can exert in his or her leadership position, as shown in table 1.1. In general, high-control situations (I, II, and III) call for task-oriented leadership because they allow the leader to take charge. Low-control situations

Table 1.1.   Decision-Making Processes

For Individual Problems	*For Group Problems*
AI. You solve the problem or make the decision yourself, using information available to you at that time.	AI. You solve the problem or make the decision yourself, using information available to you at the time.
AII. You obtain any necessary information from the subordinate, then decide on the solution to the problem yourself. You may or may not tell the subordinate what the problem is, in getting the information from him. The role played by your subordinate in making the decision is clearly one of providing specific information that you request, rather than generating or evaluating alternative solutions.	AII. You obtain any necessary information from subordinates, then decide on the solution to the problem yourself. You may or may not tell subordinates what the problem is, in getting the information from them. The role played by your subordinates in making the decision is clearly one of providing specific information that you request, rather than generating or evaluating solutions.
CI. You share the problem with the relevant subordinate, getting his ideas and suggestions. Then, you make the decision. This decision may or may not reflect your subordinate's influence.	CI. You share the problem with the relevant subordinates individually, getting their ideas and suggestions without bringing them together as a group. Then you make the decision. This decision may or may not reflect your subordinates' influence.
GI. You share the problem with one of your subordinates, and together you analyze the problem and arrive at a mutually satisfactory solution in an atmosphere of free and open exchange of information and ideas. You both contribute to the resolution of the problem with the relative contribution of each being dependent on knowledge rather than formal authority.	CII. You share the problem with your subordinates in a group meeting. In this meeting you obtain their ideas and suggestions. Then, you make the decision, which may or may not reflect your subordinates' influence.
DI. You delegate the problem to one of your subordinates, providing him or her with any relevant information that you possess, but giving responsibility for solving the problem independently. Any solution that the person reaches will receive your support.	GII. You share the problem with your subordinates as a group. Together you generate and evaluate alternatives and attempt to reach agreement (consensus) on a solution. Your role is much like that of chairman, coordinating the discussion, keeping it focused on the problem, and making sure that the crucial issues are discussed. You do not try to influence the group to adopt "your" solution and are willing to accept and implement any solution that has the support of the entire group.

(VII and VIII) also call for task-oriented leadership because they require rather than allow the leader to take charge. Moderate-control situations (IV, V, VI, and VII), in contrast, call for relationship-oriented leadership because the situations challenge leaders to get the cooperation of their subordinates.

Despite extensive research to support this theory, critics have questioned the reliability of the measurement of leadership style and the range and appropriateness of the three situational components. This theory, however, is particularly applicable for those who believe that individuals are born with a certain management style, rather than management style being learned or flexible (Fiedler and Garcia, 1987).

CONTEMPORARY SITUATIONAL LEADERSHIP

Current research suggests that the effect of leader behavior on performance is altered by such intervening variables as the effort of subordinates, their ability to perform their jobs, the clarity of their job responsibilities, the organization of the work, the cooperation and cohesiveness of the group, the sufficiency of resources and support provided to the group, and the coordination of work group activities with those of other subunits.

Thus leaders must respond to these and broader cultural differences in choosing an appropriate style. A leader-environment-follower interaction theory of leadership notes that effective leaders first analyze deficiencies in the follower's ability, motivation, role perception, and work environment that inhibit performance and then act to eliminate these deficiencies (Biggart and Hamilton, 1987).

PATH-GOAL THEORY

According to path-goal theory, the leader attempts to influence subordinates' perceptions of goals and the path to achieve them. Leaders can then choose among four styles of leadership: directive, supportive, participative, and achievement-oriented. In selecting a style, the leader acts to strengthen the expectancy, instrumentality, and valence of a situation, respectively, by providing better technology or training for the employees; reinforcing desired behaviors with pay, praise, or promotion; and ensuring that the employees value the rewards they receive (House, 1971; House and Mitchell, 1974).

Choosing a style requires a quality diagnosis of the situation to decide what leadership behaviors would be most effective in attaining the desired outcomes. The appropriate leadership style is influenced first by subordinates' characteristics, particularly the subordinates' abilities and the likelihood that the leader's behavior will influence subordinates' satisfaction now or in the future, and second by the environment, including the subordinates' tasks, the formal authority system, the primary work group, and organizational culture. The most desirable leadership style helps the subordinate achieve satisfaction, meet personal needs, and accomplish goals, while complementing his or her abilities and the characteristics of the situation.

Application of the path-goal theory, then, requires first an assessment of the situation, particularly its participants and environment, and second, a determination of the most congruent leadership style. Even though the research on path-goal theory has yielded mixed results, it can provide a leader with help in selecting an effective leadership style.

THE VROOM-YETTON MODEL

The Vroom-Yetton model involves a procedure for determining the extent to which leaders should involve subordinates in the decision-making process. The manager can choose one of five approaches that range from individual problem solving with available information, to joint problem solving, to delegation of problem-solving responsibility. Table 1.1 summarizes the possibilities (Vroom and Yetton, 1973; Vroom and Jago, 1988).

Selection of the appropriate decision process involves assessing six factors: (1) the problem's quality requirement, (2) the location of information about the problem, (3) the structure of the problem, (4) the likely acceptance of the decision by those affected, (5) the commonality of organizational goals, and (6) any likely conflict regarding possible problem solutions.

To make a decision, the leader asks each question, A through H, corresponding to each box encountered from left to right, unless questions may be skipped because the response to the previous question leads to a later one. For example, a *no* response to question A allows questions B and C to be skipped; a *yes* response to question B after a *yes* response to question A allows question C to be skipped. Reaching the end of one branch of the tree results in the identification of a problem type (numbered 1 through 18) with an accompanying set of feasible decision processes.

When the set of feasible processes for group problems includes more than one process (e.g., a *no* response to each question results in problem type 1, for which every decision style is feasible), the final selection of a single approach can use number of hours as a secondary criterion (group processes AI, AII, CI, CII, and GII are preferred, in that order). A manager who wishes to make the decision in the shortest time possible, and for whom all processes are appropriate, will choose AI (solving the problem himself or herself using available information) over any other process.

A manager who wishes to maximize subordinate involvement in the decision making as a training and development tool, for example, will choose DI or GII (delegating the problem to the subordinate, or working together with subordinates to reach a decision) if all processes are feasible and if time is not limited. Similar choices can be made when analyzing individual problems. Research has shown that decisions made using processes from the feasible set result in more effective outcomes than those not included (Field, 1982).

Suppose, for example, that the teacher evaluation instrument in your institution was in need of revision. Using the decision tree, we would ask the first question: Is there a quality requirement such that one solution is likely to be more rational than another? Our answer would have to be yes. Do I have sufficient information to make a high-quality decision? The answer is no. Is the problem structured? Yes. Is acceptance of the decision by subordinates critical to effective implementation? Yes. If I were to make the decision myself, is it reasonably certain that it would be accepted by my subordinates? No. Do subordinates share the organizational goals to be attained in solving this problem? Yes. Is conflict among subordinates likely in preferred solutions? Yes. Do subordinates have sufficient information to make a high-quality decision? Yes.

Following this procedure, the decision tree indicates that GII would be the proper approach for revising the teacher evaluation form. GII indicates that the leader should share the problem with his or her faculty. Together they generate and evaluate alternatives and attempt to reach agreement on a solution. The leader's role is much like that of a chairperson coordinating the discussion, keeping it focused on the problem, and making sure the critical issues are discussed. You do not try to influence the group to adopt your solution, and you are willing to accept and implement any solution which has the support of the entire faculty.

The recent reformulation of this model uses the same decision processes AI, AII, CI, CII, GI, GII, and DI as the original model, as well as the criteria of decision quality, decision commitment, time, and subordinate development. It differs by expanding the range of possible responses to include probabilities, rather than yes or no answers, and it uses a computer to process the data. Although both formulations of this model provide a set of diagnostic questions for analyzing a problem, they tend to oversimplify the process. Their narrow focus on the extent of subordinate involvement in decision making also limits their usefulness.

THE HERSEY-BLANCHARD MODEL

In an attempt to integrate previous knowledge about leadership into a prescriptive model of leadership style, the Hersey-Blanchard model cites the readiness of followers, defined as their ability and willingness to accomplish a specific task, as the major contingency that influences appropriate leadership style (Hersey and Blanchard, 1988). Follower readiness incorporates the follower's level of achievement motivation, ability and willingness to assume responsibility for his or her own behavior in accomplishing specific tasks, and education and experience relevant to the task. The model combines task and relationship behavior to yield four possible styles.

Leaders should use a telling style, providing specific instructions and closely supervising performance, when followers are unable, unwilling, or insecure. Leaders should use a selling style, explaining decisions and providing opportunity for clarification, when followers have moderate-to-low readiness. Leaders should use a participating style, sharing ideas and facilitating decision making, when followers have moderate-to-high readiness. And, finally, leaders should use a delegating style, giving responsibility for decisions and implementation to followers, when followers are able, willing, and confident.

Although some researchers have questioned the conceptual clarity, validity, robustness, and utility of the model, as well as the instruments used to measure leadership style, others have supported the utility of the model. For example, the Leadership Effectiveness and Description (LEAD) Scale and related instruments, developed to measure leadership style by life-cycle researchers, are widely used in industrial training programs. This model can easily be adapted to educational administration, as well as other types of leadership positions, and can be used analytically to understand leadership deficiencies and, combined with the path-goal model, to prescribe the appropriate style for a variety of situations.

REFRAMING LEADERSHIP

Lee Bolman and Terrence Deal have developed a unique situational leadership theory that analyzes leadership behavior through four frames of reference: structural, human resource, political, and symbolic. Each of the frames offers a different perspective on what leadership is and how it operates in organizations. Each can result in either effective or ineffective conceptions of leadership (Bolman and Terrance, 1991).

Structural leaders develop a new model of the relationship of structure, strategy, and environment for their organizations. They focus on implementation. The right answer helps only if it can be implemented. These leaders emphasize rationality, analysis, logic, facts, and data. They are likely to believe strongly in the importance of clear structure and well-developed management systems. A good leader is someone who thinks clearly, makes good decisions, has good analytical skills, and can design structures and systems that get the job done.

Structural leaders sometimes fail because they miscalculate the difficulty of putting their designs in place. They often underestimate the resistance it will generate, and they take few steps to build a base of support for their innovations. In short, they are often undone by human resource, political, and symbolic considerations. Structural leaders do continually experiment, evaluate, and adapt, but because they fail to consider the entire environment in which they are situated, they sometimes are ineffective.

Human resource leaders believe in people and communicate that belief. They are passionate about "productivity through people." They demonstrate this faith in their words and actions and often build it into a philosophy or credo that is central to their vision of their organization. They believe in the importance of coaching, participation, motivation, teamwork, and good interpersonal relations. A good leader is a facilitator and participative manager who supports and empowers others. Human resource leaders are visible and accessible. Peters and Waterman popularized the notion of "management wandering around," the idea that managers need to get out of their offices and interact with workers and customers (Gordon, 1993, 345). Many educational administrators have adopted this aspect of management.

Effective human resource leaders empower, that is, they increase participation, provide support, share information, and move decision making as far down the organization as possible. Human resource leaders often like to refer to their employees as "partners" or "colleagues." They want to make it clear that employees have a stake in the organization's success and a right to be involved in making decisions. When such leaders are ineffective, however, they are seen as naive or as weaklings and wimps.

Political leaders believe that managers and leaders live in a world of conflict and scarce resources. The central task of management is to mobilize the resources needed to advocate and fight for the unit's or the organization's goals and objectives. They emphasize the importance of building a power base, including allies, networks, and coalitions. A good leader is an advocate and negotiator who understands politics and is comfortable with conflict. Political leaders clarify what they want and what they can get. Political leaders are realists above all. They never let what they want cloud their judgment about what is possible. They assess the distribution of power and interests.

The political leader needs to think carefully about the players, their interests, and their power; in other words, he or she must map the political terrain. Political leaders ask questions such as whose support do I need? How do I go about getting it? Who are my opponents? How much power do they have? What can I do to reduce the opposition? Is the battle winnable? However, if ineffective, these leaders are perceived as being untrustworthy and manipulative.

The symbolic frame provides still a fourth turn of the kaleidoscope of leadership. In this frame, the organization is seen as a stage, a theater in which every actor plays certain roles and attempts to communicate the right impressions to the right audiences. The main premise of this frame is that whenever reason and analysis fail to contain the dark forces of ambiguity, human beings erect symbols, myths, rituals, and ceremonies to bring order, meaning, and predictability out of chaos and confusion. Symbolic leaders believe that the essential role of management is to provide inspiration. They rely on personal charisma and a flair for drama to get people excited and committed to the organizational mission.

A good leader is a prophet who uses symbols, tells stories, and frames experience in ways that give people hope and meaning. Transforming leaders are visionary leaders, and visionary leadership is invariably symbolic. Examination of symbolic leaders reveals that they follow a consistent set of practices and rules.

Transforming leaders use symbols to capture attention. When Diana Lam became principal of the Mackey Middle School in Boston, she knew that she faced a substantial challenge. Mackey had all the usual problems of urban public schools: decaying physical plant, lack of student discipline, racial tension, troubles with the teaching staff, low morale, and limited resources. The only good news was that the situation was so bad that almost any change would be an improvement.

In such a situation, symbolic leaders will try to do something visible, even dramatic, to let people know that changes are on the way. During the summer before she assumed her duties, Lam wrote a letter to every teacher to set up an individual meeting. She traveled to meet teachers wherever they wanted, driving two hours in one case. She asked teachers how they felt about the school and what changes they wanted.

She also felt that something needed to be done about the school building, because nobody likes to work in a dumpy place. She decided that the front door and some of the worst classrooms had to be painted. She had few illusions about getting the bureaucracy of the Boston public school system to provide painters, so she persuaded some of her family members to help her do the painting. When school opened, students and staff members immediately saw that things were going to be different, if only symbolically. Perhaps even more importantly, staff members received a subtle challenge to make a contribution themselves.

Each of the frames captures significant possibilities for leadership, but each is incomplete. In the early part of the century, leadership as a concept was rarely applied to management, and the implicit models of leadership were narrowly rational. In the 1960s and 1970s, human resource leadership became fashionable. The literature on organizational leadership stressed openness, sensitivity, and participation.

In recent years, symbolic leadership has moved to center stage, and the literature now offers advice on how to become a visionary leader with the power to transform organizational cultures. Organizations do need vision, but it is not their only need and not always their most important one. Leaders need to understand their own frame and its limits. Ideally, they will also learn to combine multiple frames into a more comprehensive and powerful style.

It is this Bolman-Deal leadership theory on which we will base our conclusions regarding the leadership behavior of the eleven historical figures profiled in this book. Before leaving our discussion of Bolman and Deal's approach, however, let us reinforce the point that balance needs to occur both *among* and *within* the frames. That is to say that, in addition to utilizing all four frames, the effective leader needs to be careful not to behave in the extreme within any one frame. Striving for the golden mean is the goal.

TRANSFORMATIONAL LEADERSHIP

A charismatic or transformational leader uses charisma to inspire his or her followers and is an example of a person who acts primarily in the symbolic frame of leadership as outlined above. He or she talks to followers about how essential their performance is, how confident he or she is in them, how exceptional they are, and how he or she expects the group's performance to exceed expectations. Lee Iacocca and Jack Walsh, in industry, and the late Marcus Foster and Notre Dame's Reverend Theodore Hesburgh, in education, are examples of this type of leader. Among the leaders profiled in this book, virtually all of them were found to be transformational leaders. Such leaders use dominance, self-confidence, a need for influence, and conviction of moral righteousness to increase their charisma and consequently their leadership effectiveness (House, 1977).

A transformational leader changes an organization by recognizing an opportunity and developing a vision, communicating that vision to organizational members, building trust in the vision, and achieving the vision by motivating organizational members. The leader helps subordinates recognize the need for revitalizing the organization by developing a felt need for change, overcoming resistance to change, and avoiding quick-fix solutions to problems.

Encouraging subordinates to act as devil's advocates with regard to the leader, building networks outside the organization, visiting other organizations, and changing management processes to reward progress against the competition can also help subordinates recognize a need for revitalization. Individuals must disengage from and disidentify with the past, and they must view change as a way of dealing with their disenchantments with the status quo. The transformational leader creates a new vision and mobilizes commitment to it by planning and educating others. He or she builds trust by demonstrating personal expertise, self-confidence, and personnel integrity.

The charismatic leader can also change the composition of the team, alter management processes, and help organizational members reframe the way they perceive an organizational situation. The charismatic leader must empower others to help achieve the vision. Finally, the transformational leader must institutionalize the change by replacing old technical, political, cultural, and social networks with new ones. For example, if an administrator wishes to make an innovative program acceptable to the faculty and the school community, he or she should follow the above plan and identify influential individuals and groups who would agree to champion the new program, develop a plan to gain the support of others in the community through personal contact or other means, and develop a monitoring system to assess the progress of the effort (Willner, 1984; Conger and Kanungo, 1987).

A transformational leader motivates subordinates to achieve beyond their original expectations by increasing their awareness of the importance of designated outcomes and ways of attaining them; by getting workers to go beyond their self-interest to that of the team, the school, the school system, and the larger society; and by changing or expanding the individual's needs. Subordinates report that they work harder for such leaders. In addition, such leaders are judged higher in leadership potential by their subordinates as compared to the more common transactional leader.

One should be cognizant, however, of the negative side of charismatic leadership, which may exist if the leader overemphasizes devotion to himself or herself, makes personal needs paramount, or uses highly effective communication skills to mislead or manipulate others. Such leaders may be so driven to achieve a vision that they ignore the costly implications of their goals.

The superintendent of schools that over-expands his or her jurisdiction in an effort to form an "empire," only to have the massive system turn into a bureaucratic nightmare, is an example of transformational leadership gone sour. A business that expands too rapidly in order to satisfy the ego of the CEO, and as a result loses its quality control, is another example. Nevertheless, recent research has verified the overall effectiveness of the transformational leadership style.

DEVELOPING A VISION

A requisite for transformational leadership is a vision. Although there seems to be a sense of mystery on the part of some individuals regarding what a vision is and how to create one, the process for developing a vision is not at all complex. Using education as an example, the first step is to develop a list of broad goals. "All children achieving" is an example of such a goal. These goals should be developed in conjunction with representatives from all segments of the school community; otherwise there will be no sense of ownership, the absence of which will preclude successful implementation.

The next step in the process is to merge and prioritize the goals and to summarize them in the form of a short and concise vision statement. The following is an example of a typical vision statement:

> Our vision for the Exeter School System is that all of our graduating students, regardless of ability, will say, "I have received an excellent education that has prepared me to be an informed citizen and leader in my community." Our students will have a world view, and as a result of their experience in the Exeter School System, will be committed to a process of lifelong learning and the making of a better world by living the ideals of fairness and justice through service to others.

The key concepts in the above vision are student achievement, excellence, leadership, multiculturalism, lifelong learning, values, and community service. It is these concepts that the transformational leader stresses in all forms of communication and in all interactions with the school community.

The final step in the process is institutionalization of the educational vision. This step ensures that the vision endures when the leadership changes. Operationalizing and inserting the important concepts of the vision into the official policies and procedures of the school system is one way of helping to institutionalize the educational vision and incorporate it into the school culture. As we will see, virtually all of the eleven historical figures profiled in this book had a clear vision of what they wanted to achieve and convinced their followers to accept ownership of what would ultimately become their shared vision.

IMPLICATIONS FOR LEADERS

The implications of leadership theory for educational and other administrators are rather clear. The successful leader needs to have a sound grasp of leadership theory and the skills to implement it. The principles of the situational and transformational leadership theories are guides to effective administrative behavior. The leadership behavior applied with an inexperienced faculty member may be significantly different from that applied with a more experienced and tested faculty member. Task behavior may be appropriate in dealing with a new teacher, while relationship behavior may be more appropriate when dealing with a seasoned teacher.

In particular, the four frames of leadership discussed by Bolman and Deal may be helpful to school leaders and to leaders in general. Consideration of the structural, human relations, political, and symbolic implications of leadership behavior can keep an administrator attuned to the various dimensions affecting appropriate leadership behavior.

With the need to deal with collective bargaining entities, school boards, and a variety of other power issues, the considerations of political frame may be particularly helpful in understanding the complexity of the relationships that exist between administrators and these groups. Asking oneself the questions posed earlier under the political frame can be an effective guide to appropriate leadership behavior when dealing with these groups.

SUMMARY

Recently, a plethora of research studies have been conducted on leadership and leadership styles. The overwhelming evidence indicates that there is no single leadership style that is most appropriate in all situations. Rather, an administrator's leadership style should be adapted to the situation, so that task behavior or relationship behavior might be appropriate at different times. At other times and in other situations, various degrees of both task and relationship behavior may be most effective.

The emergence of transformational leadership has seen leadership theory come full circle. Transformational leadership theory combines aspects of the early trait theory perspective with the more current situational or contingency models. The personal charisma of the leader, along with his or her ability to formulate an organizational vision and communicate it to others, determines the transformational leader's effectiveness.

Since the effective leader is expected to adapt his or her leadership style to an ever-changing environment, administration becomes an even more complex and challenging task. However, a thorough knowledge of leadership theory can make some sense of the apparent chaos that administrators face on an almost daily basis.

Among scholars, there is the assertion that theory informs practice and practice informs theory. This notion posits that to be an effective leader, one must base his or her practice on some form of leadership theory. On the other hand, when a leader utilizes theory-inspired behavior that is continually ineffective, perhaps the theory should be modified to account for this deficiency. In this case, practice would be informing theory.

In this book, we will examine the leadership behavior of eleven great leaders in history to ascertain whether their behavior conforms to the principles of Bolman and Deal's situational leadership theory, and if not, whether their practice needs to be modified to fit the theory or the theory needs to be modified to reflect effective practice. We will also examine how these leaders' practices can be applied to our own leadership behavior to make it more effective. However, before doing so, we will explore the *art* of leadership, or what I call leading with heart.

Chapter 2

Leading with Heart

Do unto others as you would have them do unto you.

—The Golden Rule

How a leader utilizes the concepts described in chapter 1 depends largely on one's philosophy regarding how human beings behave in the workplace. The two extremes of the continuum might be described as those leaders who believe that human beings are basically lazy and will do the very least they need to do to get by in the workplace and those who believe that people are basically industrious and if given a choice would opt for doing a quality job. I believe that today's most effective leaders hold the latter view.

I agree with Max DePree, owner and CEO of the highly successful Herman Miller Furniture Company. Writing in his book, *Leadership Is an Art*, he says that a leader's function is to "liberate people to do what is required of them in the most effective and humane way possible" (DePree, 1989). Instead of catching people doing something wrong, our goal as enlightened leaders is to catch them doing something right. I suggest, therefore, that in addition to a rational approach to leadership, a truly enlightened leader leads with heart.

Too often, leaders underestimate the skills and qualities of their followers. I remember Bill Faries, the chief custodian at a high school at which I was assistant principal in the mid-1970s. Bill's mother, with whom he had been extraordinarily close, had passed away after a long illness. The school was a religiously affiliated one, and the school community went all out in its remembrance of Bill's mother. We held a religious service in which almost three thousand members of the school community participated. Bill, of course, was very grateful. As a token of his gratitude, he gave the school a six-by-eight-foot quilt that he had personally sewn. From that point on, I did not know if Bill was a custodian who was a quilt maker or a quilt maker who was a custodian.

The point is that it took the death of his mother for me and others to realize how truly talented our custodian was. Our effectiveness as leaders begins with an understanding of the diversity of people's gifts, talents, and skills. When we think about the variety of gifts that people bring to organizations and institutions, we see that leading with heart lies in cultivating, liberating, and enabling those gifts.

LEADERSHIP DEFINED

The first responsibility of a leader is to define reality through a vision. The last is to say thank you. In between, the leader must become the servant of the servants. Being a leader means having the opportunity to make a meaningful difference in the lives of those who allow leaders to lead. This summarizes what I call leading with heart. In a nutshell, true leaders don't inflict pain; they bear pain.

Whether one is a successful leader can be determined by looking at the followers. Are they reaching their potential? Are they learning? Are they able to change without bitterness? Are they able to achieve the institution's goals and objectives? Can they manage conflict among themselves? Where the answers to these questions is an emphatic *yes* is where a truly effective leader resides.

I prefer to think about leadership in terms of what the Gospel writer Luke calls the "one who serves." The leader owes something to the institution he or she leads. The leader is seen in this context as a steward rather than an owner or proprietor. Leading with heart requires the leader to think about his or her stewardship in terms of legacy, direction, effectiveness, and values.

LEGACY

Too many of today's leaders are interested only in immediate results that bolster their career goals. Long-range goals are left to their successors. I believe this approach fosters autocratic leadership, which oftentimes produces short-term results but militates against creativity and its long-term benefits. In effect, this approach is the antithesis of leading with heart.

On the contrary, leaders should build a long-lasting legacy of accomplishment that is institutionalized for posterity. They owe their institutions and their followers a healthy existence and the relationships and reputation that enable continuity of that healthy existence. Leaders are also responsible for future leadership. They need to identify, develop, and nurture future leaders to carry on the legacy.

VALUES

Along with being responsible for providing future leaders, leaders owe the individuals in their institutions certain other legacies. Leaders need to be concerned with the institutional value system which determines the principles and standards that guide the practices of those in the organization. Leaders need to model their value systems so that the individuals in the organization can learn to transmit these values to their colleagues and to future employees. In a civilized institution, we see good manners, respect for people, and an appreciation of the ways we serve one another. A humane, sensitive, and thoughtful leader will transmit his or her value system through his or her daily behavior. This, I believe, is what Peter Senge refers to as a "learning organization" (Senge, 1990).

DIRECTION

Leaders are obliged to provide and maintain direction by developing a vision. The point was made earlier that effective leaders must leave their organizations with a legacy. Part of this legacy should be a sense of progress or momentum. An educational administrator, for instance, should imbue his or her institution with a sense on continuous progress, a sense of constant improvement. Improvement and momentum come from a clear vision of what the institution ought to be, from a well-planned strategy for achieving this vision, and from carefully developed and articulated directions and plans that allow everyone to participate and be personally accountable for achieving those plans.

EFFECTIVENESS

Leaders are also responsible for effectiveness by being enablers. They need to enable others to reach their potential both personally and institu-tionally. I believe that the most effective way of enabling one's colleagues is through participative decision making. It begins with believing in the potential of people, believing in their diversity of gifts. Leaders must realize that to maximize their own power and effectiveness, they need to empower others. Leaders are responsible for setting and attaining the goals in their organizations. Empowering or enabling others to achieve these goals ultimately enhances the leader's effectiveness. Paradoxically, giving up power really amounts to gaining power.

EMPLOYEE OWNERS

We often hear managers suggest that a new program does not have a chance of succeeding unless the employees take ownership of the program. Most of us agree with the common sense of such an assertion. But how does a leader promote employee ownership? Let me suggest four steps as a beginning. I am certain that you can think of several more.

1. *Respect people.* As indicated earlier, this starts with appreciating the diverse gifts that individuals bring to your institution. The key is to dwell on the strengths of your coworkers, rather than their weaknesses. Try to turn their weaknesses into strengths. This does not mean that disciplinary action or even dismissal will never become necessary. What it does mean, however, is that we should focus on the formative aspect of the employee evaluation process before we engage in the summative part.
2. *Let belief guide policy and practice.* We spoke earlier of developing a culture of civility in your institution. If there is an environment of mutual respect and trust, I believe that the organization will flourish. Leaders need to let their belief or value system guide their behavior. Style is merely a consequence of what we believe and what is in our hearts.
3. *Recognize the need for covenants.* Contractual agreements cover such things as salary, fringe benefits, and working conditions. They are part of organizational life, and there is a legitimate need for them. But in today's organizations, especially educational institutions, where the best people working for these institutions are like volunteers, we need covenantal relationships. Our best workers may choose their employers. They usually choose the institution where they work based on reasons less tangible than salaries and fringe benefits. They do not need contracts; they need covenants. Covenantal relationships enable educational institutions to be civil, hospitable, and understanding of individuals' differences and unique charisms. They allow administrators to recognize that treating everyone equally is not necessarily treating everyone equitably and fairly.

4. *Understand that culture counts more than structure.* An educational institution that I have been associated with recently went through a particularly traumatic time when the credibility of the administration was questioned by the faculty and staff. Various organizational consultants were interviewed to facilitate a healing process. Most of the consultants spoke of making the necessary structural changes to create a culture of trust. We finally hired a consultant whose attitude was that organizational structure has nothing to do with trust. Interpersonal relations based on mutual respect and an atmosphere of good will is what creates a culture of trust. Would you rather work as part of a school with an outstanding reputation or as part of a group of outstanding individuals? Many times these two characteristics go together, but if one had to make a choice, I believe that most people would opt to work with outstanding individuals.

IT STARTS WITH TRUST, RESPECT, AND SENSITIVITY (HEART)

These are exciting times in education. Revolutionary steps are being taken to restructure schools and rethink the teaching-learning process. The concepts of empowerment, total quality management, the use of technology, and strategic planning are becoming the norm. However, while these activities have the potential to influence education in significantly positive ways, they must be based upon a strong foundation to achieve their full potential.

Achieving educational effectiveness is an incremental and sequential improvement process. This process begins by building a sense of security within each individual so that he or she can be flexible in adapting to changes within education. Addressing only skills and techniques, such as communication, motivation, negotiation, or empowerment, is ineffective when individuals in an organization do not trust its systems, themselves, or each other. An institution's resources are wasted when invested only in training programs that assist administrators in mastering quick-fix techniques that at best attempt to manipulate, and at worst reinforce, mistrust.

The challenge is to transform relationships based on insecurity, adversarialism, and politics to ones based on mutual trust. Trust is the beginning of effectiveness and forms the foundation of a principle-centered learning environment that places emphasis upon strengths and devises innovative methods for minimizing weaknesses. The transformation process requires an internal locus of control that emphasizes individual responsibility and accountability for change and for promoting effectiveness.

TEAMWORK

For many of us, there exists a dichotomy between how we see ourselves as persons and how we see ourselves as workers. Perhaps the following words of a Zen Buddhist will be helpful:

> The master in the art of living makes little distinction
> between his work and his play, his labor and his leisure,
> his mind and his body, his education and his recreation,
> his love and his religion. He hardly knows which is which.
> He simply pursues his vision of excellence in whatever he does, leaving
> others to decide whether he is working or playing. To him, he is always
> doing both.

Work can be and should be productive, rewarding, enriching, fulfilling, and joyful. Work is one of our greatest privileges, and it is up to leaders to make certain that work is everything it can and should be.

One way to think of work is to think of how a philosopher would lead an organization, rather than how a businessman or businesswoman would lead an organization. Plato's *Republic* speaks of the "philosopher-king," where the king would rule with the philosopher's ideals and values.

Paramount among the ideals that leaders need to recognize in leading an organization is the notion of teamwork and the valuing of each individual's contribution to the final product. The synergy produced by an effective team is greater than the sum of its parts.

The foundation of the team is the recognition that each member needs every other member, and no individual can be successful without the cooperation of others. As a young boy, I was a very enthusiastic baseball fan. My favorite player was the Hall of Fame pitcher Robin Roberts of the Philadelphia Phillies. During the early 1950s, his fast ball dominated the National League. My uncle, who took me to my first ballgame, explained that opposing batters were so intimidated by Roberts' fastball that they were automatic outs even before they got to the plate. My uncle claimed that Roberts was unstoppable. Even as a young boy, I intuitively knew that no one was unstoppable by himself. I said to my uncle that I knew how to stop Robin Roberts: "Make me his catcher."

EMPLOYEES AS VOLUNTEERS

Our institutions do not amount to anything without the people who make them what they are. And the individuals most influential in making institutions what they are essentially are volunteers. Our very best employees can work anywhere they please. So, in a sense, they volunteer to work where they do. As leaders, we would do far better if we looked upon and treated our employees as volunteers. The point was made earlier that we should treat our employees as if we had a covenantal relationship rather than a contractual relationship with them.

Alexander Solzhenitsyn, speaking to the 1978 graduating class of Harvard College, said this about legalistic relationships:

> A society based on the letter of the law and never reaching any higher fails to take advantage of the full range of human possibilities. The letter of the law is too cold and formal to have a beneficial influence on society. Whenever the tissue of life is woven of legalistic relationships, this creates an atmosphere of spiritual mediocrity that paralyzes men's noblest impulses. . . . After a certain level of the problem has been reached, legalistic thinking induces paralysis; it prevents one from seeing the scale and the meaning of events. (Solzhenitsyn, 1978, 17–19)

Covenantal relationships, on the other hand, induce freedom, not paralysis. As the noted psychiatrist William Glasser (1984) explains, "Coercion only produces mediocrity; love or a sense of belonging produces excellence." Our goal as leaders is to encourage a covenantal relationship of love, warmth, and personal chemistry among our employee volunteers. Shared ideals, shared goals, shared respect, a sense of integrity, a sense of quality, a sense of advocacy, a sense of caring—these are the basis of an organization's covenant with its employees.

THE VALUE OF HEROES

Leading with heart requires that an organization have its share of heroes, both present and past. We have often heard individuals in various organizations say that so-and-so is an "institution" around here. Heroes such as these do more to establish the organizational culture of an institution than any manual or handbook of policies and procedures ever could.

The senior faculty member who is recognized and respected for his or her knowledge as well as for his or her humane treatment of students is a valuable asset to an educational institution. He or she is a symbol of what the institution stands for. It is the presence of these heroes that sustains the reputation of the institution and allows the workforce to feel good about itself and about where it works. The deeds and accomplishments of these heroes need to be promulgated and need to become part of the folklore of the institution.

The deeds of these heroes are usually perpetuated by the "tribal storytellers" in an organization (Bolman and Deal, 1991). These are the individuals who know the history of the organization and relate it through stories of its former and current heroes. An effective leader encourages the tribal storytellers, knowing that they are serving an invaluable role in an organization.

These tribal storytellers work at the process of institutional renewal. They allow the institution to continuously improve. They preserve and revitalize the values of the institution. They mitigate the tendency of institutions, especially educational institutions, to become bureaucratic. These concerns are the concerns of everyone in the institution, but they are the special province of the tribal storyteller. Every institution has heroes and storytellers. It is the leader's job to see to it that things like manuals and handbooks do not replace them.

EMPLOYEE OWNERS

If an educational institution is to be successful, everyone in it needs to feel that he or she "owns the place." Everyone should think, "This is not the school district's school; it is not the school board's school; it is my school." Taking ownership is a sign of one's love for an institution. In his book *Servant Leadership*, Robert Greenleaf (1977) says, "Love is an undefinable term, and its manifestations are both subtle and infinite. It has only one absolute condition: unlimited liability!" Although it may run counter to our traditional notion of American capitalism, employees should be encouraged to act as if they own the place. It is a sign of love.

THE SIGNS OF HEARTLESSNESS

Up to now, we have dwelled on the characteristics of a healthy organization. In contrast, here are some of the signs that an organization is suffering from a lack of heart:

- When there is a tendency to merely "go through the motions."
- When a dark tension exists among key individuals.
- When a cynical attitude prevails among employees.
- When finding time to celebrate accomplishments becomes impossible.
- When stories and storytellers cease.
- When there is the view that one person's gain needs to be at another's expense.
- When mutual trust and respect erode.
- When leaders accumulate power rather than distribute it.
- When attainment of short-term goals becomes detrimental to the attainment of long-term goals.

- When individuals abide by the letter of the law, but not its spirit.
- When people treat students or customers as impositions.
- When accidents become more important than the substance.
- When a loss of grace, style, and civility occurs.
- When leaders use coercion to motivate employees.
- When administrators dwell on individuals' weaknesses rather than strengths.
- When individual turf is protected to the detriment of institutional goals.
- When diversity and individual charisms are not respected.
- When communication is only one-way.
- When employees feel exploited and manipulated.
- When arrogance spawns top-down decision making.
- When leaders prefer to be served rather than to serve.

LEADERSHIP AS A MORAL SCIENCE

Here we address how educational administrators and other leaders should be educated and trained for such a position. Traditionally, there has been only one answer: practicing and studying educational administration in order to learn the scientific basis for decision making and to understand the scientific research that underlies proper administration.

Universities train future administrators with texts that stress the scientific research done on administrative behavior, review various studies of teacher and student performance, and provide a few techniques for accomplishing educational goals. Such approaches instill a reverence for the scientific method but an unfortunate disregard for any humanistic and critical development in the art of administration (Foster, 1986). These approaches teach us how to lead with our minds, but not necessarily with our hearts.

I am suggesting a different approach. Although there is certainly an important place for scientific research in providing empirical support for administrative behavior, I suggest that educational administrators be *critical humanists* and also lead with their hearts. Humanists appreciate the usual and unusual events of our lives and engage in an effort to develop, challenge, and liberate human souls. They are critical because they are educators and are therefore not satisfied with the status quo; rather, they hope to change individuals and institutions for the better and to improve social conditions for all. I will argue that an *administrative* science be reconstructed as a *moral* science.

An administrative science can be empirical, but it also must incorporate hermeneutic (the science of interpreting and understanding others) and critical dimensions. Social science has increasingly recognized that it must be informed by moral questions. The paradigm of natural science does not always apply when dealing with human issues. As a moral science, the science of administration is concerned with the resolution of moral dilemmas. A critical and literary model of administration helps to provide us with the necessary context and understanding wherein such dilemmas can be wisely resolved, and we can truly actualize our potentials as administrators and leaders.

One's proclivity to be a critical humanist oftentimes depends on one's philosophy of how human beings behave in the workplace, whether one holds that human beings are basically lazy or basically industrious. As described by DePree (1989), instead of catching people doing something *wrong*, our goal as enlightened leaders is to catch them doing something *right*. Such an orientation is reflective of a leader who is in the humanist tradition, if not also in the critical tradition.

THE CRITICAL TRADITION

A post-positivist leader combines the humanist tradition with critical theory. Dissatisfaction with current administrative approaches to examining social life stems from administrations' inability to deal with questions of values and morality and its inability to fulfill its promise.

For example, Griffiths and Ribbins (1995) criticize orthodox theories because they "ignore the presence of unions and fail to account for the scarcity of women and minorities in top administrative positions." Erickson (1984) asks, "Why has educational research had so few real implications for educational policy?" An answer modeled on the natural sciences fails to address issues of understanding and interpretation. This failure precludes researchers from reaching a genuine understanding of the human condition. It is time, Erickson (1984) argues, to treat educational research as a moral science. The science of administration can also be a moral one, a critically moral one.

The term *moral* is being used here in its cultural, professional, spiritual, and ethical sense, not in a religious sense. The moral side of administration has to do with the dilemmas that face us in education and other professions. All educators face three areas of dilemmas: control, curriculum, and societal.

Control dilemmas involve the resolution of classroom management and control issues, particularly the issue of who is in charge and to what degree. Control dilemmas center around four questions: (1) Do you treat the child as a student, focusing narrowly on cognitive goals, or as a whole person, focusing more broadly on intellectual, aesthetic, social, and physical dimensions? (2) Who controls classroom time? In some classrooms, children are given latitude in scheduling their activities; in others, class activities follow a strict and mandatory schedule. (3) Who controls operations or the larger context of what it means to be human and how we resolve the inevitable conflicts that go on in the classroom? And (4) who controls standards and defines success and failure?

Similar dilemmas occur in the curricular domain and relate to whether the curriculum is considered as received, public knowledge, or whether it is considered private, individualized knowledge, of the type achieved through discoveries and experiments. These curricular difficulties also depend on whether one conceives of the child as a customer or as an individual. The customer receives professional services generated from a body of knowledge, whereas the individual receives personal services generated based on his or her particular needs and context.

A final set of dilemmas has to do with what children bring to school and how they are to be treated once there. One dilemma concerns the distribution of teacher resources. Should one focus more resources on the less talented, in order to bring them up to standards, or on the more talented, in order for them to reach their full potential? The same question arises in regard to the distribution of justice. Should classroom rules be applied uniformly, without regard to the differing circumstances of each child, or should family background, economic factors, and other sociological influences be considered? Should a teacher stress a common culture, or should ethnic differences and subculture consciousness be emphasized?

Much of teaching involves resolving such dilemmas by making a variety of decisions throughout the school day. Such decisions can be made, however, in a reflective or unreflective manner. An unreflective manner means simply teaching as one was taught, without giving consideration to available alternatives. A reflective approach involves an examination of the widest array of alternatives. Thus reflective teaching suggests that dilemmas need not be simply resolved but can be transformed so that a higher level of teaching expertise is reached.

This same logic can be applied to administration. Administration involves the resolution of various dilemmas, that is, the making of moral decisions. One set of dilemmas involves control. How much participation can teachers have in the administration of the school? How much participation can parents and students have? Who evaluates and for what purpose? Is the role of administration collegial or authority centered? The area of the curriculum brings up similar questions. Is the school oriented to basic skills, advanced skills, social skills, or all three? Should the curricula be teacher made or national, state, or system mandated? Should student evaluation be based on teacher assessment or standardized tests? What is authentic assessment?

Finally, an additional set of dilemmas pertains to the idea of schooling in society. Should schools be oriented toward ameliorating the apparent deficits that some students bring with them, or should they see different cultures and groups as strengths? Should schools be seen as agents of change, oriented toward the creation of a more just society, or as socializers that adapt the young to the current social structure?

Oftentimes, these questions are answered unreflectively and are simply resolved on an as-needed basis. This approach often resolves the dilemma but does not foster a real transformation in one's self, role, or institution. If administration and leadership encompass transformation, and I argue that it should, then an additional lens of structural functionalism must be found through which these questions can be viewed. We suggest that the additional lens be in the form of critical humanism and the Ignatian vision. In this context, then, administrative leadership can be viewed as a moral science.

THE IGNATIAN VISION

In addition to the critical humanist lens, another lens through which we can view leadership behavior is the Ignatian vision. More than 450 years ago, Ignatius of Loyola, a young priest born to a Spanish aristocratic family, founded the Society of Jesus, the Jesuits, and wrote his seminal book, *The Spiritual Exercises* (Ravier, 1987).

In this book, Ignatius suggested a way of life and a way of looking at things that has been propagated by his religious community and his other followers for almost five centuries. His principles have been utilized in a variety of ways. They have been used as an aid in developing one's own spiritual life, they have been used to formulate a way of learning that has become the curriculum and instructional method employed in the sixty high schools and the twenty-eight Jesuit colleges and universities in the United States, and they have been used to develop one's own administrative style. Together, these principles comprise the Ignatian vision.

There are five Ignatian principles we will explore here as a foundation for developing an administrative philosophy and leadership style: (1) Ignatius's concept of the *magis*, or "the more"; (2) the process of inquiry or discernment; (3) the implications of his notion of *cura personalis*, or "care of the person"; (4) the development of men and women for service to others; and (5) solidarity with the underserved and marginalized, or his concept of social justice.

At the core of the Ignatian vision is the concept of the *magis*, or "the more." Ignatius spent the greater part of his life seeking perfection in all areas of his personal, spiritual, and professional life. He was never satisfied with the status quo. He was constantly seeking to improve his own spiritual life, as well as his secular life as leader of a growing religious community. He was an advocate of "continuous improvement" long before it became a corporate slogan, long before people like Edwards Deming used it to develop his Total Quality Management approach to management, and long before Japan used it to revolutionize its economy after World War II.

The idea of constantly seeking "the more" implies change. The *magis* is a movement away from the status quo, and moving away from the status quo defines change. The Ignatian vision requires individuals and institutions to embrace the process of change as a vehicle for personal and institutional improvement. For his followers, frontiers and boundaries are not obstacles or ends, but new challenges to be faced, new opportunities to be welcomed.

Thus change needs to become a way of life. Ignatius further implores his followers to "be the change that you expect in others." In other words, we are called to model desired behavior, to live out our values, to be of ever fuller service to our communities, and to aspire to the more universal good. Ignatius had no patience with mediocrity. He constantly strove for the greater good.

The *magis* principle, then, can be described as the main norm in the selection and interpretation of information. Every real alternative for choice must be conducive to advancement toward perfection. When some aspect a particular alternative is *more* conducive to reaching perfection than other alternatives, we have reason to choose that alternative. Earlier, we spoke of the dilemmas that educators face every working day. The *magis* principle is a way of seeing that can help us in selecting the better alternative.

At first hearing, the *magis* principle may sound rigid and frightening. It is absolute, and Ignatius is unyielding in applying it, but not rigid. On the one hand, he sees it as the expression of our love of humanity, which inexorably seeks to fill all of us with a desire to not be content with what is less good for us.

On the other hand, he sees that humanity has not only its particular gifts, but also its limitations and different stages of growth. Making a choice that in the abstract would be more humane than it would be in concrete application would not be seen as adhering to the *magis* principle. For example, tracking students according to ability can be seen as humane in the abstract, but in concrete application it can be dehumanizing. Ignatius would advise us to focus on the concrete in resolving this dilemma.

In every case, then, accepting and living by the *magis* principle is an expression of our love of humanity. So, whatever the object for choice, the measure of our love for our neighbor will be the fundamental satisfaction we find in choosing and acting by the *magis* principle. Whatever one chooses by this principle will always be what one would most want as a moral and ethical member of the human race, no matter how undesirable the choice is in some other respect.

Closely related to the principle of the *magis* is the Ignatian principle of *inquiry* and *discernment*. In his writings, Ignatius urges us to challenge the status quo through the methods of inquiry and discernment. This is very similar to one of the tenets of critical theory. In fact, the Ignatian vision and critical theory share a number of beliefs.

For Ignatius, the reason for entering into inquiry and discernment is to determine God's will. However, this process is of value for the purely secular purpose of deciding on which horn of a dilemma one should come down. To aid us in utilizing inquiry and discernment as useful tools in challenging the status quo and determining the right choice to be made, Ignatius suggests that the ideal disposition for inquiry and discernment is humility. The disposition of humility is especially helpful when, despite one's best efforts, the evidence that one alternative is more conducive to the betterment of society is not compelling.

When the discerner cannot find evidence to show that one alternative is more conducive to the common good, Ignatius calls for judgment in favor of what more closely assimilates the discerner's life to the life of poverty and humiliation. Thus, when the *greatest* good cannot readily be determined, the *greater* good is more easily discerned by its position on humility. These are very demanding standards, but they are consistent with the *magis* principle and the tenets of critical humanism.

In addition to the *magis* principle, taking into account what has just been said about the norm of humility as a disposition for seeking the greater good, the relationship of the greater good norm to the greatest good norm can be clarified. The latter is absolute, overriding, and always primary. The greater good norm is secondary. It can never, in any choice, have equal weight with the first *magis* principle. It can never justify a choice of actual poverty and humiliation over riches and honors if the latter are seen to be more for the service of humanity in a particular situation, with all its concrete circumstances, including one's responsibilities to others and one's own stage of psychological and spiritual development. In other words, if being financially successful allows one to better serve the poor and underserved, that would be preferred to actual poverty.

Ignatius presents us with several other supplemental norms for facing our dilemmas. In choices that directly affect the individual person and the underserved or marginalized, especially the poor, Ignatius urges us to give preference to those in need. This brings us to his next guiding principle, *cura personalis*, or care of the person.

Another of Ignatius' important and enduring principles is his notion that, despite the primacy of the common good, the need to care for the individual person should never be lost. From the very beginning, the *cura personalis* principle has been included in the mission statement of virtually every high school and college founded by the Jesuits. It also impacts the method of instruction suggested for all Jesuit schools in the *Ratio Studiorum*, or the "course of study," in these institutions.

All Jesuit educational institutions are supposed to foster what we now refer to as a constructivist classroom, where the student is an active participant in the learning process. This contrasts with the transmission method of instruction, where the teacher is paramount and the student is a passive participant in the process. In the Ignatian vision, the care of the person is a requirement not only on a personal needs basis, but also on a whole person basis, which would, of course, include classroom education.

This principle also has implications for how we conduct ourselves as educational administrators. Ignatius calls on us to value the gifts and charisms of our colleagues and to address any deficiencies they might have and turn them into strengths. For example, during the employee evaluation process, Ignatius would urge us to focus on the formative or developmental stage of the evaluation far more than on the summative or employment decision stage. This would be one small way of applying *cura personalis* theory in practice.

The fourth principle that we wish to consider is the Ignatian concept of *service*. Once again, this principle has been propagated from the very outset. The expressed goal of virtually every Jesuit institution is *to develop men and women for others*. Jesuit institutions are called on to create a culture of service as one way of ensuring that the students, faculty, and staff of these institutions reflect the educational, civic, and spiritual values of the Ignatian vision.

Institutions following the Ignatian tradition of service to others have done so through community services programs and, more recently, service learning. Service to the community provides students with a means of helping others, a way of putting their value system into action, and a tangible method of assisting local communities. Although these have always been valuable benefits, until recently there was no formal integration of the service experience into the curriculum and no formal introspection concerning the impact of service on the individual.

During the last fifteen years, however, there has been a movement toward creating a more intentional academic relationship. Service has evolved from a modest student activity into an exciting pedagogical opportunity. In the past, service was viewed as a cocurricular activity; today it plays an integral role in the learning process. For example, at Saint Joseph's University in Philadelphia, accounting majors help senior citizens complete their income tax returns.

Since many institutions are situated in an urban setting, service gives them a chance to share resources with surrounding communities and allows reciprocal relationships to form between the university and local residents. Immersion in different cultures—economic, racial, educational, social, and religious—is the vehicle by which students make connections. Working side by side with people of varying backgrounds significantly impacts students, forcing them outside of their comfort zones and into the gritty reality of how others live. Through reflection, these students have the opportunity to integrate these powerful experiences into their lives, opening their eyes and hearts to the larger questions of social justice.

Peter-Hans Kolvenbach, the superior general of the Jesuit order, in his address on justice in American Jesuit universities in October 2000, used the words of Pope John Paul II to challenge Jesuit educators to "educate the whole person of solidarity for the real world," not only through concepts learned in the classroom, but also by contact with real people (Tripole, 2004).

Upon assuming the position of superior general in 1973 and echoing the words of Ignatius, Pedro Arrupe declared, "Our prime educational objective must be to form men and women for others; men and women who will live not for themselves but for others." In the spirit of these words, the service learning movement has legitimized the educational benefit of all experiential activity.

The term *service learning* means different things to different people, and debates on service learning have been around for decades, running the gamut from unstructured programmatic opportunities to structured educational philosophies. At Ignatian institutions, service learning is a bridge that connects faculty, staff, and students with community partners and their needs. It connects academic and student life views about the educational value of experiential learning. It also connects students' textbooks with human reality, and their minds and hearts with values and action. The programs are built on key components of service learning, including integration into the curriculum, a reciprocal relationship between the community agency and student, and structured time for reflection, which is very much related to the Ignatian principle of discernment discussed earlier.

Participation in service by high school and college students, whether as a cocurricular or course-based experience, correlates with where students are in their developmental process. Service work allows students to explore their skills and limitations, to find what excites and energizes them, to discover who they are and who they want to become, to put their values into action, and to use their talents to benefit others. By encouraging students to reflect on their service, these institutions assist in self-discovery. The reflection can take many forms: an informal chat, a facilitated group discussion, written dialogue, journal entries, reaction papers, or in-class presentations on articles.

By using critical reflection to integrate the service experience, the student develops self-knowledge of the communities in which he or she lives, as well as knowledge about the world that surrounds them. It is only after the unfolding of this service-based knowledge that students are able to synthesize what they have learned into their lives. Through this reflection, faculty members also have an opportunity to learn from and about their students. Teachers witness the change and growth of the students firsthand. In short, service to others changes lives.

The implications of service to others for administration are clear. Educational administrators can enhance their effectiveness not only by including the idea of service to others in their curricula, but also by modeling it in their personal and professional lives. The concept of administrators becoming the servant of the servants is what we have in mind here. Servant leaders do not inflict pain; they bear pain, and they treat their employees as volunteers, a concept explored earlier.

The Ignatian concept of service leads into his notion of solidarity with the underserved (poor) and marginalized and his principle of social justice. We begin with an attempt to achieve some measure of clarity on the nature and role of social justice in the Ignatian vision. According to some, Ignatius defined justice in both a narrow and a wide sense (Toner, 1991). In the narrow sense, it is "justice among men and women" that is involved. It is a matter of "clear obligations" among "members of the human family." Application of this kind of justice would include the rendering of not only material goods, but also immaterial goods such as "reputation, dignity, the possibility of exercising freedom" (Tripole, 1994).

Many of his followers also believe that Ignatius defined justice in a wider sense, "where situations are encountered which are humanly intolerable and demand a remedy" (Tripole, 1994). Here, the situations may be a product of explicitly unjust acts caused by clearly identified people who cannot be obliged to correct the injustices, yet the dignity of the human person requires that justice be restored. Such situations may also be caused by unidentifiable people.

It is precisely within the structural forces of inequality in society that injustice of this second type is found, where injustice is institutionalized, that is, built into economic, social, and political structures both national and international, and where people are suffering from poverty and hunger and from the unjust distribution of wealth, resources, and power. Critical theorists, of whom we spoke earlier, would likely prefer this wider definition of social justice.

It is almost certain that Ignatius did not only concern himself with injustices that were economic. He often cites injustices about "threats to human life and its quality," "racial and political discrimination," and loss of respect for the "rights of individuals or groups" (Chapple, 1993). When one adds to these the vast range of injustices enumerated in his writings, one sees that the Ignatian vision understands its mission of justice to include the widest possible view of justice, involving every area where there is an attack on human rights.

We can conclude, therefore, that although Ignatius was to some degree concerned about commutative justice (right relationships between private persons and groups) and distributive justice (the obligations of the state to render to the individual what is his or her due), he is most concerned about what today is generally called social justice, or justice of the common good. Such justice is comprehensive and includes the strict legal rights and duties described above, but it is more concerned about the natural rights and duties of individuals, families, communities, and the relationships of nations toward one another as members of the common family of human beings.

Every form of justice is included in and presupposed by social justice, but with social justice, it is the social nature of the person that is emphasized, as well as the social significance of all earthly goods, the purpose of which is to aid all members of the human community in attaining their dignity as human beings. Many of Ignatius's followers believe that this dignity is being undermined in our world today, and their main efforts are aimed toward restoring that dignity.

In the pursuit of social justice, Ignatius calls on his followers to be in solidarity with the poor. The next logical question might then be, who are the poor? The poor are usually thought to be those who are economically deprived and politically oppressed. Thus we can conclude that the promotion of justice means to work to overcome the oppressions or injustices that cause the poor to be poor.

The fallacy here, however, is that the poor are not necessarily oppressed or suffering injustice, and so Ignatius argues that our obligation toward the poor must be understood to refer to "inhuman levels or poverty and injustice," not "those possessing only modest resources," even though those of modest means are often poor and oppressed. So we conclude that the poor are those who are wrongfully impoverished or dispossessed (Society of Jesus, 1995).

An extended definition of the poor, one that Ignatius would espouse, would include any of the following types of people: (1) first are those who are economically deprived and socially marginalized and oppressed, especially, but not limited to, those with whom one has immediate contact and is in a position to positively affect; (2) the second group includes the poor in spirit, that is, those who lack a value system or an ethical and moral sense; (3) the third group includes those who are emotionally poor, those who have psychological and emotional shortcomings and are in need of comfort.

In defining the poor in the broadest way, Ignatius exhorts us to undertake social change in our role as leader, to do what we can do to bring an end to inequality, oppression, and injustice. Once again, we can see the close connection between the Ignatian principles of social justice and the main tenets of critical theory.

IMPLICATIONS FOR ADMINISTRATION

Each of the principles of the Ignatian vision noted above has a variety of implications for leaders. The *magis* principle has implications for administrators in that it calls for us to continually seek perfection in all that we do. In effect, this means that we must seek to continually improve. And, since improvement implies change, we need to be champions of needed change in our institutions. This means that we have to model a tolerance for change and embrace not only our own change initiatives, but also those in other parts of the organization. In effect, the Ignatian vision prompts us not to be merely leaders but transformational leaders.

The Ignatian principle of discernment requires educational administrators to be reflective practitioners. It calls on us to be introspective regarding our administrative and leadership behavior. We are asked to reflect on the ramifications of our decisions, especially in light of their cumulative effect on the equitable distribution of power and on the marginalized individuals and groups in our communities. In effect, the principle of discernment galvanizes the other principles embodied in the Ignatian vision. During the discernment process, we are asked to reflect upon how our planned behavior will manifest the *magis* principle, *cura personalis*, and service to the community, especially the underserved, marginalized, and oppressed.

The principle of *cura personalis* has additional implications. To practice the Ignatian vision, one must treat people with dignity under all circumstances. *Cura personalis* also requires us to extend ourselves by offering individual attention to the needs of all those with whom we come in contact. Being sensitive to the individual's unique needs is particularly required. Many times in our efforts to treat people equally, we fail to treat them fairly and equitably. Certain individuals have greater needs than others, and many times these needs require exceptions to be made on their behalf.

For example, if an adult student does not hand in an assignment on time but the tardiness is due to the fact that he or she is going through some personal or family trauma at the moment, the principle of *cura per-*

sonalis calls on us to make an exception in this case. It is likely that some would consider such an exception to be unfair to those who made the effort to complete the assignment in a timely manner, or that we cannot possibly be sensitive to the special needs of all of our students and colleagues. However, as long as the exception is made for everyone in the same circumstances, Ignatius would not perceive this exception as being unfair. In fact, the exception would be expected if one is practicing the principle of "care of the person."

The development of men and women for others requires one to have his or her own sense of service toward those with whom one interacts and that one also develop this spirit of service in others. The concept of servant leadership requires us to encourage others toward a life and career of service and to assume the position of being a servant of the servants. Ignatius thinks about leadership in terms of what the Gospel writer Luke calls the "one who serves." The leader owes something to the institution he or she leads. The leader is seen in this context as steward rather than owner or proprietor.

The implications of Ignatius' notion of social justice are myriad for the leader. Being concerned about the marginalized among our constituencies is required. We are called on to be sensitive to those individuals and groups that do not share equitably in the distribution of power and influence. Distinctions according to race, class, and gender should be corrected. Participative decision making and collaborative behavior is encouraged among administrators imbued with the Ignatian tradition.

Equitable representation of all segments of the school community should be provided whenever feasible. Leadership behavior such as this will assure that the dominant culture is not perpetuated to the detriment of the minority culture, rendering the minorities powerless. We will find in the succeeding chapters that the most effective figures of history incorporated many of the Ignatian concepts in their leadership behavior.

In my view, therefore, the Ignatian Vision completes situational leadership theory. Left on its own, situational leadership theory is secular and amoral. Utilizing situational leadership theory alone is as likely to produce a leader like Adolph Hitler as it is to produce a leader like Mahatma Gandhi. But by using the additional lens of the Ignatian vision through which to view situational leadership, we will ensure that we have more Gandhis and fewer Hitlers in the world.

SUMMARY

We began this book by suggesting that leaders are made, not born. We posited that if one could master the skills involved in effective leadership, one could become a successful administrator. In this chapter, however, we make the assertion that learning the skills involved in effective leadership is only part of the story. Leadership is as much an art, a belief, a condition of the heart, as it is mastering a set of skills and understanding leadership theory. A truly successful leader, therefore, is one who leads with both the *mind* and the *heart*.

When we look at the leadership behavior of the eleven individuals included in this study, we should observe not only whether their leadership practices conform to Bolman and Deal's situational leadership theory, but also whether they are leading with heart. I believe we will find that those leaders who are most comfortable operating in Bolman and Deal's human resource frame of leadership are most likely to be leading with heart. At any rate, the most effective leaders will be those who lead with both mind (structural and political frames) and heart (human resource and symbolic frames) and view their leadership behavior through the lens of the Ignatian vision or some similar moral compass.

Chapter 3

Jane Addams

Let us have faith that right makes might, and in that faith, let us to the end dare to do our duty as we understand it, with malice towards none, with charity for all, with firmness on the right as God gives us to see the right, let us strive on.

—Abraham Lincoln

BACKGROUND

Jane Addams was born in Cedarville, Illinois, at the dawn of the Civil War in 1860. She is remembered primarily as a founder of the Settlement House Movement. She and her friend Ellen Starr founded Hull House in the slums of Chicago in 1889. She was also the first American woman to receive the Nobel Peace Prize.

Addams was a pioneer in the areas of labor reform, especially laws that governed the working conditions for children and women, and was a charter member of the National Association for the Advancement of Colored People (NAACP).

Addams was especially devoted to her father. He taught her tolerance, philanthropy, and a strong work ethic. He encouraged her to pursue higher education, but not at the expense of losing her femininity. She attended the Rockford Seminary for women and excelled in her studies. She also developed strong leadership traits and her classmates admired her and followed her example.

Her parents decided that the best course was to take her and a few of her friends on a grand tour of Europe for a year or two. Perhaps Addams would discern a career or vocation for herself.

A couple of years later, Addams headed back to Europe. She did a lot of the usual sightseeing, but just by chance, while in England, she was introduced to the founders and the workings of Toynbee Hall, an all-male settlement house in the slums of London. It did not immediately strike her that social work was to be her calling. After this experience, she and her traveling companion, Ellen Starr, committed themselves to the idea of starting a settlement house in Chicago. Within a few years, Hull House was founded, offering medical care, child care, and legal aid to poor immigrants. It also provided classes for immigrants to learn English, vocational skills, music, art, and drama.

Addams realized that there would be no end to poverty and need if laws were not changed. The workers joined Addams in lobbying the state of Illinois to examine laws governing child labor, the factory inspection system, and the juvenile justice system. They worked for legislation to limit the working hours of women, mandate schooling for children, recognize labor unions, and provide for industrial safety.

Addams supplemented Hull House funding with revenue from lecture tours and the numerous articles that she wrote. She began to enjoy international acclaim. Her first book was published in 1910 and others followed biennially. Her biggest success in writing came with the release of the book *Twenty Years at Hull House*. It became her autobiography and brought her wealth.

Addams was also an ardent pacifist. In 1915, in an effort to avert war with Germany, she organized the Women's Peace Party and the International Congress of Women. This latter organization met at The Hague and made serious diplomatic attempts to thwart the war. In 1919 she was elected first president of the Women's International League for Peace and Freedom. She was a founding member of the American Civil Liberties Union (ACLU). These positions earned her much criticism, and she was accused of being a socialist, an anarchist, and a communist.

However, after World War I and especially during the Great Depression, her reputation was reinstated; she received numerous awards during this time including, in 1931, the Nobel Peace Prize. That year her health began to fail but she continued her work until her death in 1935 (Davis, 1973; Diliberto, 1999).

SITUATIONAL LEADERSHIP ANALYSIS

Situational models of leadership differ from earlier trait and behavioral models in asserting that no single way of leading works in all situations. Rather, appropriate behavior depends on the circumstances at a given time. Effective managers diagnose the situation, identify the leadership style or behavior that will be most effective, and then determine whether they can implement the required style.

Jane Addams was very adept at adapting her leadership behavior to the situation. Addams's basic and well-known image as a compassionate, self-effacing, and gentle woman could easily be misleading. When necessary, she was very capable of engaging in political frame leadership behavior, for example, in order to gain some advantage for the settlement movement or one of her many other causes.

In actuality, Jane Addams engaged in all five leadership frames. She expressed structural leadership behavior with her considerable business acumen; human resource behavior in her concern for humanity; political behavior as a fund-raiser and with her genius for compromise; symbolic behavior as a persuasive public speaker and writer; and moral behavior in the transformative effect she had on society in the area of social justice.

Jane Addams and her lifelong co-worker and friend, Ellen Gates Starr, made a great team because each possessed different but complementary traits that allowed them when working together to adapt their leadership behavior to any given situation. Addams was an introvert, while Starr was gregarious. Jane was more cerebral and Ellen was more intuitive. Together, they were an amazing team because they balanced their leadership skills so that between them they could respond effectively to virtually every situation they encountered.

Addams believed that the ability to adapt one's leadership behavior to the situation depended at least somewhat on one's gender. According to her, men and women were born with different leadership talents. "Woman," she often declared, "wishes not to be a man, nor like a man, but she claims the same right to independent thought and actions." On the other hand, she continued, "We still retain the old ideal of womanhood—the Saxon lady whose mission it was to bring bread unto her household. So we have planned to be bread givers throughout our lives believing that labor alone is happiness and that the only true and honorable life is one filled with good works and honest toil. We strive to idealize our labor and thus happily fulfill women's highest mission" (Diliberto, 1999, 74).

Lastly, Addams readily admitted that "life cannot be administered by definite rules and regulations" (Diliberto, 1999, 204). In order to address the concerns, dreams, and hopes of an individual or a group, one needs to really know what makes them tick. In other words, an effective leader cannot apply the same behavior in every situation. One needs to adapt his or her leadership behavior to the readiness or maturity level of one's followers. Jane Addams knew instinctively that one size did not fit all.

THE STRUCTURAL FRAME

Structural frame leaders seek to develop a new model of the relationship of structure, strategy, and environment for their organizations. Strategic planning, extensive preparation, and effecting change are priorities for them. Although Jane Addams was primarily thought of as a human-resource leader, we shall see that she made extensive use of structural frame leadership behavior.

Upon graduation from Rockford College, Addams wanted desperately to make her mark upon the world. She dreamed of leading her life differently from the stereotypical female of her day. To realize her dream, however, she knew that she had to utilize structural frame leadership behavior and devise a plan to attain it.

There was always an aura around Addams that separated her from other girls of her age. At Rockford College her dormitory room was known as "an available refuge from all perplexities" (Diliberto, 1999, 69). There was always a sense of gravitas surrounding Addams.

Displaying structural leadership behavior, Addams was a passionate college debater. In one particularly momentous debate, she finished just behind a fellow named William Jennings Bryan. Bryan, of course, became a U.S. congressman, a presidential candidate, and secretary of state, and would go on to become one of the most famous orators in American history. So Addams was in good company, indeed.

In another display of structural behavior, Addams was named class valedictorian. Her speech topic was Cassandra, the Trojan woman who had the gift of prophesy but was not taken seriously by her countrymen because she was a woman. Addams utilized structural leadership behavior and prepared herself so that she would not suffer Cassandra's fate.

Addams read George Eliot, Victor Hugo, John Ruskin, and Thomas Carlyle. Together, these authors influenced her thoughts on society's obligation to address the agonies of poverty and human suffering. As a result, Addams eventually settled in the urban slums of Baltimore and it was her experiences there that led to her interest in social work. In typical structural leadership fashion, she prepared herself for this work by visiting various other charitable organizations including London's Toynbee Hall, the world's first settlement house, which she had visited when in Europe.

During her second visit to Toynbee Hall, Addams had an epiphany. This experience was the defining moment in her decision to establish Hull House. It seems that while Addams was entertained by the bullfight spectacle she attended in Spain, her friends were appalled by it and by Addams's seemingly blasé attitude toward it. Almost as a penance for her ambivalence toward violence, Addams decided to dedicate her life to the settlement house movement.

Until the 1880s, most charities and philanthropic endeavors were based on giving relief in the form of food, money, clothes, shelter, and other services, based on the Good Samaritan Bible story. But typical of her structural leanings, Addams decided to approach charity in a very different way. She would go beyond providing the poor with material resources and provide them with the education, skills, and know-how that would allow them to rise above the cycle of poverty. She would not only give them fish, but also teach them how to fish.

In typical structural leadership style, Addams prepared herself well to carry on her social work. She attended Sunday school lectures on the subject, volunteered her services to various missions in Chicago, and taught social work at the Industrial Arts School there. So by the time she opened Hull House she was an expert in her chosen field. At Hull House she immediately established the first kindergarten in the city and started an adult education program that focused on job preparation and training.

Being the pragmatic structural leader that she was, Addams defied her critics and insisted that the Hull House residents fit into the American melting pot as soon as possible, believing that doing so was the immigrants' best chance to be assimilated into the American mainstream and attain the "good life."

As a result of Addams's use of structural leadership behavior, Hull House was a magnificent success, and the settlement movement in the United States flourished. When Hull House was founded in 1892, there were only six settlement houses in the nation. By 1910 there were more than a hundred, and their services were sorely needed in that workman's compensation and social security were still years away.

Perhaps this anecdote about Jane Addams's idiosyncrasies sums up her reliance on structural leadership behavior. It seems that in the preparation of her many speeches Addams had the habit of cutting up her pages of notes and rearranging the paragraphs and then piecing them together with straight pins—all this in the midst of the phenomenal and distracting activity always taking place around her. Thus, we have seen that Jane Addams utilized structural frame leadership behavior quite extensively and effectively.

THE HUMAN RESOURCE FRAME

Human resource leaders believe in people and communicate that belief. They are passionate about productivity through people. Considering her concern for social justice, it is difficult to imagine Jane Addams not extensively utilizing human resource leadership behavior. She expressed her human resource tendencies when she said, "I am a great admirer of Platonic love or rather pure sacred friendship. I think it is so much higher than what is generally implied in the word love" (Diliberto, 1990, 76).

There are myriad examples of Addams's use of human resource behavior. One of them involved an instance where she took the side of a known criminal. Addams was a friend of Flora Guiteau, whose insane half brother, Charles, assassinated President James Garfield. After the shooting, Flora had been a pariah in the community. Jane, however, demonstrated human resource leadership behavior and remained loyal to Flora.

In another instance, Addams urged an out-of-work shipping clerk to take a construction job that he was reluctant to take for health and safety reasons. Two days into the job, the man contracted pneumonia and died. The grieving Addams remained in touch with his wife and children and helped fund their living and educational expenses.

In a letter to her college friend and Hull House cofounder, Ellen Starr, Addams wrote, "I am convinced every day that friendship is after all the main thing in life. And friendship and affection must be guarded and taken care of just as other valuable things" (Diliberto, 1999, 99). In still another example of Addams engaging in human resource behavior, upon visiting one of her shelters for African Americans, she observed, "I had such a pleasant afternoon yesterday with the old women in the Colored Shelter. They are so responsive and confidential and begin to know me well enough now to be perfectly free" (Diliberto, 1999, 118). Addams was particularly sensitive to race and class distinctions. She was a pioneer in recognizing the value of ethnic pride, which led her to host a number of ethnic-themed dinner parties at Hull House.

Unlike most of the social elite of her time, Addams believed all children, even the poor, had the capacity to be productive citizens. This human resource-type conviction led her into the most successful battle of her early career, the outcome of which was the establishment of the first juvenile court system in the United States. Up to then, juvenile criminals were tried, convicted, and jailed as adults

Perhaps the way to end this section on Jane Addams's propensity for utilizing human resource leadership behavior is to note what her friend and co-worker Ellen Starr once said of Addams's faith in humanity, "Jane, if the devil himself came riding down Halsted Street with his tail waving out behind him, you'd say, 'What a beautiful curve he has in his tail'" (Davis, 1973, 115).

THE SYMBOLIC FRAME

In the symbolic frame, the organization is seen as a stage, a theater in which every actor plays certain roles and the symbolic leader attempts to communicate the right impressions to the right audiences. Like most successful leaders, Jane Addams made frequent and effective use of symbolic frame leadership behavior.

Addams used symbolic leadership behavior to establish her feminist image. Early on it became obvious to her that the only way to significantly impact society was to acquire women's right to vote. So, after some delay, she became a woman's suffrage exponent.

Addams drew strength in her endeavors from Abraham Lincoln's words at New York's Cooper Union in 1860: "Let us have faith that right makes might, and in that faith, let us to the end dare to do our duty as we understand it, with malice towards none, with charity for all, with firmness on the right as God gives us to see the right, let us strive on" (Diliberto, 1999, 211).

Using symbolic leadership behavior, Addams consciously chose to establish Hull House in the middle of an immigrant ghetto. It was to become an oasis in a desert—a place where young females dedicated themselves to social work, and poor immigrants could gain refuge from the horrors of the streets.

In another symbolic leadership move, Addams encouraged the publication of a cartoon in the Chicago newspapers depicting the "Hull House Revolution." A series of six black-and-white contrasting drawings showed the after-Hull House transformation of two immigrants, a man and a woman, from disheveled, slack-jawed new arrivals to prosperous, neatly attired citizens (Diliberto, 1999, 160).

Addams's generosity became part of her legend. It is said that her seamstress resorted to monogramming everything so she would be less likely to give it away. As a result, she became a nationally and internationally recognized symbol for rich liberal women. And Hull House became the beacon of hope on the hill.

Women felt a common bond with one another and Addams was their icon. In an example of political correctness, 1890s style, Addams struggled to avoid using the term *young lady*, favoring instead *sister*, and apologizing once to a friend for a lapse into "false social distinction, a remnant of former prejudice" (Diliberto, 1999, 180).

Addams was careful to use symbolic behavior to build up the image of the settlement house and social movements. For example, she made certain that she was one of the five people chosen to lead the Civic Federation of Chicago to try to settle the famous Pullman Strike of 1894. This appointment was precipitated by a speech to the Ethical Culture Society and published in the prestigious *International Journal of Ethics*. Addams also used this occasion to attack corrupt Chicago alderman John Powers. These two events helped put Jane Addams in the national spotlight.

In 1911, after the John Powers incident, in yet another symbolic move, Addams became keenly aware of the power of the vote and finally joined America's suffrage efforts, becoming vice president of the National American Woman Suffrage Association (NAWSA). In that same year, she starred in a silent movie with Anna Howard Shaw, president of NAWSA.

Through Addams's effective application of symbolic behavior through her publications and speeches, her reputation began to spread both nationally and internationally to the point where she had no trouble getting an appointment with President William McKinley in 1899 to get her friend Florence Kelly the job of general secretary of the newly formed National Consumers League in New York.

As the photograph at the beginning of this chapter depicts, with her graying hair pulled back into a bun she reflected the image of a very proper woman and one of great credibility—an image she consciously cultivated.

John Dewey, the legendary educator and philosopher, thought so much of Addams that he named his daughter after her. Their respect for one another was mutual, as a newspaper reporter once remarked:

"Dewey's faith in democracy as a guiding force in education took on both a sharper and deeper meaning because of Hull House and Jane Addams" (Davis, 1973, 97). And, according to most reporters, Jane Addams was the epitome of the nineteenth-century heroine who had "never had a selfish thought," "who was wonderfully gentile" and sexually pure and innocent, and who was thus in a sense superior to men. She was an early version of Mother Teresa (Davis, 1973, 103).

Her national reputation grew to the point where, "with a flag-waving, foot-stomping crowd cheering her every word, Addams stood at the podium of Chicago Coliseum on August 7, 1912, to second the nomination of Theodore Roosevelt for president on the Progressive Party ticket" (Diliberto, 1999, 260). This symbolic leadership behavior was prompted by Roosevelt's running on a platform "calling for the abolition of child labor; an eight-hour, six-day workweek for adults; housing reform; and the vote for women . . . all the things I was fighting for," said Addams (Diliberto, 1999, 260).

As a result of her effective use of symbolic leadership behavior, by 1914 her reputation was at its zenith. Her popular speeches and her best-selling books made her one of the most famous women in America. Honors came her way from every direction and she became the first woman to be awarded an honorary doctorate by Yale University.

Addams's almost universal popularity temporarily ended, however, when World War I broke out in Europe in 1914 and she strenuously opposed American involvement. As chairperson of the Women's Peace Party she became one of America's most ardent pacifists. Even her old friend Teddy Roosevelt denounced her as "one of the shrieking sisterhood," referring to her as "Poor Bleeding Jane" and "Bull Mouse" (Diliberto, 1999, 261).

Another public relations disaster was her support of Henry Ford's ill-fated "Peace Ship." Ironically, even though Addams was sick and did not sail on the Ford Peace Ship, her name was closely associated with the failure. Ford's promise that he'd "get our boys home by Christmas" never happened (Davis, 1973, 242). Addams and her friend Woodrow Wilson were now at odds. The country followed Wilson and not Addams. This turned out to be one of the only times that Jane did not use political frame leadership behavior and compromise—and it cost her.

A few years later, when the Red Scare captivated the nation, Addams's reputation lost even more of its luster. Because of her support of labor unions and the right of free speech, she was denounced as a communist. She was first on the list of subversives on the War Department's chart—a latter-day Jane Fonda.

However, Addams's popularity and influence were resurrected in the 1930s. The Great Depression had created doubts about the effectiveness and fairness of capitalism as an economic and political system.

Addams's commitment to the poor during the Depression made her once again an admired figure, and in the last years of her life, she was once again treated like a saint. In May 1931, Jane Addams was awarded the Nobel Peace Prize for her efforts to bring about world peace. Suffice it to say that Jane Addams's reputation as a role model for women everywhere was to a large degree the result of her astutely applied symbolic leadership behavior.

THE POLITICAL FRAME

Leaders operating out of the political frame clarify what they want and what they can get. Political leaders are realists above all. They never let what they want cloud their judgment about what is possible. They assess the distribution of power and interests. Among Jane Addams's considerable leadership skills was the ability to utilize political frame leadership behavior when appropriate.

Jane Addams had a natural ability to make friends and influence people. Her lifelong friend Ellen Gates Starr marveled at her ability to get along with almost anyone. Addams protested, "Ellen always overestimates my influence" (Diliberto, 1999, 123). But the reality was that Addams consciously utilized political frame behavior in order to advance the goals of the settlement movement and the other causes she championed. She even suddenly decided to join an established church because she knew a baptismal certificate would give her credibility with Chicago's most powerful clergymen, the city's reformists, and those she would need for ensuring the continuing existence of Hull House.

Addams's most notable trait was that of conciliation. She was no unyielding ideologue. She frequently engaged in political frame behavior and almost always sought a reasonable compromise. Her position in the textile strike of 1910 was perhaps typical. The strike began as an unorganized walkout of the Hart, Schaffner, and Marx factories in Chicago and spread to other plants. Addams played an important role in bringing the two sides together, but when the arbitration board was selected, her name was missing because there were those on *both* sides who felt she was too committed to the other side.

Addams was called "the Henry Clay (the Great Compromiser) of Chicago. She was by nature a conciliator who preferred the middle ground" (Davis, 1973, 134). Through her writing and her speaking, she created the image of being a great moral leader. She was credited with being the "feminine conscience of the nation" (Davis, 1973, 134).

Addams's political connections allowed her to attract Chicago's leading lights to lecture and support Hull House. Among them were the famous muckraker, Henry Demarest Lloyd, Clarence Darrow, Frank Lloyd Wright, and educator/philosopher John Dewey.

Addams became an intrepid fund-raiser for her varied causes. She once asked Helen Culver, the former owner of Hull House, to pay for two new bathrooms and repair of the front piazza of Hull House. Culver sent her one hundred dollars, and Addams responded in another display of political frame behavior by threatening to have the beautiful but crumbling piazza torn down if Culver did not increase her gift—which she did, of course.

In another example of her political skill, in a widely publicized 1891 internecine battle between women's suffrage advocates Bertha Palmer and Phoebe Couzins, which ended up in court, Addams consciously stayed out of the conflict, maintaining good relationships with all the women involved. Thus, despite their differences regarding suffrage strategies, they all remained ardent supporters of Hull House in particular and the settlement movement in general.

As mentioned earlier, Addams made it her goal to depose the powerful and corrupt Chicago alderman, John Powers. But, because of the political favors Powers was able to bestow on his constituents, she was not successful in getting him unseated. Powers wielded influence by bailing out constituents from jail, handing out patronage jobs, and providing turkeys to voters at Christmas. Addams learned the valuable lesson that, in order to achieve any political gains, women needed the right to vote. So she engaged in yet more political leadership behavior and at long last became a suffrage advocate.

THE MORAL FRAME

The moral frame is my own contribution to situational leadership theory. In my view, the moral frame completes situational leadership theory. Without it, leaders could just as easily use their leadership skills for promoting evil as for promoting good. Leaders operating out of the moral frame are concerned about their obligations and responsibilities to their followers. Moral frame leaders use some type of moral compass to direct their behavior. They practice what has been described as servant leadership and are concerned with those individuals and groups that are marginalized in their organizations and in society. In short, they are concerned about social justice.

The moral frame was one of Jane Addams's strongest . Even at the early age of fifteen, she was a devotee of the writings of Ralph Waldo Emerson, whose work appealed to her because, like her father, he celebrated "the demise of religious dogma and the rise of religion based on moral duty" (Diliberto, 1999, 52). She asserted that "the test of righteousness is good works, not divine election" (Diliberto, 1999, 52).

As the last quote would indicate, Addams was not necessarily a religious person, but her actions were guided by moral philosophy. In her religious quandaries, Addams was greatly influenced by the works of the humanists John Ruskin, Thomas Carlyle, Matthew Arnold, and Ralph Waldo Emerson. Their advocacy of the Golden Rule moved her.

In this regard, Addams was a typical late-Victorian intellectual who was suspicious of organized religion. She confessed that she could not accept the divinity of Christ. "I can work myself into a great admiration of his life, and occasionally I can catch something of his philosophy, but he doesn't bring me any nearer the deity," she remarked. "I feel a little as I do when I hear very fine music—that I am incapable of understanding" (Diliberto, 1999, 68).

Nevertheless, as we have seen, after years of religious questioning, she finally decided to be baptized in the Protestant faith. "At that moment something persuasive within made me long for an outward symbol of fellowship, some bond of peace, some blessed spot where unity of spirit might claim right of way over all differences" (Diliberto, 1999, 136).

Addams came to see that addressing the needs of the underserved was a moral issue. Underlying her ideologies was her moral commitment to the basic equality of all human beings. In this, she was ahead of her times in many ways, but especially in her views of diversity and social justice (Davis, 1973; Diliberto, 1999).

CONCLUSION

Jane Addams no longer provides an ideal role model for young women. For better or worse, her insistence on the special intuitive nature of women and her Victorian attitudes toward sex have partially separated her from the present generation. Her reform ideas and her attempt to promote peace often seem naive from the vantage point of the early twenty-first century. Yet her struggle to overcome the traditional image of women as solely housekeepers and her attempts to serve society still have meaning for all of us today.

In addition, those seeking to improve urban schooling and promote social justice and peace in the world can build on what Addams and her co-workers constructed. For educational leaders and others, we cannot help but be impressed by the life of Jane Addams. And one cannot ignore the journeys that led to her being perceived as a saintly heroine, and then a villain, and then finally a saint again. In all of this, Addams was very much the situational leader. She utilized all five frames of leadership behavior in almost equal measure. There is much to be learned from this "woman of the ages."

BEST DEAL

*Save 54%**

Name _____

Address _____

City _____ State _____ Zip _____

Email _____ (Include your email address to get notification of new features and offers.)

☐ **Payment Enclosed** ☐ **Bill Me Later**

Alaska

magazine

CHECK ONE:

☐ **20 Issues for $46**

☐ **10 Issues for $24**

Please allow 6-8 weeks for delivery. This offer good for new U.S. orders only.

*Based on regular newsstand price of $4.99 when you order 20 issues.

Visit our website at
www.**alaskamagazine**.com

BUSINESS REPLY MAIL

FIRST-CLASS MAIL   PERMIT NO. 22120   ESCONDIDO CA

POSTAGE WILL BE PAID BY ADDRESSEE

ALASKA
PO BOX 469013
ESCONDIDO CA 92046-9300

Chapter 4

Walt Disney

When you wish upon a star, your dreams come true!

—Walt Disney

BACKGROUND

Walt Disney was born in 1901 in Chicago, but almost immediately his family moved to a farm in Marceline, Missouri, where he lived out most of his childhood. He had a very early interest in drawing and art, selling small sketches and drawings to nearby neighbors for spending money when he was only seven years old.

The Santa Fe Railroad ran past the Disney farm, and Disney would often put his ear to the tracks to listen for approaching trains. These early experiences led to a lifelong fascination with trains and railroads. Later in life, he enjoyed inviting visitors to ride on his pride and joy—the miniature train he had built that ran through the grounds of his Hollywood home.

Eventually, the Disney family moved to Kansas City, where Walt continued to develop and enhance his talent for artistic drawing in the form of animated cartoon characters. His first real job involved producing short animated films for local businesses. However, Disney encountered financial difficulties and his company, Laugh-O-Grams, went bankrupt. The ever-optimistic Disney took the bankruptcy in stride and headed for Hollywood to start a new business. At the tender age of twenty-one, he joined his brother Roy, who was already living in California. Roy offered Walt moral support, and, as importantly, financial help. Pooling their human and financial resources, they launched their first business, working out of their uncle's garage.

In 1925, Disney married one of his first employees, Lillian Bounds. Three years later, he created what was to become his signature character, Mickey Mouse. Mickey Mouse made his screen debut in *Steamboat Willie*, which premiered at a small theater in New York on November 18, 1928. Mickey, who was initially named Mortimer, was an immediate hit and Disney's career took off as a result.

In 1937, *Snow White and the Seven Dwarfs*, the first full-length animated musical feature in the history of films, premiered in Hollywood. *Snow White* was followed by such Disney full-length animated classics as *Pinocchio, Fantasia, Dumbo, Bambi, Cinderella,* and *101 Dalmatians*.

In 1940, construction was completed on his Burbank Studio and Disney's staff grew to over a thousand, enabling him to branch out into nonanimated films. In 1945 the musical *The Three Caballeros* premiered, becoming the first film to combine live action with cartoon animation. Disney used the same process successfully in such other films as *Song of the South* and *Mary Poppins*.

In 1955, Disney's dream of a theme-based amusement park came true when Disneyland opened in Anaheim, California. Disney spent more than five years of his life developing and promoting the park. At the same time, however, being a master at multitasking, Disney ventured into nonanimated films such as *20,000 Leagues under the Sea*, *The Shaggy Dog*, *Old Yeller*, and *The Parent Trap*. In addition, he defied his film-making counterparts by branching out into television, hosting a weekly series named *Disneyland*, which along with serving as a hour-long commercial for Disneyland, spawned another of his most famous characters, Davy Crockett. In 1955, the studio's first daily television show, *The Mickey Mouse Club*, debuted. Disney, always a heavy smoker, died of lung cancer in 1966.

Today, Walt Disney's studios and theme parks have developed into a multibillion-dollar television, motion picture, vacation destination, and media corporation that carries his name. The company has annual revenue of over $40 billion, and as Disney often observed, it all started with a mouse (Gabler, 2006).

SITUATIONAL LEADERSHIP ANALYSIS

Situational models of leadership differ from earlier trait and behavioral models in asserting that no single way of leading works in all situations. Rather, appropriate behavior depends on the circumstances at a given time. Effective managers diagnose the situation, identify the leadership style or behavior that will be most effective, and then determine whether they can implement the required style. There are a number of indications in Walt Disney's professional and personal life that he practiced situational leadership.

Disney showed a penchant for practicing situational leadership in partnering with Ubbe Iwerks to found what would ultimately become Walt Disney Productions. Disney and Iwerks were polar opposites. Whereas Disney was gregarious and able to make friends and influence people very easily, Iwerks was the socially awkward visionary that complemented Disney perfectly. So if Disney lacked the leadership style needed in a certain situation, he depended on Iwerks to get him through.

Later in his career, Disney used his brother Roy to complement his leadership behavior in the same way he had utilized Iwerks. Roy Disney had worked in the financial industry his whole life. So Walt used Roy in business matters, considering himself the expert in animation and art, and Roy the expert in finances. Together they built Walt Disney Productions into the multibillion-dollar concern it has become.

In another instance of Disney's situational leadership thinking, he adapted his cartoons to the new trend of so-called realism in animation.

Disney was one of the first animators to supplant cartoon caricatures with more human caricatures. Realism convinced Disney to be more situational and move from exclusively short cartoon production to full-length animated movies like *Snow White* and *Cinderella*. And with realism came color. Disney became one of the pioneers of Technicolor animations. His first color release was the enormously successful *The Three Little Pigs*.

Disney was most situational in his leadership behavior when he perceived that one of his practices or characters was wearing thin with the public. For example, in the late 1940s, when interest in the cartoon character Mickey Mouse was beginning to fade in popularity, the Disney studio needed a new star. Disney decided upon what was to become the anti-Mickey, Donald Duck, who possessed many of the traits that Mickey Mouse had not. Of course, Disney once again displayed his situational tendencies when in the late 1950s he made Mickey Mouse more lifelike and the character experienced a colossal resurgence.

Disney was also situational in the way he dealt with employee relations. Initially, Disney was a very progressive employer, paying top dollar and providing benefits and working conditions far superior to anyone else in the industry. However, after an animators' strike in 1941, Disney once again practiced situational leadership. After the strike, Disney treated his employees in a more traditional way, stressing structural leadership behavior and eliminating human resource leadership behavior almost completely. Whereas there had been a benign friendliness in the past, there was now a fear of Disney among his employees.

During World War II, with entertainment films no longer a priority, Disney used situational leadership and negotiated with the U.S. government for their training-film and propaganda-film business. At this time, without traditional films to make but with a studio to maintain, he had become less a filmmaker and more of a salesman and public relations man. He attracted government work simply because of who he was. As a result, his public image changed from artist to CEO.

In a final example of how Walt Disney practiced situational leadership by varying his leadership behavior, once he assumed more control over the design and opening of Disneyland, he yielded some control of Walt Disney Productions. "I feel what's wrong is there's been too much of me. I feel like a dirty heel the way I pound, pound, pound" (Gabler, 2006, 539). As a result of adapting his leadership style in this way, over time, television, theme parks, and merchandizing, rather than motion pictures, accounted for almost 70 percent of Walt Disney Production's revenue.

The bottom line is that Disney refused to be fixated on one leadership paradigm. He constantly moved on to new and different things. For example, he was not particularly interested in building another amusement park on the East Coast. So when he built Disney World in Orlando,

Florida, along with the Magic Kingdom, he concentrated on building the prototype of a utopian town, an Experimental Prototype Community of Tomorrow, or EPCOT.

THE STRUCTURAL FRAME

Structural frame leaders seek to develop a new model of the relationship of structure, strategy, and environment for their organizations. Strategic planning, extensive preparation, and effecting change are priorities for them. Although he left much of the structural leadership decisions to his brother Roy, Walt Disney engaged in a fair amount of structural leadership behavior himself.

His service in World War I was sort of an epiphany for Disney as far as the use of structural behavior was concerned. He enlisted in the Red Cross and was stationed in Paris. Like many of his fellow G.I.s, he returned after the war more mature and serious. "I was settled," was the way he later put it (Gabler, 2006, 42). In his first animation job, for example, he was so intent on being successful that in his first week he never left his drawing board, not even to go to the men's room.

Adopting the cloak of structural leadership, Disney was very serious, almost obsessed, with whatever project he was working on at the moment. Initially, animation was his passion. Later, realism, full-length animated films, nonanimated films, and theme parks struck his fancy.

Disney also demonstrated his structural leadership in dealing with the quality of his animations. He was obsessive about the quality of anything that had the Disney name attached to it. Thus, he received consistently outstanding reviews for the quality of his animations. Regarding *Steamboat Willie*, *Variety* wrote, "Not the first animated cartoon to be synchronized with sound effects, but the first to attract favorable attention. This one represents a high order of cartoon ingenuity, cleverly combined with sound effects" (Gabler, 2006, 127). Even the *New York Times* called it "an ingenious piece of work with a good deal of fun" (Gabler, 2006, 127).

Again displaying his structural frame tendencies, Disney constantly expressed his belief that his success would be in making products that were so superior to his competitors that the public would all but demand to see and attend no other than Disney productions. His vision in this regard was particularly prophetic.

In the quest for domination of the animation industry, Disney displayed structural behavior as he sought to displace Felix the Cat with Mickey Mouse as the most recognizable cartoon character in America. He was able to do so because he was capable of more structural leadership behavior than Pat Sullivan, Felix's creator was. By 1930, Felix was displaced by Mickey Mouse mostly because Disney worked harder than Sullivan and created more positive changes to his cartoon character.

Again demonstrating his structural behavior tendencies, Disney never left the studio at five o'clock like the rest of the staff. He stayed until seven and often returned after dinner and continued his preparation, planning, analysis, and creativity.

Being the workaholic that he was, Disney would drive several of his animators to downtown Los Angeles to attend night classes at the Chouinard Art Institute. Not wanting to waste any time, he would return to the studio to work until it was time to pick them up. Eventually, Disney brought the training in-house to "the great Disney Art School." Disney hired a Stanford professor, Don Graham, to operate his school (Gabler, 2006, 174).

As his company grew and the plot lines for his stories no longer originated with Disney, he once again demonstrated his tendencies toward structural leadership behavior. He remained the "last word" on all of the scripts, but his real insight was his ability almost to inhabit his characters. He thought like them. As a result, his animators saw Disney as an inspiration. One of his animators said of him, "His greatest ability was to make people feel that what he wanted done was a terribly important thing to be done" (Gabler, 2006, 210).

Disney described in his own words his structural behavior leanings. "Believe it or not," he said, "I'd prefer to work harder and make less money, if I knew my efforts were going into pictures that were carefully planned and properly made" (Gabler, 2006, 225). As a result of this attitude, he attracted some of the best animators in the business. After making this statement, Disney operationalized his sentiments by facing his next challenge, which was the making of an animated feature set to classical music. *Fantasia* was the product of an unlikely collaboration between Disney and the great conductor and composer Leopold Stokowski.

In the same way that he utilized structural leadership behavior to continually blaze new trails in the film industry, Disney also did so in the entertainment industry in general. When he decided to build a theme park, he did so with the same dynamism and attention to detail with which he had labored over the making of *Snow White*, the first full-length animated film. "Look," he said, "the thing that's going to make Disneyland unique and different is the detail. If we lose the detail, we lose it all" (Gabler, 2006, 527). This attention to detail was displayed at the opening ceremonies of Disneyland, when it was said that Disney actually counted the number of rockets set off during the fireworks display to make sure that he got his money's worth. Suffice it to say, Walt Disney made frequent use of structural frame leadership behavior.

THE HUMAN RESOURCE FRAME

Human resource leaders believe in people and communicate that belief. They are passionate about productivity through people. Walt Disney was basically a kind and gentle man whose instinct was to frequently utilize human resource leadership behavior. We shall see, however, that because the situation changed somewhat, he used less of it in the latter part of his career than he had earlier. He became jaded after the 1941 animators' strike and made less frequent use of human resource behavior, especially with his employees, than he had in the past.

Still, even while Disney was struggling with finances and with Universal Studios over the production rights of his characters, he was utilizing human resource leadership behavior with his staff, which by 1926 had increased to ten. Disney has been described as a sociable, fun-loving, and sensitive person. In effect, he was a grown-up kid. On the job, he was the same way, often socializing with his animators and their families after hours.

Disney's passion for his work was an inspiration to his employees. "We'd hate to go home at night, and we couldn't wait to get to the office in the morning," said Disney's early partner, Ubbe Iwerks. "We all loved what we were doing and the enthusiasm got onto the screen" (Gabler, 2006, 136).

Even after the Disney staff increased to two hundred, he retained a sense of community. Working for him made them all feel "as if we were members of the same class at West Point" (Gabler, 2006, 157).

One of Disney's writers depicted the esprit de corps at the studio in the following way: "I couldn't understand it, but you'd do anything to get his approval. You'd work like a dog, like a little kid saying, 'Hey look at me, I'm doing something pretty terrific.' You'd do anything for a smile" (Gabler, 2006, 212).

Ever the human resource leader, Disney was always on the lookout for an employee who was being underpaid. He would then instruct the payroll office to make a salary adjustment. "His ambition," wrote a reporter, "is to pay his employees well enough for them to save for old age and still enjoy living as they go along" (Gabler, 2006, 241).

Disney believed that he was building the organization for his employees as well as for himself. Although this attitude could be described pejoratively as a form of paternalism, it is consistent with his lifelong quest for the utopia that he hoped that working at Walt Disney Productions would become.

But, as mentioned earlier, this attitude was forever altered after the 1940s animators' strike. Seeing it as a betrayal, Disney never again trusted his employees to give him the blind loyalty that he had cultivated and expected from them. From then on, he employed structural leadership behavior with his employees far more often than human resource behavior.

In a sense, however, he was appropriately utilizing the principles of situational leadership theory by varying his leadership behavior according to the situation and readiness level of his followers.

THE SYMBOLIC FRAME

In the symbolic frame, the organization is seen as a stage, a theater in which every actor plays certain roles, and the symbolic leader attempts to communicate the right impressions to the right audiences. In light of his profession, one could easily argue that Walt Disney's most prominent leadership frame was the symbolic one.

Walt Disney dedicated his life to show business, which by its very nature is the institutionalization of symbolic behavior, and he was magnificent at it. Detractors called his effect on American culture *Disneyfication*, meaning the substitution of a fake or symbolic world for the real one—but that was his intent. His mantra, "When you wish upon a star, your dreams come true," said it all. His cartoon characters, his movie heroes, and even his theme parks reflected the image that he consciously promoted—good, wholesome family entertainment at its finest.

Virtually every American alive has been impacted by Disney's symbolism. Whether it was through such characters as Mickey Mouse, Donald Duck, Davy Crockett, or Bambi, Disney has been able to leave an imprint on most people through his characters and their stories. Though he frequently reminisced about his Midwestern roots, Disney was right at home in Hollywood where he had the opportunity to operationalize his hope-filled philosophy of life.

As early as 1930, the Mickey Mouse Club was established as a symbolic vehicle for perpetuating the Disney vision and image. In that same year, Disney granted his first license to use Mickey Mouse on school writing tablets and pencils, again influencing young people in a subtle and symbolic way.

Although it was said that Mickey Mouse's persona was modeled on two of the stars of the day, Charlie Chaplin and Douglas Fairbanks, Mickey would eventually become a reflection of Disney himself. Disney described the image that he intended Mickey Mouse to project to young people: "He is never mean or ugly. He never lies or cheats or steals. He is a clean, happy little fellow who loves life and folks. He never takes advantage of the weak and we see to it that nothing ever happens that will curb his conviction that the world is just a big apple pie" (Gabler, 2006, 200).

By the time Disney got around to building theme parks, they, too, became a reflection or symbol of his creativity and his eternal optimism and hopefulness. He astutely used the weekly television show that he hosted,

The Wonderful World of Disney, not only to promote his theme parks but also to hone his public image.

On the show, he reinforced his image as "Uncle Walt," the calm, unpretentious, homespun, and charming relative who had come home to visit—"the perfect guest to have in one's living room each week "(Gabler, 2006, 512). Thus, virtually everything that Disney did, from making motion pictures, to creating and drawing cartoon characters, to creating theme parks, to creating his own personal image, was an example of symbolic frame leadership put into action—and he was a master at it.

THE POLITICAL FRAME

Leaders operating out of the political frame clarify what they want and what they can get. Political leaders are realists above all. They never let what they want cloud their judgment of what is possible. They assess the distribution of power and interests before they act. Although far from his dominant frame, Walt Disney used the political frame on the rare occasion when it was appropriate.

Disney demonstrated his astute use of the political leadership frame in one of his first negotiations, with film distributor Margaret Winkler, regarding the distribution rights for *Alice's Wonderland*. Winkler made her first offer to Disney, and in political frame style, he promptly rejected it, threatening to take his film to another distributor. The reality was that there was no such competitor. His ploy worked, however, and Winkler increased her offer. This pattern of negotiation was repeated many times during Disney's career.

Disney was not as successful, however, in his political machinations regarding *The Alice Comedies*. Virginia Davis, the actress who played Alice, was on an annual salary and Disney, in a cost-cutting measure, proposed that she be paid per project instead. Davis vehemently objected to the new arrangement and threatened to quit. Davis was so identified with the character that Disney was forced to capitulate for fear of losing his audience.

In another political episode, Disney learned his lessons well with the Charles Mintz situation at Universal Studios, where he had lost the rights to Oswald the Rabbit. So when he was negotiating with Universal for the distribution rights to *Steamboat Willie*, one of his first Mickey Mouse cartoons, he made certain to have some imaginary competitors in the wings as leverage. In fact, they weren't so imaginary, since he ultimately took his business to another studio.

In the late 1930s, Disney decided in typical political frame style to monopolize the animation industry and establish Walt Disney Studios as its acknowledged and unchallenged leader. The timing was right since

Mintz had lost his Universal contract, and the Fleischers, Disney's other major competitor, had lost theirs. "Now is our chance to get a hold on the industry," he told his brother Roy. "So let's take advantage of the situation" (Gabler, 2006, 130).

Later, Disney sensed that his new distributor, Columbia Pictures, was recalcitrant in its efforts to promote Disney cartoons, not to mention that it was skimming some of the Disney profits. But this time Disney was determined not to be hoodwinked the way he had been with Mintz and Universal Studios. Instead, he engaged in his own version of political frame behavior and began negotiating with the much larger United Artists Studios even before his contract with Columbia had ended.

In still another instance of utilizing political frame leadership behavior, in preparing for *Snow White*, Disney set his sights on a particularly good animator, Bill Tytla. After a year of negotiating with no sign of a favorable outcome, Disney decided to use some reverse psychology, indicating that it might be best if Tytla did not come to Disney Studios, because "to bring a stranger in without rating his ability with the others, would be an injustice to members of our own animating staff" (Gabler, 2006, 226). Presented with this challenge, Tytla immediately took the job with Disney, and at a lower rate of pay than he was currently making.

At about this same time, Charlie Chaplin offered to give his friend Disney all his "records and experience," and his ledgers from the classic silent movie *Modern Times*, which allowed Disney to pressure RKO Pictures to "go out and ask Chaplin prices." Disney subsequently wrote to Chaplin, "Your records have been our Bible—without them, we would have been as sheep in a den of wolves" (Gabler, 2006, 271).

As mentioned earlier, in the late 1930s unionization in the animation industry had begun to rear its ugly head. Whereas Disney's paternalism was well received up to that point, from then on employees began to see it as exploitation. The 1941 animators' strike, led by one of Disney's most trusted employees, jolted Disney and he never again had the same attitude toward his employees. From then on, he used political and structural behavior rather than human resource behavior toward them.

Disney used political frame behavior in financing his theme park idea. He had found a source of funding in the unlikely form of television, which was commonly thought of as the enemy of Hollywood. He promptly negotiated a contract with ABC for a weekly broadcast of a show he hosted, *The Wonderful World of Disney*. He used the proceeds from the weekly series to finance Disneyland and also used the series as an extended commercial so that the park was filled from its grand opening to the present day.

In one final instance of Disney's wise use of political frame leadership behavior, in 1954, with *Lady and the Tramp* due to be released, neither of the Disney brothers wanted to leave its success to the vagaries of the financially and otherwise shaky RKO Pictures. Thus, they formed their own distribution company, Buena Vista, and were finally able to control their own destiny.

THE MORAL FRAME

The moral frame is my own contribution to situational leadership theory. In my view, the moral frame completes situational leadership theory. Without it, leaders could just as easily use their leadership skills for promoting evil as for promoting good. Leaders operating out of the moral frame are concerned about their obligations and responsibilities to their followers. Moral frame leaders use some type of moral compass to direct their behavior. They practice what has been described as servant leadership and are concerned with those individuals and groups that are marginalized in their organizations and in society. In short, they are concerned about care of the person, equality, fairness, and social justice.

It is obvious from examining Walt Disney's leadership behavior that he operated out of the moral frame in virtually all of his personal and professional activities. We have seen how, at least initially, he paid his employees significantly more than his competitors paid theirs. He was a devoted family man who, with his lifelong mate, Lillian, raised his children, instilling in them the traditional values that he cultivated in his screen characters and in himself. Given the fact that he was and is recognized as the King of Family Entertainment, it is obvious that he faithfully followed a moral compass (Gabler, 2006).

CONCLUSION

Walt Disney's success in the entertainment business was no accident. He consciously utilized a variety of leadership behaviors in making Walt Disney Studios the dominating entity it has become. He utilized structural leadership behavior in meticulously planning what he wanted to achieve in animation, full-length pictures, and later his theme parks. Until the 1941 animators' strike, he effectively utilized human resource leadership behavior to engender loyalty in his employees. After the strike, he astutely adjusted his leadership behavior to include more structural behavior and less human resource behavior in dealing with his employees.

Disney's use of symbolic leadership was a requisite for success in the entertainment business, and his success was amazing. We saw how he learned the value of political frame leadership the hard way, through harsh experience. However, he learned his lesson well, and by the end of his career he had become a master in its use. He could be considered the poster boy for the use of situational leadership theory. There is much for leaders and aspiring leaders to learn from examining and emulating the leadership behavior of Walt Disney.

Chapter 5

Thomas Edison

If a man can write a better book, preach a better sermon, or make a better mousetrap than his neighbor, though he build his house in the woods, the world will make a beaten path to his door.

—Ralph Waldo Emerson

BACKGROUND

Thomas Edison was born in 1847 in Milan, Ohio. He did not have traditional classroom education, being home-schooled by his mother, who was previously a teacher. Edison was partially deaf from childhood and became a telegraph operator as a result of saving little Jimmie Mackenzie from being hit by a derailed train. Jimmie's father, stationmaster J. U. Mackenzie, was so grateful that he hired Edison as his apprentice and taught him to be a telegraph operator. Edison's deafness was a blessing in disguise as it prevented him from being disturbed by the other telegraph machines in the room.

This early training enabled Edison to experience a long string of inventive and entrepreneurial successes. These talents eventually led him to found General Electric and thirteen other companies. He earned his first patent in 1869 with the invention of the first electric voting machine.

In 1871, Edison married Mary Stilwell, whom he had met as an employee at one of his shops. They had three children, but Mary died young, in 1884. In 1886, Edison married twenty-year-old Mina Miller. They had three children and remained married until Edison's death.

The invention that made Edison famous was the phonograph machine, which he invented in 1877. His first phonograph was recorded on tinfoil around a grooved cylinder and had poor sound quality and could only be replayed a few times. Nevertheless, the phonograph was so novel and affordable that it captivated the nation.

His most significant innovation, however, was the establishment of the first research-and-development laboratory. It was the first industrial complex built to ensure the continuous production of technological innovations and improvements. At this laboratory, located in Menlo Park, New Jersey, Edison invented the first commercially viable, incandescent light bulb.

Edison's incandescent light bulb consisted of a high-resistance light bulb in a total vacuum with a tungsten filament that would burn for hundreds of hours. Also around this same time, Edison invented and developed the carbon microphone, which was used in all telephones, along with the Bell receiver, until the 1880s. The carbon microphone was also used in radio broadcasting and public address systems through the 1920s.

Edison patented an electric distribution system in 1880, which was essential if his invention of the light bulb was to be maximally profitable. He established his Pearl Street station in New York, which in 1882 provided direct electric current to its first fifty-nine customers in lower Manhattan.

Another invention that Edison patented was the fluoroscope, or X-ray machine. German physicist Wilhelm Röntgen's screens were capable of producing only very faint images. The fundamental design of Edison's fluoroscope is still in use today. Coincidentally, Edison nearly lost his eyesight while developing the fluoroscope.

On a personal level, along with his home in West Orange, New Jersey, Edison bought property in Fort Myers, Florida, and built a winter retreat and laboratory there in the 1880s. His next-door neighbor was his good friend Henry Ford. They had a symbiotic relationship, with Edison providing technological advice for Ford's automobiles, and Ford providing manufacturing advice to Edison. They remained friends throughout Edison's life.

Active in business right up to his passing, Edison died on October 18, 1931, in his home in West Orange at the age of eighty-four (Baldwin, 1995).

SITUATIONAL LEADERSHIP ANALYSIS

Situational models of leadership differ from earlier trait and behavioral models in asserting that no single way of leading works in all situations. Rather, appropriate behavior depends on the circumstances at a given time. Effective managers diagnose the situation, identify the leadership style or behavior that will be most effective, and then determine whether they can implement the required style.

Although we will find that Thomas Edison was basically a structural leader who was constantly developing new models of the relationship of structure, strategy, and environment for his company, there is much evidence that he saw the value in practicing situational leadership and varying his leadership behavior depending on the circumstances. In addition to structural leadership behavior, he displayed human resource, symbolic, and political frame behavior when the need arose.

Early in his career, Edison separated his invention activities from his manufacturing efforts because of their different focus. He was always trying to find a better way to be a more creative and effective inventor. Then, he continually sought the most efficient method to implement his ideas, in conformity with his will and the production process.

In this manner, Edison was defining, delineating, and examining the dynamics of what we now refer to as R & D—research and development. The key being that he and all around him had to remain open and flexible to any emerging paradigm. Thus Edison was keenly cognizant of the need not only to utilize all of the four leadership frames described by Lee Bolman and Terrance Deal (1991), but also to seek moderation *within* each of the frames.

Edison often used the invention of the automobile as a metaphor for the need to be situational and farsighted in responding to anything new. Although he saw the automobile as having an overall positive effect on society, almost prophetically, he declared, "Automobiles will change every detail of movement in our cities and thus present one of the biggest *problems* in the modern city" (Baldwin, 1995, 373).

At that time in history, Edison held that we had only barely begun to envision the monumental impacts of the automobile. In that light, he was the first to suggest "express streets," overpasses, and underpasses, and other innovations to relieve traffic congestion. He also anticipated the urban sprawl and global warming that would eventually accompany the automobile. He suggested that we never get locked into a certain paradigm. As a result of his situational thinking, Edison always seemed to have an innovative response for every question that arose (Baldwin, 1995).

However, there are indications that Edison acquired his situational mindset the hard way—through unfortunate experiences. For example, while watching phonograph cylinder sales plummet by 90 percent, he stubbornly refused to allow his son to purchase a record-making company, failing to see that the situation had changed and that the phonograph record would eventually replace his phonograph cylinder. A similar instance of not being situational took place when Edison failed to see the advantages of alternating current over direct current. Still, despite these rather minor lapses, Edison was an enthusiastic disciple of situational leadership theory well before it became codified by the likes of Bolman and Deal.

THE STRUCTURAL FRAME

Structural frame leaders seek to develop a new model of the relationship of structure, strategy, and environment for their organizations. Strategic planning, extensive preparation, and effecting change are priorities for them.

As noted above, Thomas Edison could be described as the quintessential structural frame leader. He was the author of the often repeated adage that "Those who can, do, and those who can't, teach." There are many examples that show him as an industrious, passionate, and conscientious man not limited by the twenty-four-hour day and his strong preference for structural frame leadership behavior. "I was small and industrious," he wrote. "I could fill the position all right. . . . Night jobs suited me as I could have the whole day to myself. . . . I seldom reached home before 11:30 at night" (Baldwin, 1995, 37).

Edison continued to utilize structural behavior in both his professional and personal life. As a telegraph operator for Western Union in New York City when he was only nineteen years old, Edison began the faithful recording of every technological advancement that he discovered. As a result, he is justly known and revered for having registered more than one thousand patents in the course of his sixty-year career.

His use of structural behavior crossed over from his inventor's role to his management role. Edison was a hands-on manager. He refused to leave the telegraph office because he needed to "watch the men and give instructions" (Baldwin, 1995, 50). He set very specific and oftentimes unreasonable standards for himself. "Sleep," he said, "was a scarce article" for him at the time (Baldwin, 1995, 51).

Nevertheless, Edison's six-day, ten-hours-a-day work week paid off with the invention of the phonograph and incandescent light bulb. Rather than springing fully formed from the workshop of his imagination, however, the phonograph and the light bulb had been gradually developed through many hours of plain hard work. His persistence, industriousness, and other such traits are associated with a structural frame leader. "Nature contains certain materials which are capable of satisfying human needs," he would say, "but those materials must, with rare and minor exceptions, be won by labor, and must be fitted to human use by more labor" (Baldwin, 1995, 127).

When Edison finally developed the long-lasting tungsten filament and patented the light bulb, he distinguished himself from other inventors by monopolizing the production of the dynamos that generated the electricity and the wiring that carried the electricity to his light bulbs. The Edison Electric Light Company (later General Electric) was organized "to own, manufacture, operate and license the use of various apparatus used in producing light, heat, or power by electricity" (Baldwin, 1995, 103).

Edison even took a structural frame approach to nonwork related issues. In his later years, the Wizard of Menlo Park was asked about his thoughts on ending wars. He replied that peace conferences and the League of Nations alone would not do it. He believed that the key to ending wars was "preparation." The way to make war impossible, he declared, was for nations to go on experimenting and keeping up to date with inventions, so that war would be unthinkable. In effect, he was forecasting the "atomic age," when leaders would be reluctant to wage war in light of the probable consequences. Suffice it to say, there were a plethora of instances in Thomas Edison's life that showed him to be a prototypical structural frame leader (Baldwin, 1995).

THE HUMAN RESOURCE FRAME

Human resource leaders believe in people and communicate that belief. They are passionate about productivity through people. Although human resource leadership behavior could never be construed as one of Thomas Edison's greatest strengths, there is evidence that he used it when the situation called for it.

One needs to remember that during the post–Industrial Revolution era of the late 1800s and the early 1900s, human resource behavior was not as expected by one's followers as it is in today's age of political correctness—the *situation*, indeed, has changed. Still, Edison did not have the reputation for exploiting his employees that many of his counterparts had, the reason being that he frequently applied human resource leadership behavior when appropriate.

Edison began applying human resource behavior and becoming more collegial as his career progressed. While working for Western Union, he joined his coworkers to form the local chapter of the National Telegraphic Union. The NTU was founded to give the telegraph operators a voice in their industry and a way of addressing the many work grievances that they encountered in this unregulated era. In the process of his union organizing he was to find the love of his life, Mary Stilwell, whom he married on Christmas Day in 1871.

Edison used human resource behavior in cultivating his relationship with Charles Batchelor. Batchelor was one of Edison's first collaborators and friends and remained so for over twenty-five years. Batchelor referred endearingly to Edison as "The Old Man," although a number of their co-workers were older than Edison.

While, on the one hand, he maintained a classically hierarchal structure in order to efficiently make what needed to be made and maintain his authority, Edison was "compelled," as he put it, to apply a human resource dimension by democratically wandering up and down the aisles. His ubiquitous presence was encouraging to the welders and die cutters bent over their wooden workbenches (Baldwin, 1995, 57).

In a community atmosphere at Menlo Park, where Edison also lived, his colleagues in upper management shared houses on the property. To improve morale and encourage camaraderie, he hired a distant relative to run a boarding house on site, where the single men would have a home away from home with a family atmosphere.

Edison also practiced human resource behavior in his personal life. Although he somewhat neglected his wife and children because of his workaholic nature, when he was with them, he showed his human touch. Marion, his daughter, loved to make surprise visits to the laboratory, which she saw as an exotic playland. There she doted on her father until he gave her a dime to buy some candy. When his second wife, Mina, made an appearance in the lab, he would conduct whimsical experiments with her.

Many of his closest colleagues were drawn to Edison because of his penchant for human resource behavior. Francis Upton, who was instrumental in the development of the light bulb, being the first to place a filament in a vacuum, was attracted to Edison by his sensitivity toward others. A typical day for Edison would include a good measure of both structural and human resource behavior. He would start at dawn, work through lunch at his roll-top desk, then go on to dinner, and then share more laughs with his crew at Delmonico's in Manhattan.

Compared to the robber barons of his generation, Edison paid his employees well. He also respected them, empowering them to be creative and make independent decisions. He constantly pointed out to his audiences that "when you honor me, you are also honoring the vast army of workers, but for whom my work would have gone for nothing" (Baldwin, 1995, 397).

Finally, Edison demonstrated his human resource behavior inclinations in his relationship with his lifelong friend and confidant, carmaker Henry Ford. They had mutual respect for one another. Edison honored the younger Ford for his knowledge of the production process. Likewise, Ford respected Edison for his creativity. Their friendship became so close that they purchased homes next door to one another in Fort Myers, Florida.

THE SYMBOLIC FRAME

In the symbolic frame, the organization is seen as a stage, a theater in which every actor plays certain roles, and the symbolic leader attempts to communicate the right impressions to the right audiences. Thomas Edison was quite astute at creating and sustaining his positive image through the thoughtful and strategic use of symbolic leadership behavior.

One of Edison's favorite quotes, and the one that we began this chapter with, was Ralph Waldo Emerson's "If a man can write a better book, preach a better sermon, or make a better mousetrap than his neighbor, though he build his house in the woods, the world will make a beaten path to his door." Although he truly believed the sentiments expressed in these words, he was not one to wait patiently for folks to come to his door.

On the contrary, he was very proactive in promulgating his image as the Great Inventor. Relocating his research facility to Menlo Park was symbolic in that Edison wanted to move from Port Huron, Michigan, where he had been bullied as a child, a place where his mother was buried, where he had spent thousands of dollars helping his aimless brother avoid bankruptcy, to the idyllic environs of New Jersey.

Edison frequently used symbolism in his advertisements for his products. For example, an ad for his electric pen, which duplicated letters, was romantically portrayed. The pen was not shown in the ad. Rather, an embracing couple was seen, surrounded by words floating overhead: "Like kissing, every succeeding impression is as good as the first, endorsed by everyone who tried it! Only a gentle pressure used" (Baldwin, 1995, 71).

Edison often used symbolic behavior in coining memorable phrases. A classic Edison maxim is: "Genius is 1 percent inspiration and 99 percent perspiration." He also gave this standard advice to young people: "Don't go to college; get into a shop and work out your own salvation," echoing Benjamin Franklin's declaration to the American worker: "Keep your shop and your shop will keep you" (Baldwin, 1995, 51).

In his competitive efforts to outdo Alexander Graham Bell and other inventors, Edison offered the press an adversarial image that would become all too familiar. He projected the image of a young man so often ridiculed that it had no effect except to motivate him to want to excel even more. In effect, he portrayed himself as the unappreciated underdog.

So, because of his symbolic leadership behavior, it was "Professor" Thomas Edison, the Wizard of Menlo Park, the New Jersey Columbus, the Napoleon of Invention, that the masses were coming to see at Menlo Park, or as it came to be known, Monte Cristo's Cave. Although he would never admit it, Edison had a steak of P. T. Barnum in him.

To add to his budding reputation, Edison became a member of the National Academy of Sciences at an early age. Viewing the stars through the mighty telescope, Edison identified strongly with Galileo and his subsequent excommunication from the Catholic Church and the way Edison's invention of the phonograph was considered by many to be but a popular toy. On one of his visits to the Observatory in Washington, D.C., Edison was invited to the White House by President Rutherford B. Hayes for a private phonograph session. Of course, in what had become his symbolic frame style, Edison made certain that the press was also invited.

So established had Edison's image become, that his staff at a Christmas party at Menlo Park, in the midst of the development of the light bulb, composed a tribute to their boss, set to the tune of Gilbert and Sullivan's *H.M.S. Pinafore*:

> I am the Wizard of the electric light
> And a wide-awake Wizard, too.
> I see you're rather bright and appreciate the might
> Of what I daily do.
> Quadruplex telegraph or funny phonograph,

It's all the same to me;
With ideas I evolve and problems that I solve
I'm never ever stumped, you see.
What, never?
No, never!
What, never?
Well, hardly ever! (Baldwin, 1995, 114)

Menlo Park, at Edison's direction, now became an electric showplace. Further demonstrating his symbolic frame tendencies, Edison had transformed Menlo Park into a symbol of his huge impact on America and the rest of the world.

Even when immersed in his work, Edison was quick to respond and never too preoccupied with research to engage in image building. In fact, he was one of the first captains of industry to hire a public relations director, John Michels, a former *New York Times* writer (Baldwin, 1995).

In an era of atheistic and agnostic scientists, Edison was careful to project the image of a believer. He held that man's intelligence came from a greater power. When asked if he believed in an intelligent Creator and personal God, Edison replied, "Certainly!" His belief in "intelligent design" was depicted in the opening scene of the MGM classic *Edison the Man*. Spencer Tracy, as Edison, is surrounded by a group of children asking questions, and with great humility he smiles and looks up, saying, "That's the real Inventor!"(Baldwin, 1995, 172).

Edison also used symbolic leadership behavior in his running feud with George Westinghouse over whose electric dynamo was better. Once, Westinghouse demonstrated the effectiveness of his dynamo by generating the electricity necessary to execute a criminal in the electric chair. After that, Edison referred to prisoners who were executed this way as "being Westinghoused" or having been "condemned to the Westinghouse" (Baldwin, 1995, 202).

In another instance of using symbolic behavior, Edison's name was removed from the Edison General Electric Company letterhead because of corporate infighting. Even though he was still salaried and on the board of directors of General Electric, he led the public to think that the white-haired Wizard of Menlo Park was once again being taken advantage of by the hated robber barons.

Another incident that added to the Edison folklore took place at his winter home in Florida. At Fort Myers, the spring training facility for the Philadelphia Athletics, Kid Gleason challenged Edison to hit his curve ball. Having missed the first pitch, Edison hit a blooper into the outfield on his second try. Gleason yelled, "Sign him up, Connie [Mack]! After missing the first curveball, he must have *invented* a way to hit the second one" (Baldwin, 1995, 369).

Edison continued inventing until he was eighty-five, during which time he created his greatest invention of all—his final persona.

THE POLITICAL FRAME

Leaders operating out of the political frame clarify what they want and what they can get. Political leaders are realists above all. They never let what they want cloud their judgment about what is possible. They assess the distribution of power and interests. As we shall see, Thomas Edison made frequent and intelligent use of the political frame.

Even with his earliest underwriters, Edison set the tone and terms for the ways in which he needed to do business and conduct his work. The fact that he held an astounding 1,093 U.S. patents is testimony to his astute use of political behavior.

For example, in 1875, while working for Western Union, Jay Gould offered Edison the staggering sum of $30,000 for the right to his laboratory. Under some financial strains at the time, Edison believed that it was in his best interest to sign the contract, which he did. Out the door went any loyalty to Western Union.

As mentioned earlier, Alexander Graham Bell and Edison were fierce competitors. Edison found that Bell's telephone messages could only be sent a short distance. There had to be a way to make the sound travel farther. If Edison could find the way, he could successfully circumvent Bell's patent. Eventually Edison found that way and, outwitting Bell, ended up with the patent for the telephone *receiver*, a version of which is used to this day. However, as was his practice in patent disputes, Edison displayed some human resource leadership behavior and reached a settlement with Bell, to the benefit of both great inventors, resulting in the United Telephone Company of Great Britain.

Edison even outwitted the unions by using political frame behavior. He withstood the threat of a strike, whereby all the lights in New York would have been in danger of burning out, by threatening to relocate and consolidate major manufacturing functions outside of the big cities like New York, where unionization was less likely to take place. This tactic worked, as the union capitulated.

Yet another example of Edison's savvy use of political behavior was his relationship with the great inventor Nikola Tesla. Knowing talent when he saw it, Edison moved swiftly to co-opt Tesla, who invented alternating current, and hired him at a low salary before he became famous. Even after he left Edison's employ, Edison maintained a share of his patent. As a result, Tesla became one of Edison's few critics.

And, in true political frame manner, Edison was not beyond ingratiating himself to a potential customer. At the Paris International Exhibition in 1889, seeking French business over his competitors in England, he pointed out to the French that the Eiffel Tower was a great idea. "The glory of Eiffel is in the magnitude of the conception and the nerve of its execution. I like the French," he said. "They have big conceptions. The English ought to take a leaf out of their books. What Englishmen would have this idea? What Englishmen could have conceived of the Statue of Liberty?" (Baldwin, 1995, 205).

Finally, Edison's long kiln for making cement turned out to be one of his most profitable and sustained inventions. Into the 1920s, he was receiving a royalty of one cent on every barrel of cement produced by other companies through the long-kiln method. He was happy to point out to anyone who would listen that Yankee Stadium was not really the house that Ruth built. Rather, it was the house that Edison built—after all, it was 180,000 bags of his concrete.

THE MORAL FRAME

The moral frame is my own contribution to situational leadership theory. In my view, the moral frame completes situational leadership theory. Without it, leaders could just as easily use their leadership skills for promoting evil as for promoting good. Leaders operating out of the moral frame are concerned about their obligations and responsibilities to their followers. Moral frame leaders use some type of moral compass to direct their behavior. They practice what has been described as servant leadership and are concerned with those individuals and groups that are marginalized in their organizations and in society. In short, they are concerned about equality, fairness, and social justice.

By all accounts, Thomas Edison was a thoroughly decent man. His leadership behavior is full of instances where he demonstrated an ethic of caring and a concern for the "little guy" (which ironically he considered himself to be) and the more marginalized individuals in society. He was fair to his competitors and sought to arrive at a mutually beneficial outcome to their negotiations. He treated his employees with dignity and respect, compensating them at a higher rate than most of his competitors. In general, Edison seemed to view his leadership behavior through a moral lens that was most likely ingrained in him in his youth. The available evidence indicates that Thomas Edison was as active in the moral frame as he was in the other four frames of leadership behavior (Baldwin, 1995).

CONCLUSION

Thomas Edison's rise to fame as perhaps the most successful inventor and entrepreneur in history was no accident. He practiced situational leadership long before it became popular to do so. Although he was basically a structural frame leader, being a workaholic of major proportions, he effectively utilized the other situational leadership theory frames as required and appropriate.

We saw how Edison was ahead of his time in his application of human resource leadership behavior. He paid his employees considerably more than the competition did. He respected his workforce, oftentimes complimenting them to the press and crediting them for his success. He was close enough to his employees that they felt comfortable parodying him in their rendition of *H.M.S. Pinafore*.

Edison's use of symbolic leadership behavior was also extensive. He cultivated his image as the Wizard of Menlo Park, the New Jersey Columbus, and the Napoleon of Invention. He depicted himself as the homespun Professor Edison who was continually victimized by avaricious robber barons.

Edison also made effective use of political frame leadership behavior, especially among his major competitors like Alexander Graham Bell and Henry Westinghouse. However, he used the political frame in moderation, always trying to create a win-win situation whereby both parties benefited.

Finally, it seems obvious that Edison was also active in the moral frame. He seemed to view his behavior through the lens of the Golden Rule—do unto others as you would have them do unto you. Thus, his credibility and integrity were rarely questioned.

There is much to be learned from studying the leadership behavior of Thomas Edison. Leaders and aspiring leaders would be well served to emulate his ability to balance his leadership behavior both across and within the five leadership frames explored here. In my view, Thomas Edison is an exemplary leader in the situational leadership theory tradition.

Chapter 6

Henry Ford

You can have any color Model T you want, so long as it's black.

—Henry Ford

BACKGROUND

Automobile manufacturer Henry Ford was born in 1863 on his family's farm in Dearborn, Michigan. From the time he was a young boy, the future great carmaker enjoyed tinkering with machines. By 1896, Ford had constructed his first horseless carriage, which he sold in order to finance work on an improved model.

Ford incorporated the Ford Motor Company in 1903. By 1908, he had produced the first Model Ts and priced them at an affordable $950. Over the Model T's nineteen years of production, its price decreased to $280 and nearly 16 million were sold in the United States alone.

Ford married Clara Ala Bryant in 1888. They had only one child, Edsel. In 1891, Ford became an engineer at Thomas Edison's Edison Illuminating Company. After his promotion to chief engineer in 1893, he devoted his attention to experiments on gasoline engines. As a consequence of this early connection, Ford and Thomas Edison became friends and remained so for the rest of their lives.

Ford revolutionized the manufacturing process. By 1914, his Highland Park, Michigan, plant, using innovative production techniques, could turn out a complete automobile almost ten times faster than his nearest competitor. Using the moving assembly line, division of labor, and careful coordination of operations, Ford realized huge efficiencies in production.

In 1914, Ford began paying his employees five dollars a day, nearly doubling the wages offered by other manufacturers. He reduced the workday from nine to eight hours in order to convert the factory to a three-shift workday. Incredibly, Ford's mass-production techniques would eventually turn out a Model T every twenty-four seconds.

Later in life, Ford became deeply involved in philanthropy, founding the Ford Foundation. In ill health, at the age of eighty-one, Ford finally ceded the presidency of the Ford Motor Company to his grandson, Henry Ford II, and retired. By the time of his death two years later, he was one of the most famous men in the world and remains so even today (Lacey, 1986).

SITUATIONAL LEADERSHIP ANALYSIS

Situational models of leadership differ from earlier trait and behavioral models in asserting that no single way of leading works in all situations. Rather, appropriate behavior depends on the circumstances at a given time. Effective managers diagnose the situation, identify the leadership style or behavior that will be most effective, and then determine whether they can implement the required style.

Although, like most business persons, we will see that Henry Ford was basically a structural frame leader, he intuitively knew that he had to vary his leadership style to maximize his effectiveness. For example, the Reverend Samuel Marquis, Ford's minister, got very close to him. Working beside Ford in his Sociological Department (a precursor to today's Human Resources Department), Marquis had come to see that along with Ford's strong work ethic (i.e., structural behavior), his moral qualities and impulses were "some of the highest and noblest I have ever known" (Lacey, 1986, 178). But Marquis also saw another, dark, side of Ford. "There rages in him," he wrote, "an endless conflict between ideals, emotions and impulses as unlike as day and night" (Lacey, 1986, 178).

Ford was quick to recognize his limitations and to vary his leadership behavior by using the talents of others. His son, Edsel, took on the role, in many respects, that Ford's founding partner, James Couzens, had played. Edsel was in charge of the business and human resources side of the company, while Henry concentrated on the engineering aspects. Later in his career, Ford observed, "There is altogether too much reliance on good feeling in our business organizations. A great business is really too big to be human" (Lacey, 1986, 247).

These Darwinian sentiments were inconsistent with the mindset of a man who, ten years earlier, had pioneered the establishment of the Sociological Department. But the intervening ten years had changed Henry Ford. We will see that incidents like the ill-fated Peace Ship, the Dodge brothers dispute, the *Chicago Tribune*, and the pressure of the postwar recession, amounted to new and different situations that required different applications of leadership.

In a further recognition of the situational nature of leadership, Ford once said, "It could almost be written down as a formula that when a man begins to think that he has at last found the method, he had better begin a most searching examination of himself to see whether some part of his brain has not gone to sleep" (Lacey, 1986, 283).

In another example of his situational nature, Ford initially defended the utilitarian approach that he and other carmakers took in the early years with his famous aphorisms, "You can have any color Model T you want, so long as it's black" and "A Ford will take you anywhere except into society." However, times were changing. Style rather than practicality was taking over the industry. And, although Ford mightily resisted, he too finally saw the light in 1928 with his Model A, which was stylized and came in many colors.

Responding to the flexible installment plan of General Motors was another instance of Ford's flexibility. Ford finally had to sell cars on credit to continue to compete. Consumers did not have complaints about the Model T's performance; they just got bored with it and had trouble financing it, so Ford had to adjust his leadership behavior to the new situation.

THE STRUCTURAL FRAME

Structural frame leaders seek to develop a new model of the relationship of structure, strategy, and environment for their organizations. Strategic planning, extensive preparation, and effecting change are priorities for them. As mentioned earlier, Henry Ford felt most comfortable operating out of the structural leadership frame.

Even at an early age, Henry Ford showed structural frame tendencies. He had a reputation as a tinkerer and was forever dismantling, investigating, and generally displaying his mechanical genius.

Ford further demonstrated his structural frame leanings when he realized that the internal combustion engine relied on electricity for its firing cycle. In typical structural frame fashion, he set out to acquire the knowledge that he lacked. So, searching the Detroit area, he secured a job with the Edison Illuminating Company as a mechanical engineer. In the process, he formed a lifelong, close relationship with Thomas Edison. As was mentioned in the previous chapter, the two men purchased vacation homes next door to each other in Fort Myers, Florida.

Even in this, his first significant job, Ford had the knack of running an efficient shop. He managed to simplify things in a way that everyone could understand and made life for his co-workers less complicated. For example, he devised a boring bar which greatly eased the boring out of clogged cylinders. As a result of his inefficiencies, his employers gave him more latitude and leisure time to ponder his innovations.

Ford was the first to see that decreasing the weight of the first cars would make a significant difference. "Fat men cannot run as fast as thin men," he declared. "I cannot imagine where the delusion that weight means strength came from." This insight allowed him to build his cars cheaper, while increasing their performance. Lightness, speed, reliability, and low price were Ford's central ideas that would enable him to engineer a car for the masses.

By 1903, Ford had teamed up with James Couzens and in typical structural leadership form immediately developed a business plan for the manufacture and sale of his first mass-produced car, the Model A. They produced 658 cars in 1904, and averaged twenty-five cars a day the next year. Ford and Couzens worked out the balance sheet to the penny. The basic machinery for the engine would cost $250. Body, and other parts, including labor, came to an additional $154. They earmarked $150 for marketing costs, and the car would sell for $750, leaving a margin of $196 per unit.

The traditional market for the early motorcars was the affluent upper and middle classes. But Ford sensed that a larger and potentially richer market lay in the lower classes. At forty-two years old and already successful with the Model A, Ford decided to build "the car for the masses" (Lacey, 1986, 79).

Ford wrestled with the problem of price for the Model T and, because of his structural frame thinking, had come to see that the secret to reducing the production costs was in streamlining the production process. Thus he came up with the ingenious idea of a moving assembly line. Another way of reducing costs would be to use a lighter metal which led to the use of vanadium steel, an alloy that was lighter and stronger than regular steel.

By using vanadium instead of steel, and the moving assembly line as opposed to the fixed assembly line, Ford was able to build a car that was not only less expensive than the competition, but also more reliable and efficient. So, when the Model T came out in 1908, it was an instant success, and deservedly so.

Another of Ford's innovations inspired by the structural leadership frame thinking was the interchangeability of parts. Before his time, each part of the motorcar was manufactured individually by a craftsman. Often the parts were slightly different in size and were therefore not interchangeable. They had to be filed and refined to fit. Ford pioneered the process whereby each piece was machined so that every part was exactly the same size, and thus interchangeable. This innovation saved innumerable man-hours on the assembly line.

Being the structural leader that he was, Ford subscribed wholeheartedly to the science of Taylorism, developed by Frederick Taylor, the father of scientific management. Ford studied Taylor's time-and-motion techniques and as a result doubled his output of Model Ts in one year. After making a success of the Ford Motor Company, Ford's structural frame leanings compelled him to expand his interests somewhat. He had always had a multitrack mind and now devoted it to social engineering, saving the birds, and trying to stop America's entrance into World War I. But these other interests never prevented him from continuing to improve his cars.

For example, in 1932, when he was seventy, Ford perfected the V-8 engine. He was particularly proud of one accomplishment: Bonnie and Clyde Barrow's beige-grey Desert Sand V-8 Ford Deluxe was stolen seventy-five hundred miles earlier and riddled with 107 bullets from the rifles and automatic shotguns of the ambushing lawmen; but when the bloodstained bodies of the bandits were removed from the car and the local Ford dealer was called to drive it away, the V-8 engine turned over the first time the key was put in the ignition. Suffice it to say, Henry Ford was a prototypical structural frame leader (Lacey, 1986).

THE HUMAN RESOURCE FRAME

Human resource leaders believe in people and communicate that belief. They are passionate about productivity through people. During Ford's era, scientific management, which encouraged structural frame leadership, dominated American industry. Nevertheless, among the successful industrialists of his time, Ford was widely known to utilize human resource frame leadership far more often than his peers.

Ford showed his human side in his relationship with his only son, Edsel. Ford was as active and as attentive as a parent could be. He loved gadgets, and he loved showing Edsel how to use them. He was also somewhat of a shutterbug, and his snapshots were full of clowning and horseplay. For example, there is a photo of Ford, when he was forty-four, turning a cartwheel for Edsel's benefit on the beach at Atlantic City.

Ford also showed his human resource tendencies in the unlikely friendship he had with one of his first partners, James Couzens. Even though they were both strongly opinionated, Ford found a way to be tolerant of Couzens's forceful approach, to the point where they became lifelong friends and collaborators.

The automobile industry during Ford's time would routinely lay off employees during down times. One of the perennial down times in the motorcar industry was the Christmas season. One year, upon observing his laid-off employees trudging off despairingly to their homes, Ford decided to use some human resource frame behavior and begin the practice of not only paying laid-off employees through Christmas vacation but also more than doubling their pay to the unheard-of figure of five dollars a day—a policy that would make national headlines.

The company had earned huge profits from the labor of these men, Ford observed, and not only because of the stockholders or the board of directors. Thus he explained that the five-dollars-a-day policy was merely a case of enlightened self-interest, a view he acquired by reading the works of Ralph Waldo Emerson.

In leadership behavior that had both human resource and symbolic implications, Ford employed more women and minorities than most other employers in Detroit, and at better wages. He was even more progressive when it came to the employment of people with disabilities. He instructed his human resource department that the only reason not to hire a person with a disability was if he or she had a contagious disease.

In another demonstration of his human resource tendencies, Ford became friendly with some of his business counterparts of the era. In one of his excursions, which were to become an annual tradition, Ford and John Burroughs, the great naturalist, were joined in bird-watching by Thomas Edison and Harvey Firestone, the tire maker. They were sometimes joined by John D. Rockefeller.

In 1921, in still another instance of his human resource leanings, the Ford Motor Company was heading for record profits, and in a moment of largesse, Ford announced that he would be happy to devote some of his profits and energies to rescuing Henry M. Leland, whose Lincoln Motor Company was on the verge of bankruptcy.

Even during the Great Depression, Ford's first reaction was to increase salaries. Consequently, the Detroit area fared relatively well during the Great Depression. Ford reduced the prices of his cars and raised his minimum wage to seven dollars per hour. So, during an era when human resource behavior was rare in business and industry, Henry Ford practiced more than his fair share of it.

THE SYMBOLIC FRAME

In the symbolic frame, the organization is seen as a stage, a theater in which every actor plays certain roles, and the symbolic leader attempts to communicate the right impressions to the right audiences. Although not his strongest frame, Henry Ford seemed to know instinctively of the need to establish a certain image of himself and his fledgling company.

Ford spoke in symbolic terms when he colorfully described his first encounter with the moving steam engine. He related it to the New Testament story of St. Paul being knocked from his horse on his way to Damascus by the vision of God. Ford knew immediately what he wanted to do in his life. He wanted to be a carmaker. So that very day he walked nine miles to Detroit to find a job in the fledgling auto industry.

Ironically, Henry Ford considered himself a farmer by nature. Thus his first mechanical inclinations were to build a tractor. His beliefs remained very much that of the Michigan farmer: temperance (he was a teetotaler), mistrust of the East Coast establishment, and a deep suspicion of Wall Street. And he did all that he could to perpetuate his "common man" image.

Ford made certain through the frequent use of symbolic leadership behavior that, along with Bell and the telephone, Edison and the light bulb, and the Wright brothers and the airplane, he and his motorcars were thought of in the same way. As we know, Ford did not invent the motorcar. His great contribution to American industry was the moving assembly line, but that accomplishment was too obscure for Ford. He wanted to be identified with something more tangible like the automobile.

In the early years of the auto industry the only way carmakers could obtain some publicity was by winning motorcar races. Being the symbolic frame leader that he was, Ford took full advantage of these opportunities. He won a famous victory in 1901 over Alexander Winton at a Detroit track and the victory put Ford on the auto-making map. It was not long after that he formed the Ford Motor Company. Less than a year later, Ford won his second big victory in a car driven by the legendary Barney Oldfield, who went on to a successful career as one of the first great race-car drivers.

"Home of the Celebrated Ford Automobile," proclaimed a huge white-lettered sign that ran along the side of the new Ford factory, which stands to this day in Detroit. With that sign and his compelling rhetoric, Ford was becoming a master in the use of symbolic leadership behavior.

"I will build a motorcar for the great multitude," he declared. "It will be large enough for the family, but small enough for the individual to run and care for it. It will be constructed of the best materials, by the best men to be hired, after the simplest designs that modern engineering can devise. But it will be so low in price that no man making a good salary will be unable to own one and enjoy with his family the blessing of hours of pleasure in God's great open spaces" (Lacey, 1986, 87). The "peoples' car" was unique for that time. Cars were associated with the rich. But Ford's everyman instincts compelled him to build a car that could be afforded by the common man—like him.

One of the symbolic attributes of the Model T was its ability to inspire affection in its owners. People gave their car a name, usually female. To Ford's great satisfaction and with his encouragement, the Model T became affectionately known to the general public as the "Tin Lizzy."

Ford also made good use of the Association of Licensed Automobile Manufacturers' (ALAM) court verdict to further enhance his image. The ALAM, many of whose members were Ford's competitors in the automobile-making industry, sued Ford for patent infringement. After a six-year court battle, Ford finally prevailed. When he did, he became a folk hero for much of the American public as the David who had slain Goliath.

As mentioned earlier, Ford became a devotee of Ralph Waldo Emerson and symbolically fashioned his management philosophy on Emerson's ideas. Ford and Emerson were in accord in believing machines like the motorcar were in harmony with nature as long as they were designed and used with integrity.

Ford, whose nose for publicity had developed with his ALAM victory, knew he had a good story for the local newspapers when he announced his five-dollars-a-day pay schedule. The day after the announcement,

"Five Dollars a Day" was the story on the front pages of newspapers all over the country.

As mentioned earlier, in Ford's mind, such practices were in his own enlightened self-interest. In his words, "wage earners were wage spenders" (Lacey, 1986, 130). He was before his time in recognizing that consumption fuels economic growth. The five-dollars-a-day policy was the answer to the economists' questions at the beginning of the twentieth century of who was going to buy all the new products that were being produced. The answer was right in front of them—the workers they employed would purchase them.

In another indication of his symbolic frame leanings, Ford was a devout pacifist. He was willing to do most anything to keep America out of the war. To make his point, he chartered a ship which he christened the "Peace Ship" and sailed it around the world as a symbol of peace.

The ill-fated project failed to reach its goal of bringing about world peace, but it served to strengthen Ford's image as the modern-day Don Quixote. "It is better a thousand times to be branded a fool in the service of humanity," declared Rabbi Joseph Kranaskopf at the time, "than be hailed a hero for having shed rivers of blood" (Lacey, 1986, 145).

Although he was bitterly disappointed at the futility of the Peace Ship effort, once war was declared, Ford did his part in the war effort. He built tanks and other military vehicles for the army and promised to operate his factories without one cent of profit. To him, getting rich on the war effort was like taking blood money.

Ford resigned as CEO of the Ford Motor Company at age fifty-five to devote his energies to supporting his philanthropic interests. In another symbolic gesture, he established the Ford Foundation, which meted out money to numerous charitable causes. The Ford Foundation remains one of the most highly endowed and effective foundations in the world.

In yet another symbolic frame act, Ford purchased the *Dearborn Independent*, a newspaper he used as an organ of the Ford Motor Company. He envisioned his homespun paper being sold at newsstands across the country, rivaling the *New York Times* in distribution. It included "Mr. Ford's Own Page," where Ford wrote his idiosyncratic views on the various topic of the day.

It was largely through the *Dearborn Independent* that some of Ford's symbolic leadership behavior backfired. In an unfortunate display of inappropriate symbolic behavior, Ford's anti-Semitism first came into the open, when the *Dearborn Independent* featured an article in which Ford reinforced Nazi propaganda and blamed the Jews for virtually all of the world's problems.

Hitler, still an obscure political figure in Germany at that time, read Ford's articles and became a devotee of the great carmaker. He used

Ford's example as a reinforcement of his own anti-Semitic views and actually hung a portrait of Ford on his office wall.

Still, because of his astute use of symbolic leadership behavior, the Ford image retained its luster. In 1928, Thomas Edison laid the foundation stone for the Henry Ford Museum and Ford began construction on Greenfield Village, Ford's rendition of the town of the future. The exterior of the museum was a full-scale red brick replica of three of America's most historical buildings: Independence Hall, Congress Hall, and the Old City Hall of Philadelphia. Both Greenfield Village and the Henry Ford Museum made several important contributions to the study of history.

President Herbert Hoover's dedication of the Henry Ford Museum was a high point in Ford's life, a testament to his belief that it was mechanical inventiveness and ingenuity that made America the great nation that it was.

When his reputation was beginning to fade because of his reluctance to change anything about his beloved Model T, Ford engaged in yet another round of symbolic behavior—he suddenly launched the Model A.

The Model A had all the improvements that the Model T lacked and pound for pound cost less than the Model T. Like the Model T, it was no surprise that the Model A was an instant success—it deserved to be. It was fashionable, durable, and relatively inexpensive. Ford sold 1.5 million Model As in 1929, a market share of 34 percent—fourteen points ahead of Chevrolet, his nearest competitor. Ford was on top once again.

In 1932, however, Ford received another blow to his carefully crafted image when the Ford Hunger March took place to honor those who were killed outside the Ford Motor Company after they had protested in favor of collective bargaining. The high wages that he had paid his employees became but a distant memory after this fiasco.

In 1938, Ford's reputation was further sullied when he was honored by Hitler with the Grand Cross of the German Eagle. Of course Ford was roundly criticized for accepting it. Thus, in his advancing age, Ford was losing his handle on the appropriate use of symbolic frame leadership behavior. Nonetheless, in describing Ford's symbolic behavior in a more positive light, the noted historian Arthur Schlesinger Jr. said of Ford, "Some people must dream broadly and guilelessly, if only to balance those who never dream at all" (Lacey, 1986, 132).

THE POLITICAL FRAME

Leaders operating out of the political frame clarify what they want and what they can get. Political leaders are realists above all. They never let what they want cloud their judgment about what is possible. They assess the distribution of power and interests.

Like most of the industrial leaders of his day, Henry Ford found it necessary to utilize political leadership behavior rather frequently. He used his political guile to his advantage early in his career in his fund-raising efforts. Sometime in the latter part of 1899, Ford gained an audience with a promising potential financial backer. Ford made the friendly wager that if his car could drive the financier out to Farmington, northwest of Detroit, and then back via Pontiac without a breakdown, a distance of over sixty miles, his car would be worthy of the investment. His motorcar made the trip without incident, and Ford used the investment to found an early version of the Ford Motor Company.

Citing his farmer roots, Ford professed contempt for the lack of ethics in big business. But when it came to the pursuit of his own interests, he took advantage of the situation. For example, in 1906 when the Ford Motor Company was still entangled with a majority owner who preferred more expensive and luxurious cars, Ford defiantly produced the less expensive Model N, the predecessor of the Model T. The majority owner, much to Ford's satisfaction, relinquished his shares to Ford a few months later.

In a similar power play in 1909, after the Model T had dominated the car market, the Association of Licensed Automobile Manufacturers, consisting of twenty-six of Ford's competitors in the auto industry, sued Ford for patent infringement. As we have seen earlier, after six years of litigation the courts ruled in Ford's favor. With the Model T selling so well, a settlement would have been in order. But because of principle, Ford refused to compromise.

Ford even used political frame behavior with his friend John Burroughs. The well-known naturalist, author, and poet was sent a brand-new Model T by Ford. It seems that Ford had been annoyed by Burroughs's depiction of the auto industry as desecrating American's landscape. Being proactive, Ford thought the gift might co-opt Burroughs. It worked, and Burroughs toned down his criticism and became a lifelong friend of Ford's.

In 1912, in a further pursuit of political behavior, Ford lent support to the Weeks-McLean bill, a proposal to protect migratory birds and one of John Burroughs's pet projects. Furthermore, he sent personal requests to Thomas Edison and John D. Rockefeller to use their influence. Much to Burroughs's delight, the Weeks-McLean bill became law in 1913.

In 1916, many were urging Ford to run for president. But Ford refused to be considered, throwing his public support to Woodrow Wilson's reelection campaign. Of course he was building political capital that he hoped would work to his advantage in the future. As a result, Ford was promised the president's support in his effort to purchase Muscle Shoals, Alabama, where the Wilson Dam was to be built. Ford had hopes of building a model city there. It never materialized, but it stands as another example of Ford using political behavior to advance his goals.

As a result of his frequent use of political behavior, Ford was often charged with ulterior motives for his apparent largesse. For example, in implementing his five-dollars-a-day plan, his critics claimed that his apparent generosity was no more than a way of getting back at the Dodge brothers. If he had not paid his employees that extra amount, it would have gone to the bottom line and been shared with his partners, including the Dodge brothers. Ultimately, the financially strapped Dodge brothers were forced to give up their shares of the Ford Motor Company and Ford once again prevailed.

It was noted earlier that Ford used his *Dearborn Independent* newspaper as a tool to define his public image. He also used political behavior in regard to it. When public opinion raged against the *Dearborn Independent*'s anti-Semitic articles, they stopped as abruptly as they had started. Ford ordered his editor to be more complimentary of the Jews and use future articles to push his position, and that of most Jews, on the gold-versus-silver-standard debate in hopes that the Jews would support his monetary position. In addition, he was seriously thinking of running for president in 1922 and needed to secure the Jewish vote to get nominated.

A final example of Ford's use of political frame leadership behavior (with a little symbolic behavior thrown in) is the establishment of the Ford Foundation to fund scientific, educational, and other charitable causes. Ever the political animal, Ford took full advantage of the tax implications of his foundation. As we know, donations to recognized charities are exempt from taxation. So, if the Fords were to will their Class A stock to this new foundation, they would not only retain their voting power, but also avoid having to pay income tax on 95 percent of their wealth—which is exactly what they did.

THE MORAL FRAME

The moral frame is my own contribution to situational leadership theory. In my view, the moral frame completes situational leadership theory. Without it, leaders could just as easily use their leadership skills for promoting evil as for promoting good. Leaders operating out of the moral frame are concerned about their obligations and responsibilities to their followers. Moral frame leaders use some type of a moral compass to direct their behavior. They practice what has been described as servant leadership and are concerned with those individuals and groups that are marginalized in their organizations and in society. In short, they are concerned about equality, fairness, and social justice.

There is every indication that Henry Ford used a moral compass to guide his actions. In many ways, he was a humanitarian at heart. As indicated earlier, he was a confirmed pacifist and contributed large sums to charitable causes. We saw that the automobile industry of his time would routinely lay off employees at Christmas, a notoriously slow time in auto sales. However, Henry Ford broke with tradition and, upon observing his laid-off employees sadly walking home, introduced the practice of not only paying laid-off employees through the Christmas holidays, but also more than doubling their pay to the precedent-setting figure of five dollars a day. And although he always explained the five-dollars-a-day policy as a hardheaded business decision, the fact is that it emanated from his concern for humanity and social justice (Lacey, 1986).

CONCLUSION

There is much to learn from observing the leadership behavior of Henry Ford. At a time in history when scientific management was in vogue, with its emphasis on efficiency in production, close supervision, and strong leadership—translated *autocratic*—Henry Ford was an exception. Although he was a devoted disciple of scientific management, he instinctively realized that a more situational approach was necessary for maximum effectiveness. Thus, in addition to his frequent use of structural frame leadership behavior, Ford's leadership practices included significant use of the human resource, symbolic, political, and moral frames.

We saw how Ford utilized the structural frame of leadership in his creation of the first moving assembly line in mass production. His use of human resource behavior is exemplified by his establishment of the five-dollars-a-day wage policy. We saw how he carefully honed both his own public image and that of his company through the frequent use of symbolic frame leadership behavior. And we saw his use of political behavior when he astutely maneuvered the Dodge brothers out of their shares of the Ford Motor Company and gained total control of it for himself and his family.

Finally, we saw that Ford showed signs of viewing his leadership behavior through the lens of a moral code that tended to guide his leadership toward good rather than evil. In summary, although he was eccentric at times and had his foibles, Ford was a prototypical situational leader whose example can be of great benefit to both today's and tomorrow's leaders.

Chapter 7

Mahatma Gandhi

There are many causes that I am prepared to die for, but no causes that I am prepared to kill for.

—Mahatma Gandhi

BACKGROUND

Mahatma Gandhi was born in 1869 and is considered the father of the Indian independence movement. First, Gandhi spent twenty years in South Africa working to fight discrimination. It was there that he created his concept of *satyagraha*, a nonviolent way of protesting against injustices. Later, while back in India, Gandhi's virtue and modest lifestyle endeared him to the people. He spent his lifetime working diligently to gain independence from British rule and improve the lives of India's poor classes. Many civil rights and religious leaders, including Martin Luther King Jr. and Mother Teresa, used Gandhi's concept of nonviolent protest as a model for their own struggles.

In 1888, at the age of eighteen, Gandhi left India, without his wife and newborn son, in order to study to become a lawyer in London. He passed the bar in 1891, and sailed back to India two days later. For the next two years, Gandhi unsuccessfully attempted to practice law in India. When he was offered a year-long position in South Africa, he grabbed the opportunity.

Gandhi once again left his family behind, and set off for South Africa, arriving in British-governed Natal in 1893. Gandhi's transformation into a social-justice advocate began during a business trip taken shortly after his arrival in South Africa.

Embarking on his train trip from Nepal to the South African capital Pretoria, Gandhi boarded the first-class car for his journey. Railroad officials told him that he needed to transfer to the third-class passenger car. When Gandhi, who was holding first-class passenger ticket, refused to move, a policeman came and forcibly removed him from the train.

As a result of this and other similar experiences, Gandhi spent the next twenty years working to advance Indians' rights in South Africa. In 1894, Gandhi established the Natal Indian Congress (NIC) to facilitate the process of furthering his causes. In a few short years, Gandhi had become an important leader of the Indian community in South Africa.

In 1915, Gandhi returned to India. He almost immediately entered the struggle for independence from England. He employed noncooperation, nonviolence, and peaceful resistance as his strategies in the struggle against the British. In Punjab, the Amritsar Massacre of civilians by British troops was a catalyst in the furthering of the independence movement.

In 1930 Gandhi launched a nonviolent protest against the tax on salt that the British had recently imposed, which was highlighted by his famous "salt march" to Dandi to make salt himself. Thousands of Indians joined him on this march to the sea. This campaign was one of the most successful at weakening the British hold on India.

When World War II broke out in 1939, India declared that it could not be party to a war ostensibly being fought for democratic freedom when freedom was denied to India. As the war progressed, Gandhi intensified his demands for independence, drafting a resolution that called for the British to "Quit India." Although he was instrumental in obtaining freedom from British rule in India, he did not live to see it. On January 30, 1948, Gandhi was shot and killed during his nightly public walk on the grounds of his community by a radical Hindu assassin who felt that Gandhi's compassion for the Muslims weakened the Hindus (Marcello, 2006; Pasten, 2006).

Both Mother Teresa and Martin Luther King Jr., among others, were inspired by Gandhi's life and principles, and their leadership behavior was greatly influenced by him. The leadership behavior of Martin Luther King Jr. is profiled in a separate chapter of this book, while Mother Teresa's will be compared with Gandhi's in this chapter.

SITUATIONAL LEADERSHIP ANALYSIS

Situational models of leadership differ from earlier trait and behavioral models in asserting that no single way of leading works in all situations. Rather, appropriate behavior depends on the circumstances at a given time. Effective managers diagnose the situation, identify the leadership style or behavior that will be most effective, and then determine whether they can implement the required style.

Although he is primarily known as a human resource and symbolic leader, Mahatma Gandhi was adept at utilizing all four leadership frames suggested by Bolman and Deal (1991). Furthermore, he ran virtually all of his leadership behavior through a self-imposed moral lens.

Early in his professional career, while living in South Africa, he stressed the need to be situational with his growing cadre of followers. He implored them to come together as a group, despite their varied faiths—Hindu, Parsi, Muslim, and Christian—and urged them to get out of their comfort zone and learn English so that they could better represent themselves in South African society.

Gandhi modeled the situational nature of leadership for his disciples. Among Europeans living in South Africa, Indians were seen as unclean. Gandhi was known as a "coolie barrister" in South Africa, and he knew that continuing to wear his turban would only perpetuate the image, so he changed his turban to a Western-style hat and avoided any confrontations. Later in life, after he had established his reputation, he dressed the way he wanted.

When one method did not work, Gandhi was disappointed but never disheartened. Being the situational leader that he was, he merely pursued other means of attaining his goals. For example, when structural behavior was not effective in strengthening and uniting the South African Indian community, he used a more symbolic approach and founded a weekly journal called the *Indian Opinion*, which featured educational and informational articles on such varied topics as politics, diet, health, and security issues.

Having initially tried and failed with the traditional methods of opposing laws, such as lobbying against them and threatening to vote legislators out of office, Gandhi looked for an opportunity to apply an alternative approach—*satyagraha*, or civil disobedience—to the situation. The first opportunity to do so came in 1907 after the government of Transvaal, South Africa, passed a law that became known as the Black Act. It required Indians living in Transvaal to be fingerprinted and to carry registration cards. It also imposed taxes on them and declared Hindu marriages to be illegal. An outraged Gandhi advised the Indian community to disobey the law.

When civil disobedience began to lose its impact, Gandhi moved to a different method of opposing oppression. With unemployment and salaries among the Indian population in South Africa ever worsening, Gandhi decided to go on a hunger strike. He pledged to fast until the workers' demands were met. With the press covering his actions and employers concerned that he would become a martyr for the cause, they capitulated.

Being the situational leader that he was, he was always looking for new and different ways of achieving his goals, but always within the parameters of nonviolence. He urged government officials to stop working in the service of England, and lawyers to walk out of court. He urged university students to boycott government schools, and soldiers to desert. He persuaded his followers to stop paying their taxes. Engaging in symbolic leadership behavior, he used his newspaper, *Young India*, and his speeches to garner support for the cause.

Gandhi retained the flexibility of a situational leader throughout his life. For example, even though he did not condone the violence and inhumanity of war, Gandhi wanted to help the Allies in some way, so he established an ambulance corps to transport injured men from the battlefield during World War I.

THE STRUCTURAL FRAME

Structural leaders develop a new model of the relationship of structure, strategy, and environment for their organizations. Strategic planning, extensive preparation, and effecting change are priorities for them. Although he was not primarily known as a structural leader, we shall see that, being the situational leader that he was, Gandhi depended on structural frame leadership behavior when it was appropriate to do so.

As a young man, Gandhi no sooner arrived in South Africa than he began utilizing structural leadership behavior. The government was about to pass a law depriving Indians of their right to elect members of the Natal Legislative Assembly. In effect, they would have no representation in local government. Gandhi thought the bill was extremely dangerous. "It is the first nail into our coffin," he said. "It strikes at the root of our self respect" (Pasten, 2006, 45). Gandhi cancelled his passage back to India and stayed to oppose the franchise bill by obtaining more than ten thousand signatures protesting it.

When the franchise bill passed, Gandhi was not daunted and planned continued protestation. He wanted the law vetoed. To achieve this goal, the Indians decided to create a political vehicle to operate their campaigns, the Natal Indian Congress. As few members were accustomed to public speaking, Gandhi taught them the rules of procedure and the art of public speaking. He used this type of structural leadership behavior for the remainder of his life.

Gandhi continued his focus on structural leadership behavior for the next three years as he maintained a thriving legal practice and streamlined the operations of the Natal Indian Congress, which organized opposition to injustice and discrimination.

Eventually, Gandhi's leadership behavior produced results. At a mass meeting in Johannesburg, he convinced three thousand Indians to oppose the Black Act. In typical structural frame style, he and his followers set goals and made plans to oppose what they believed was an unjust law. It was in protestation of the Black Act that the idea of *satyagraha*, or civil disobedience, was spawned.

By the time he returned to India, Gandhi had honed his use of structural leadership behavior in the form of very effective peaceful protest and civil disobedience. In response to yet another British tax, this time on imported cotton, Gandhi reacted in true structural leadership form. India had its own cotton-spinning and cotton-weaving traditions. However, they had gone out of use, with British materials so readily available. If people relearned how to spin cotton into thread, Gandhi reasoned, they would not have to import it and pay the tax.

Continuing his structural leadership behavior in protest of the salt tax, whereby Indians were mandated to buy heavily taxed salt from England, Gandhi wrote a letter to Lord Irwin, viceroy of India, proclaiming the tax evil and said, "If my letter makes no appeal to your heart, on the eleventh day of this month, I shall proceed with such co-workers of the Ashram as

I can take, to disregard the provisions of the Salt Laws" (Pasten, 2006, 81). After receiving no response, Gandhi organized his legendary Dandi salt march, in which he and thousands of his followers marched 248 miles to the sea and made salt themselves.

Later, after World War II, when the Quit India movement went into full force, Gandhi utilized the same form of structural leadership behavior and planned and organized his marches and protests down to the last detail. He also developed well-thought-out strategies, like hunger strikes, and applied them at just the right time to maximize their effectiveness. As we have seen, although Gandhi is best known for his use of the human resource, symbolic, and even political frames, he also used the structural frame of leadership to great effect.

THE HUMAN RESOURCE FRAME

Human resource leaders believe in people and communicate that belief. They are passionate about productivity through people. This frame is one of Mahatma Gandhi's strongest. He had great respect for humankind.

Gandhi valued human dignity and devoted his life to the pursuit of human rights for everyone. Virtually all of his efforts were devoted to obtaining justice for all individuals, no matter their status in society. In South Africa, he organized peasants, farmers, and urban laborers in protesting excessive land taxation and discrimination, and he did so in a nonviolent way. He led thousands in the Dandi salt march, protesting the unjust and discriminatory British salt tax.

Later, in India, he organized and led the Quit India campaign that ultimately gained Indian independence from Great Britain. Even though he was a devout Hindu, he was very ecumenical in dealing with people of other faiths. He was very much against the partition of India into India and Pakistan because he believed that, given time, the Hindus and Muslims would learn to live peaceably alongside one another. Suffice it to say, the human resource frame was at the foundation of Gandhi's leadership behavior. Next, we will see how Gandhi frequently expressed his concern for humanity through the practice of symbolic frame leadership behavior.

THE SYMBOLIC FRAME

In the symbolic frame, the organization is seen as a stage, a theater in which every actor plays certain roles, and the symbolic leader attempts to communicate the right impressions to the right audiences. One could argue that Gandhi's prolific use of symbolic leadership behavior sets him apart from many of the leaders profiled in this book.

Gandhi began his use of symbolic behavior at a very young age. Even as a schoolboy he valued personal integrity and feared telling a lie. There is an oft-related story of when he misspelled the word *kettle* during the education inspector's visit to his high school. His teacher secretly encouraged Gandhi to copy the correct spelling from his neighbor's slate. But Gandhi could not understand what was happening. It never occurred to him to copy the work of another student. So while the rest of the class easily completed the assignment, Gandhi faltered. Later in his life it was this same love for the truth that would drive him to lead millions of Indians in the fight for independence from England.

As a young lawyer in South Africa, Gandhi used symbolic behavior to make some of his points. For example, he felt the disapproval of the white classes when he entered the courts. But when the magistrate asked him to remove his turban, he became angry and walked out. Afterward, he wrote to the local newspaper defending the wearing of turbans in court on cultural grounds. The press criticized the "unwelcome visitor," but some people supported him, and the turban remained part of Gandhi's attire, at least for the time being (Pasten, 2006, 39).

Reminiscent of the *Plessy v. Ferguson* legal case in the United States, Gandhi was asked to move to a third-class seat on a train, despite having a first-class ticket. Like an early Homer Plessy, Gandhi refused to be denied. Finally he was physically thrown from the train, but in doing so, he had made his point and embellished his growing reputation.

In the process of peaceably protesting yet another unjust and discriminatory British tax in South Africa, Gandhi was met by an angry mob armed with bricks. A police superintendent's wife saved him from being badly injured. However, true to his peaceful nature, Gandhi did not press charges since it was not the attackers but the political and economic system that was responsible.

Gandhi wanted to set an example of humility and sacrifice for other Indians in South Africa, so even though he was wealthy enough to have servants, he washed and ironed his own clothes and cut his own hair. He even helped with the delivery of some of his children. He expected the whole family to share in all household tasks, even emptying the chamber pots. Once again demonstrating his penchant for acting out of the symbolic frame, Gandhi wrote two pamphlets for the purpose of propagandizing his beliefs. In the first, *An Appeal to Every Briton in South Africa*, he wrote in regard to the Indian franchise law, which imposed stringent and discriminatory voter-registration regulations on Indians. "To say that the Indian does not understand the franchise is to ignore the whole history of India. Representation in the truest sense of the term, the Indian has understood and appreciated from the earliest ages. That principle—the Panchayat—guides all the actions of the Indian. He considers himself a member of the Panchayat, which really is the whole body civic to which he belongs for the time being" (Marcello, 2006, 49). The second work, entitled *The Indian Franchise: An Appeal*, also suggested mobilizing in opposition to the Indian franchise law.

As mentioned earlier, Gandhi engaged in symbolic leadership behavior when during the Boer War between the Zulus and the British, he volunteered to become involved. He had no hostile feelings toward the Zulus, but as a British subject, he thought it disloyal to the empire to support them. Having been refused membership in the British Army, Gandhi organized an ambulance corps.

The Zulu rebellion made Gandhi ponder even more the principles guiding his life—truth, nonviolence, and community service. Understanding that a commitment to these goals meant acquiring greater spiritual strength, he publically took a vow of *brahmacharya*—control of the senses and abstinence from material goods and physical pleasures. By disciplining oneself in this way, Gandhi believed that one's inner strength could be developed to the point where one would have the fortitude to practice nonviolence and civil disobedience even though there would be severe repercussions.

As a result of his various protests, Gandhi spent much of his life in prison, sometimes doing hard labor. But he never complained. Rather, he behaved symbolically by passing his days reading and praying. He believed that the real path to happiness lay in suffering for the interests of one's country, humanity, and religion, and he modeled these desired behaviors.

Hailed by native Indians for his success in South Africa, he was warmly welcomed home in 1916. His effective use of symbolic leadership behavior in South Africa had earned him the title *Mahatma*, which means "Great Soul."

Once back in India, he began cultivating his future image by wearing clothes more typical of a laborer than a lawyer—a loincloth from an Indian mill and a cap. Taking only third-class transportation, the young man who had been expelled from his first-class compartment in South Africa now chose to share the discomfort of common passengers. He witnessed many examples of discrimination and injustice and vowed to overthrow the system that fostered these atrocities.

Gandhi was further disillusioned by the so-called Massacre of Amritsar, when a peaceful protest of British rule was met by violence. Some of the protesters dove into a well to escape the bullets and drowned. In twenty minutes, 379 people were left dead and 1,200 wounded. Afterward, General Dyer, the leader of the nearby military compound, would not let any Indians into the compound to help the wounded. He later said cavalierly, "It was not my job. Hospitals were open and they could have gone there" (Pasten, 2006, 67).

The great Indian poet Togore renounced his knighthood, stating in a letter of protest, "The time has come when the badges of honor make our shame glaring in their incongruous context of humiliation, and I for my part wish to stand shorn of all special distinctions, by the side of those of my countrymen who, for their so-called insignificance, are liable to suffer degradation not fit for human beings" (Pasten, 2006, 68).

Gandhi took his cue from Togore and engaged in some symbolic leadership behavior of his own by returning the medals he had earned for his service in the Boer War and the Zulu rebellion, and he asked Indians of all religions to join him in the fight for self-rule.

An organized campaign against the British began to take shape. There was to be a policy of civil disobedience throughout the homeland. Dressed only in his trademark dhoti, shawl, and sandals, Gandhi traveled throughout the provinces, spreading his message. Over time, Gandhi's use of symbolic frame behavior made him a hero to his followers and to the world.

Just as the Quit India movement reached its zenith, it ended abruptly after a violent clash in the town of Chauri Chaura in 1922. Fearing that the movement was about to take a turn toward violence and convinced that this would be the undoing of all his work, Gandhi called off the campaign of mass civil disobedience. He was arrested and, in a typically symbolic act, he pleaded guilty on all counts and told the court, "I should have known the consequences of every one of my acts. I know them. I knew that I was playing with fire. I ran the risk, and if I was set free, I would still do the same" (Pasten, 2006, 75).

While Gandhi was in prison, cooperation between Hindus and Muslims began to diminish. In another instance of symbolic leadership behavior, Gandhi engaged in his first great fast in order to teach the lesson of religious tolerance, even if it literally killed him. His fast had the intended result. On the twenty-first day, Muslim and Hindu leaders joined in prayer and Gandhi ended his fast by taking a sip of orange juice.

In another form of symbolism, Gandhi had the Indian National Congress issue a declaration of independence from England on January 26, 1930. However, unlike the American Revolution, Gandhi would use a peaceful means, *satyagraha*, to accomplish his aims. One of his first efforts at civil disobedience was the protestation of the salt tax with the Great Salt March to the sea. Gandhi bathed in the sea as an act of purification and then picked up some salt from the beach, which was a symbolic form of civil disobedience and, in effect, broke the law.

With no movement by the British toward Indian independence, Gandhi scheduled another series of demonstrations. The nation took a pledge to win independence or die trying. In a draft of the people's pledge, Gandhi stated that India had been ruined economically, politically, culturally, and spiritually, and he wrote, "We hold it to be a crime against men and God to submit any longer to a rule that has caused this fourfold disaster to our country" (Marcello, 2006, 140).

A few days later, Gandhi published a list of reforms required of England to avoid widespread civil disobedience. Included in the list were a reduction in military expenditures by 50 percent, a levy of a protective tariff on foreign cloth, the discharge of all political prisoners, and the abolition of the salt tax.

Upon the outbreak of World War II, Gandhi once again utilized symbolic leadership behavior. He firmly believed that violence never solved anything and wrote to Adolph Hitler, "It is quite clear that you are today the one person in the world who can prevent a war which may reduce humanity to the savage state" (Pasten, 2006, 91).

Gandhi was further distraught by Hitler's persecution of the Jews. He wrote, "If there ever could be a justifiable war in the name of and for humanity, war against Germany would be completely justified." But Gandhi continued to insist, despite Hitler's evil government, "I do not believe in any war" (Pasten, 2006, 92).

After a lifetime of seeking peace, Gandhi was assassinated by a Hindu extremist in 1948, when he was seventy-eight years old. The effectiveness of his leadership behavior, specifically his symbolic behavior, can be judged by the words of Jawaharlal Nehru, the prime minister of India, upon Gandhi's death. With his voice breaking with emotion, he addressed his new nation on the radio after he had learned of the death of his mentor.

> The light has gone out of our lives and there is darkness everywhere and I do not quite know what to tell you and how to say it. Our beloved leader, Bapu as we call him, the father of our nation, is no more. The light has gone out, I said, and yet I was wrong. For the light that shone in this country was no ordinary light. The light that has illumined this country for so many years will illumine this country for many more years, and the world will see it and it will give solace to innumerable hearts. For that light represented the living truth, and the eternal man was with us with his eternal truth reminding us of the right path, drawing us from error, and taking this ancient country to freedom. (Pasten, 2006, 109)

Gandhi's symbolic behavior was an inspiration to poor people the world over. He was a model for Martin Luther King Jr.'s integration work in the American South and for Nelson Mandela's fight against apartheid in South Africa. Gandhi asked his fellow man to "recall the face of the poorest and most helpless man you have ever seen and ask yourself if the step you contemplate is going to be of any use to him" (Pasten, 2006, 112). These words were almost exactly echoed fifty years later by Mother Teresa in her work with the world's poor.

Gandhi believed that if one freed oneself from rage, one could accomplish good for all mankind. In effect, he took Jesus's message, "love your enemy," to a whole new level. In one last example of his symbolic leadership behavior, Gandhi left the world the following message of hope: "We may never be strong enough to be entirely nonviolent, in thought, word, and deed. But we must keep nonviolence as our goal and make steady progress towards it. The truth of a few will count. The untruth of millions will vanish even like chaff before a whiff of wind" (Pasten, 2006, 120).

THE POLITICAL FRAME

Leaders operating out of the political frame clarify what they want and what they can get. Political leaders are realists above all. They never let what they want cloud their judgment about what is possible. They assess the distribution of power and interests.

Mahatma Gandhi made frequent use of political frame leadership behavior. For example, when he first came to South Africa, Gandhi's friends thought he had betrayed them by removing his head covering in court. But Gandhi explained to his followers that he was merely observing the tradition that no head covering of any kind was to be worn in the courtroom. This position of compromise and pragmatism was to become Gandhi's modus operandi.

Gandhi's political behavior paid dividends when in 1914, after much protestation, Gandhi and General Jan Christiaan Smuts reached a political agreement that all Hindu and Muslim marriages in South Africa would be recognized, and Indians would no longer be subject to unfair taxes. In a symbolic gesture, he sent General Smuts a pair of sandals he had made while in prison.

Gandhi often used political leadership behavior in assessing the readiness level of his followers for engaging effectively in nonviolent civil disobedience. In one instance, he heard about violent acts occurring in the name of *satyagraha* in Indian cities and realized that tensions were too great and the people too untrained in nonviolence for the demonstration to be organized properly and be effective. Thus he called off the protests.

The Amritsar Massacre turned Gandhi from a social activist into a political one as well. When he became the head of the Indian National Congress he changed its constitution to allow all classes of Indians to join, not just the Indian intellectuals, as had formerly been the case. In 1931, in the midst of his nonviolent protests over British rule in India, when over sixty thousand protesters had been jailed, Gandhi and the viceroy reached a political agreement that they both hoped would calm things down. In addition, Gandhi did not want to jeopardize the gains made by the earlier nonviolent salt march. The agreement included the following:

- Temporary discontinuance of the civil disobedience movement.
- The Indian National Congress's agreement to participate in a Round Table Conference with the royal government.
- Withdrawal of all governmental regulations meant to impede the Indian National Congress.
- Withdrawal of all convictions that did not pertain to violent actions on the part of the protesters.
- Release of all prisoners who had participated in the civil disobedience movement.

Typically, members of both sides felt slighted, each believing that their side had given too much. But Gandhi convinced his followers that this was the best compromise that could be agreed to under the prevailing conditions.

Gandhi used political behavior to extract concessions from England in exchange for India's participation in World War II. India would have dominion status, similar to Canada's, when the war ended. Also, after the war, the individual territories in India could withdraw from the British Commonwealth if they so wished.

However, the British insisted that India be divided into many parts to assimilate the various ethics groups. This provision turned out to be the deal breaker when Gandhi could not in good conscience accept a fragmented India, and he officially opposed the war and would not approve of India's involvement in it. Nevertheless, Gandhi's persistence proved successful when, after the war, Great Britain finally granted independence to India.

Still, with the advent of India's independence, Indian Muslims threatened to destroy India if they could not have a separate Pakistan. With no other recourse, Gandhi finally capitulated. In typical political frame thinking, Gandhi reasoned that independence for two countries was better than no independence at all.

So, on August 15, 1947, British India was divided into two nations: India and Pakistan. Gandhi's dream had been realized and the two-hundred-year reign of Britain ended. Subsequently, he was asked to be the president of India, but once again he engaged in political leadership behavior by authoring an article in *Young India* convincing his constituents that he was not the logical choice for president because of his age and potential health problems. He encouraged his mentee Nehru's election.

THE MORAL FRAME

The moral frame is my own contribution to situational leadership theory. In my view, the moral frame completes situational leadership theory. Without it, leaders could just as easily use their leadership skills for promoting evil as for promoting good. Leaders operating out of the moral frame are concerned about their obligations and responsibilities to their followers. Moral frame leaders use some type of moral compass to direct their behavior. They practice what has been described as servant leadership and are concerned with those individuals and groups that are marginalized in their organizations and in society. In short, they are concerned about equality, fairness, and social justice.

There is little question that Mahatma Gandhi was a great believer in the necessity of operating out of the moral frame. One could argue that his every action was examined through a moral lens. He developed such a moral lens through his concept of *satyagraha*—nonviolent protest. In his native language, *satya* means "truth," and *agraha* means "firmness." Using this as his guide, he engaged in a moral war against persecution and injustice.

In chapter two, it was suggested that in order to make leadership a moral science, one should consider using the Ignatian vision as a guide to one's leadership practice. The Ignatian vision posits a concern for the *magis* (the more), discernment, *cura personalis* (care of the person), service to others, and social justice. Mahatma Gandhi's leadership behavior shows evidence of a deep concern for these ideals. He sought perfection (the *magis*) in the form of truth in all of his actions, he engaged in discernment in determining the best course of action for attaining his social-justice goals, he had great respect for human dignity, he devoted his life to service of others, and he was sensitive to those like the untouchables and others who were on the margins of society. In short, Mahatma Gandhi was a model of moral frame leadership behavior (Marcello, 2006; Pasten, 2006).

CONCLUSION

In many ways, Mahatma Gandhi could be considered the prototype for situational leadership behavior. He appropriately balanced his leadership behavior both across and within the five leadership frames. Mother Teresa of Calcutta and Martin Luther King Jr. are two of many who modeled their leadership behavior after that of Mahatma Gandhi. Martin Luther King Jr. is profiled later in this book. However, since Mother Teresa, a self-proclaimed disciple of Gandhi's, is not given a full chapter in this book, it is appropriate here to recount the similarities between her leadership behavior and Gandhi's.

Like Gandhi, Mother Teresa was a situational leader, able to move across and within the five leadership frames. One of her colleagues during her Calcutta days recalled Mother Teresa's use of the human resource frame, for which she is best known, but also of the structural, symbolic, political, and of course moral frames when it was appropriate.

> I witnessed not only the love and luminous smile for which she became increasingly internationally renowned but also here practical abilities, the way in which she liked to rearrange the furniture in the sisters' houses, the efficiency which meant that somehow everything was perfectly organized and administered without any organization or administration, the lack of sentimentality and the immense shrewdness that went hand in hand with intuitive understanding, the earthly qualities which did not detract from her spirituality but which were somehow molded by it. I came to know her humor and her toughness. She was, I discovered, not only humble and small but also strong-willed, resolute, determined and totally fearless, because God was on her side. (Spink, 1997, vii)

Examples of Mother Teresa's use of the structural frame abound. "What Mother wants, she gets" was a truism widely accepted among those who knew her. Notes written in longhand and signed *Mother* gave directions relating to the most ordinary of practical details. The central courtyard of the motherhouse contained two tanks of water. "Sisters, please do not keep anything on top of the tank," a carefully handwritten note commanded (Spink, 1997, ix). Through the astute use of structural leadership behavior, Mother Teresa was able to spread her Sisters of Charity congregation to an astounding five hundred branches throughout the world.

Mother Teresa's directions to her sisters were those of a firm believer in discipline; obedience was to be "prompt, simple, blind and cheerful, for Jesus was obedient unto death." Charity was to be manifested in "words, deeds, thoughts, desires and feelings, for Jesus went about doing good." Poverty was to be applied to all "desires and attachments, in likes and dislikes, for Jesus being rich made himself poor for us." Chastity was to be lived "in thoughts and affections, in desires and attachments, for Jesus is a jealous lover" (Spink, 1997, 73).

By 1979, only fifteen years after its founding, there were 158 Sisters of Charity foundations scattered throughout the world, with almost two thousand sisters. Again utilizing structural leadership behavior, Mother Teresa established the Missionary Brothers of Charity in 1967. She reasoned that the foundation of a male order was appropriate by noting that the men and women have different but complementary gifts.

Mother Teresa showed her structural frame side in dealing with a priest who had spoken in his homily against some of the traditional beliefs held by her and her congregation, among which was genuflecting before the Blessed Sacrament, which Catholics believe to be the body and blood of Jesus Christ. The priest said there was no need to do so outside of Mass. After he had finished speaking, Mother Teresa led the priest to the door, thanked him for coming, and informed him that he need not come again. She then proceeded to refute everything he had said in an hour-long dialectic with her nuns.

As far as the use of the human resource frame was concerned, Mother Teresa was quite prolific. After all, she dedicated her very being to the service of the poor. Like Gandhi, Mother Teresa considered every person to be a reflection of God. "Every person is Christ for me," she often said. "Since there is only one Jesus, the person I am meeting is the one person in the world at that moment." She was equally concerned about the unborn, as she set about combating abortion with adoption. She sent word out to the hospitals and clinics, "Please do not destroy the child. We will take the child" (Spink, 1997, 62).

Every morning, Mother Teresa would go from one baby to the next in her children's home in Calcutta. If she noticed one who was so frail and sick that he or she seemed close to death, Mother Teresa would wrap the child in a blanket and give it to one of her helpers to hold, with the simple instruction to love the child until it died. Her concern for people went far beyond the poor. When Queen Elizabeth II presented her with the Honorary Order of Merit, Mother Teresa inquired, "And how is your grandson, Prince William?" (Spink, 1997, 180).

Like Mahatma Gandhi, Mother Teresa practiced symbolic leadership behavior with great frequency. Both were very cognizant of their image and were careful to cultivate and project behavior that would reflect their ideals. For example, Mother Teresa cultivated her image of humility by noting that "No one thinks of the pen while writing a letter. That's exactly what I am in God's hand—a little pencil" (Spink, 1997, xii).

While Gandhi had his distinctive garb, Mother Teresa followed his lead by establishing her own unique uniform. In preparation for founding the Missionaries of Charity, she purchased three saris from the local bazaar—white ones edged with three blue stripes, which would in time become the distinctive habit of the new congregation. Symbolic behavior such as this was once again manifested when Mother Teresa was presented with the white Lincoln limousine that Pope Paul VI had used during his 1964 visit to India. Mother Teresa promptly raffled it off and used the funds for the poor.

In a similar incident in 1979, she earmarked the money she received for the Nobel Peace Prize for the hungry of Norway. The ceremonial banquet was also cancelled at her request, and again the money was used, with an additional amount raised by young Norwegians, for the poor.

In preparation for Christmas at her motherhouse in Calcutta, Mother Teresa once again exhibited symbolic behavior by setting up an empty crib in the chapel. Also in the chapel was a box containing straw. The sisters were encouraged to make small personal sacrifices and then to discreetly put a piece of straw in the crib so that when the statue of the baby Jesus was laid in the manger on Christmas Day, it would be a crib warmed by their love and sacrifice.

As mentioned earlier, Mother Teresa was a great admirer of Mahatma Gandhi, although they never met. She called her new international association of lay workers the "Co-Workers of Mother Teresa," because that is how Gandhi referred to his followers. And, symbolically adhering to Gandhi's principles of nonviolence, she said, "Let us not use bombs and guns to overcome the world. Let us use love and compassion. Peace begins with a smile" (Spink, 1997, 173).

In a final example of Mother Teresa's frequent use of symbolic leadership behavior, she was criticized for giving the poor fish instead of teaching them how to fish. In response, she said, "Ah, my God, you should see these people. They have not even the strength to lift a fishing rod, let alone use it to fish. Giving them fish, I help them to recover the strength for their fishing of tomorrow." She was similarly criticized by intellectuals for not having a cutting-edge philosophy that was tied to psychology and sociology. Once asked by a professor of sociology why she cared for people the way she did, she asked him if he had a flower garden. "Do you take care of the flowers?" she asked. "Don't you think a human being is so much more than a flower?" (Spink, 1977, 246).

Like Gandhi, Mother Teresa engaged in political leadership behavior when necessary and appropriate. The municipality of Calcutta was seeking a solution to the public relations problem of the destitute dying in the streets. When Mother Teresa applied to the municipality for a house, the municipality realized that in exchange for the gift of a house, Mother Teresa was offering to soothe the consciences of Calcutta's more socially minded citizens.

When Indira Gandhi supported sterilization as a means of birth control, Mother Teresa went to the capital to confront her. Mother Teresa's power and influence with the people became evident when, shortly after Indira Gandhi continued her support for sterilization, she was defeated at the poll and was succeeded by the pro-life candidate.

In a similar incident, in reaction to the Freedom of Religion bill in India, which would discourage the activities of foreign, especially non-Hindu, missionaries, she wrote to parliament, saying, "After much prayer and sacrifices I write to you, asking you to face God in prayer, before you take a step which will destroy the joy and freedom of our people. Don't belittle our Hindu religion by saying that our Hindu people will give up their religion for a plate of rice" (Spink, 1997, 157).

Mother Teresa was by no means as politically naive or unfamiliar with the ways of the world as it sometimes suited her to appear. She was political by not being political. She knew she had influence, and she was not above using it. For instance, in support of her request to Governor Mario Cuomo of New York for the release of three AIDS sufferers in Sing Sing prison (she called these victims the *Lepers of the West*), she added the leverage of her friend Mayor Koch, who announced that he felt like "a blessed instrument to be the vehicle for making this request." He could not believe that anyone would say no to Mother Teresa (Spink, 1997, 205).

In conclusion, we can readily see that Mahatma Gandhi's and Mother Teresa's leadership styles were extremely comparable. They were both situational, and they both operated effectively across and within the various frames of leadership behavior. Leaders and aspiring leaders would do well to take a page out of Mother Teresa's and Martin Luther King Jr.'s books and model their leadership behavior after that of Mahatma Gandhi.

Chapter 8
Adolph Hitler

Today Germany, tomorrow the world.

—A popular Nazi campaign slogan

BACKGROUND

Adolph Hitler was born in 1889 in Austria. He left school at an early age to become an artist. In 1909, after his mother had died, he moved to Vienna to earn a better living and pursue his interest in art. Within a year, however, he was living in homeless shelters and eating at soup kitchens.

In 1913, still not able to gain consistent employment, Hitler moved to Munich, Germany. At the outbreak of the World War I, in 1914, he volunteered for service in the German army. He fought bravely in the war and was promoted to corporal and decorated with both the Iron Cross Second Class and First Class.

After the war, he became involved in German politics and was able to hone his oratory skills and become a member of the German Workers Party. Given responsibility for publicity and propaganda, Hitler succeeded in attracting large audiences with his often fiery speech-making. At one such meeting he presented a twenty-five-point program of ideas that was to be the basis of the party's campaign platform. The name of the party was then changed to the National Socialist German Workers Party (Nazi Party).

Hitler continued to expand his influence in the party and began to form a private group of thugs which he used to enforce Nazi Party protocols. This group subsequently became popularly known as Hitler's Brownshirts. During the summer of 1920, Hitler also chose the swastika as the Nazi Party emblem.

On November 8, 1923, Hitler led an attempt to take over the local Bavarian government in Munich in an action that became known as the Beer Hall Putsch. Hitler fled the scene and was later arrested and charged with treason. After his trial he was sentenced to five years in prison, during which he wrote the book *Mein Kampf* (My Struggle).

The Great Depression hit Germany especially hard. These desperate conditions were helpful to Hitler and his Nazi Party in gaining power, and by 1933 the Nazi Party became the largest in the Reichstag. At that point, Hitler demanded that he be made chancellor but was offered only the position of vice-chancellor in a coalition government, which he refused. Finally on January 30, 1933, President Hindenburg, under great pressure, decided to appoint Hitler chancellor. By the end of 1933, Hitler passed a law making the Nazi Party the only political party in Germany. When Hindenburg died, in 1934, Hitler was named both president and chancellor.

During the years following Hitler's consolidation of power, he set about the Nazification of Germany. Among other things, all youth associations were abolished and reformed as a single entity known simply as the Hitler Youth. As part of the Nazification movement, the Jewish population was increasingly persecuted and ostracized from society.

Hitler and the Nazi Party pursued a foreign policy based on the goal of providing *Lebensraum* (living space) for the German people. The first significant implementation of this policy was the German invasion of Poland in 1939 which caused the British and French to declare war on Germany, leading to the outbreak of World War II.

Eventually Germany and her major allies, Italy and Japan, were defeated and by 1945 Germany was in ruins. Hitler's vision of territorial conquest and racial subjugation caused the deaths of tens of millions of people, including the systematic genocide of an estimated six million Jews in what is known as the Holocaust.

On April 30, 1945, with the Allies breathing down his neck, Hitler committed suicide, shooting himself while also swallowing a cyanide capsule (Redlich, 1998).

SITUATIONAL LEADERSHIP ANALYSIS

Situational models of leadership differ from earlier trait and behavioral models in asserting that no single way of leading works in all situations. Rather, appropriate behavior depends on the circumstances at a given time. Effective managers diagnose the situation, identify the leadership style or behavior that will be most effective, and then determine whether they can implement the required style. Despite his over-reliance on some frames and under-reliance on others, there is much evidence to conclude that Adolph Hitler practiced situational leadership.

After his failed Beer House Putsch in 1923, when he attempted to overturn the German government by force, Hitler learned the value of situational leadership. He realized that he had to bring both the German bourgeoisie and conservatives to his side. He needed—at least for the time being—an alliance with them that would require him to be flexible in his leadership behavior.

The unsuccessful putsch was a turning point in Hitler's life. He decided to change his tactics and achieve power in Germany not through armed revolution but by convincing the masses of the German people that in their hearts they knew he was right. He realized it was time to abandon structural frame leadership behavior and embrace the human resource, symbolic, and political frames.

Another notable instance of Hitler's use of situational leadership came in 1936. That year saw him shift his emphasis from domestic to foreign matters and preparations for war. The real Hitler was being revealed.

What he could not achieve by persuasion and bullying, he would acquire through military means. The military buildup would no longer be hidden. Hitler began to openly express what he had always felt in his heart: that a war to accomplish his goals was necessary. But he knew enough that the timing had to be right. By 1936, he believed the situation was right.

One would never accuse Adolph Hitler of being a human resource leader. However, he was situational enough to know that he could not depend exclusively on structural and political behavior to be successful. Once again, when the situation called for it, he could adjust and practice human resource and symbolic leadership behavior and be a seductive prophet to the German people. Carl Jung called him "the loudspeaker that magnified the inaudible whispers of the German soul" (Redlich, 1998, 302).

THE STRUCTURAL FRAME

Structural frame leaders seek to develop a new model of the relationship of structure, strategy, and environment for their organizations. Strategic planning, extensive preparation, and effecting change are priorities for them. It is fair to say that Hitler spent a good deal of his time operating out of the structural frame of leadership.

Hitler, we are told, was a man with a rudimentary intellect devoid of scruples, an individual with no respect for God or humankind. He owed his success to two outstanding qualities: his rhetorical skills and his theatrical delivery. Despite these obvious symbolic frame strengths, however, he utilized a good deal of structural frame leadership behavior

Hitler often spoke of the primacy of mind over matter, the will over the flesh—a typical structural behavior approach. In *Mein Kampf*, he wrote about a visit to the local government offices where he was shocked by the amount of laziness, apathy, and corruption—all characteristics that he abhorred.

In contrast to what he witnessed in the government, Hitler continually displayed the characteristics of a structural frame leader. His associates agreed that he possessed an exceptionally good memory. He was able to store and retrieve a large body of knowledge, citing figures of gun calibers and ship tonnage with great accuracy.

Hitler distained formal education, but in true structural frame fashion, he was an avid reader and devoured books, pamphlets, and other reading material. And he was a great fan of the great German composer Wagner—especially appreciating his military compositions. However, he had a very limited knowledge of the famous German philosophers like Schopenhauer and Nietzsche.

Being knowledgeable about military matters was of the utmost importance to Hitler. According to the generals who worked under him, as well as military historians, Hitler's knowledge of military science was impressive. In addition, he was by and large perceived to have good judgment. During the long years of successful operations, Hitler made few mistakes

In an extreme use of structural behavior, any questionable lack of judgment was rationalized away. In the Bormann papers, for example, Hitler offered the following explanations: (1) The putsch had not been successful because he had no choice but to act; (2) the destruction of the Czech state was not a mistake; instead he had acted too late; (3) he did not pursue the British at Dunkirk because he did not want to humiliate the British, who he hoped would join him in his fight against the Bolsheviks; (4) the attack on Russia was not a mistake because the conquest of Russian soil and mineral reserves was of the utmost importance to his ultimate goal of world domination; he blamed Stalingrad on the lack of fighting spirit in his generals; and (5) he admitted misjudgment on his declaration of war on the United States, but he lauded Japan for attacking the United States at his urging and making it divide its forces on two fronts (Redlich, 1998, 296).

Hitler's belief in racial superiority led him to believe that the Germans should establish European hegemony and ultimately rule the world. This ultimate goal, and the plans to achieve it, was outlined very clearly in *Mein Kampf*. Thus he went about his pursuit of these goals in a very structural frame way. He had an elaborate and well-thought-out plan.

Hitler's economic achievements in his first years as führer, such as the abolition of unemployment, the military buildup, and the elimination of the last vestiges of the Treaty of Versailles, were just preliminary steps on the way to his real goal, which was to rule the world. Because, he believed, the Germans did not possess the resources necessary for their survival, they would have to obtain those resources from other nations, and if other nations were not willing to give up their resources, the Germans would acquire them through force.

Hitler pursued his goals in a very structural way—methodically, and with forethought. For example, to obtain purity of race, he had a law passed stipulating compulsory sterilization by surgical procedure for those carrying genetic illness. On another front, to Hitler, education and schooling meant first and foremost indoctrination in the spirit of National Socialism. He put training in physical education first and character formation second, because they were prerequisites for military training, and general education a distant third.

Although Hitler was very conservative in his preference for an agrarian society over an industrialized one, in sharp contrast, he advocated technical change, particularly in automotive transportation—he was responsible for the autobahn and the Volkswagen—but also in modern city planning, protection of the environment, and even modernization of household equipment to improve the lot of the German housewife. He used structural leadership behavior to make these dreams a reality.

As part of his long-term plan to dominate the world, one of Hitler's major short-term goals was to forge an alliance among Germany, Italy, and Great Britain against Russia. A secondary goal was to undermine the relationship between Great Britain and France. Of course he was never able to fully achieve either the ultimate goal or many of the intermediate goals, but having such a systematic plan is endemic to a structural frame leader.

As is often the case when a leader practices structural frame behavior to the extreme, Hitler considered himself to be irreplaceable. "I am convinced," he declared, "of the power of my brain and decisiveness. I have the greatest experience in all questions of armament; I will not shy away from anything and will destroy anybody who is against me" (Redlich, 1998, 303).

THE HUMAN RESOURCE FRAME

Human resource leaders believe in people and communicate that belief. They are passionate about productivity through people. Needless to say, this will be a very brief section because Hitler's leadership behavior was notoriously bereft of the human touch.

According to Percy Schramm, an early acquaintance of Hitler's, he did have some human sensitivity, but it was often subverted by a darker side. According to Schramm, Hitler was "the friend of women, children and animals—this was one face of Hitler neither acted nor feigned, but entirely genuine. There was, however, a second face which he did not show to his table companions, though it was no less genuine" (Machtan, 2001, 69).

Albert Speer, Hitler's notorious armament chief, had become an important member of the inner circle by the beginning of World War II. Speer's statement that if Hitler had been capable of having a friend, he would have been his friend is probably accurate (Redlich, 1998, 188). However, there were many more instances of Hitler lacking the capacity to express human resource behavior than there were of the reverse.

Hitler's relationship with his general staff was always one of aloofness, especially when the assassination attempts increased. Apart from his relationships with his companion Eva Braun, young people, and animals, he did not display much by way of human resource frame behavior.

Although officers as well as enlisted men described Hitler in very complimentary terms during his World War I days, he was also considered to be aloof, brooding, and restless. He read abridged editions of philosophical works and wandered around at night shooting rats, of all things.

By most accounts, Hitler was a self-aggrandizing narcissist. However, narcissism is a characteristic trait of nearly all outstanding political leaders. Hitler just took his narcissism to the extreme, which left him almost incapable of operating out of the human resource frame when it would have been appropriate to do so.

THE SYMBOLIC FRAME

In the symbolic frame, the organization is seen as a stage, a theater in which every actor plays certain roles, and the symbolic leader attempts to communicate the right impressions to the right audiences. One could argue that in addition to the political frame, Hitler's skill in effectively utilizing the symbolic frame was one of his great strengths.

One of the reasons that Hitler was so effective in his use of the symbolic frame was that he possessed the ability to become completely absorbed in his role of the moment and to believe in the truth of what he happened to be saying at the time. This helped him to convince others of his sincerity and successfully conceal his obsession with the acquisition of power and influence. Hitler cultivated a myth around himself and employed it to his own ends.

Hitler used symbolic leadership behavior in supporting his efforts toward implementing the doctrine of social Darwinism in Germany and beyond. "National Socialism," he said, "is nothing but applied biology." In *Mein Kampf*, he wrote, "It is a half measure to let incurably sick people steadily contaminate the remaining healthy ones. This is in keeping with the humanitarianism which, to avoid hurting one individual, lets a hundred others perish. The demand that defective people be prevented from propagating equally defective offspring is a demand of the clearest reason and, systematically executed, it represents the most human act of mankind" (Redlich, 1998, 113). Although logically convoluted, this argument convinced many Germans of the validity of social Darwinism, because of Hitler's way with symbolic leadership behavior.

Hitler also used symbolic leadership behavior to garner allegiance from the young people of Germany by establishing propagandizing youth clubs. His alternative to support for education in Germany was establishment of Hitler Youth, along with the League of German Girls. By 1939, an amazing seven million young people were members of these clubs.

The familiar Nazi symbol of the swastika and the salute of "Heil Hitler" were but two examples of Hitler's use of the symbolic frame. He copied much of the organization of the militia from the leisure organization Dopo Lovore, and the fascist greeting of an outstretched arm from Mussolini. Italians called Hitler *"Il Imitatore"* (the Imitator). The title of the leader, *Duce I Capo di Governimiento*, was translated by the Germans as *Führer* and *Reichskanzler*. Hitler admitted that there would never have been Brownshirts without there first being Blackshirts (Redlich, 1998, 137).

In another display of symbolic behavior, Hitler insisted that the armistice with France be staged in the forest of Compiègne, and in the same dining car in which the Treaty of Versailles was signed in 1919.

Two additional incidents demonstrated Hitler's flair for the dramatic. In 1942, he expressed to Heinrich Himmler one of his favorite comparisons, equating Jews to bacilli: "It is one of the greatest revolutions of the world. The Jew will be recognized. The same fight that Koch and Pasteur had to fight will be waged by us. Innumerable illnesses have been caused by this bacillus: the Jew," he asserted (Redlich, 1998, 185). In a similar display of symbolic behavior, after an assassination attempt in 1944, Hitler took Mussolini to the wrecked room and dramatically remarked, "After today's miraculous escape, I am more convinced than ever that I am destined to bring our great task to a happy ending" (Redlich, 1998, 185).

Even in defeat, Hitler managed to utilize symbolic behavior. "If fate has decreed that we should be crushed by a superior force, then let us go down with our head held high and secure in the knowledge that the honor remains without blemish," he said. He was referring to the proud stand of the Greek leader Leonidas and the three hundred Spartans who fought to the death to hold off a superior force until the Spartan army could be reinforced (Redlich, 1998, 190).

Hitler's understanding of the masses and his exceptional ability to relate to them is well documented. The responses of large groups of people, in mass meetings and at the national congresses, contributed more than any other factor to his identity as a charismatic leader. At the end, Hitler lost his strength as a leader because, being sequestered, he could no longer touch the masses. Nevertheless, Hitler was successful largely because, like the true situational leader that he was, he correctly gauged the readiness level of the German people for his message.

Two German authors, Alexander Mitscherlich and Peter Hofstatter, both believed that the Germans were receptive to such symbolic behavior. They opined that a charismatic leader need not actually be a strong leader as long as his followers believe he is strong—perception becomes reality. And, as we have seen, Hitler was expert at projecting an omniscient and confident image through the masterful application of symbolic leadership behavior (Redlich, 1998).

THE POLITICAL FRAME

Leaders operating out of the political frame clarify what they want and what they can get. Political leaders are realists above all. They never let what they want cloud their judgment about what is possible. They assess the distribution of power and interest. As stated above, along with the symbolic frame, the political frame was Hitler's strongest. His perceptions were keen when it involved human weakness, deception, and bluffing, resulting in a basically cynical and mistrustful view of human beings. These traits made Hitler expert in the effective use of political frame leadership behavior.

In *Mein Kampf*, Hitler describes himself as fundamentally a political frame leader of the most extreme kind. He was a self-proclaimed Machiavellian who was concerned solely with accumulation of power and was prepared to destroy his adopted country to retain it. He was not motivated by any formal ideology but was driven to acquire power for power's sake.

Hitler recognized early on in Vienna that life is not ruled by the principles of humanity but by victory and defeat. His belief was that the stronger and abler will always win. So, in 1926, he fought and won office against the radical opposition by using political frame behavior and agreeing to vote in favor of a restitution of properties to the former German princes that had been taken from them in 1918, a cause dear to the older German conservatives. Again in 1932, he knew that in order to come to power, he had to appeal to the anticommunism of the German conservatives. So he warned Hindenburg that "the Bolshevization of the masses proceeds rapidly" (Lukacs, 1997, 87). He knew this was not true, but he also knew that this kind of argument would impress Hindenburg and the conservatives.

Hitler even used sports to his political advantage. His only physical workouts were expander exercises that enabled him to endure giving the familiar Nazi greeting with an outstretched arm during the endless parades. His interest in spectator sports was once again politically motivated, the most famous example being his use of the 1936 Olympics for propaganda purposes to show the world his benign leadership of a civilized country and to demonstrate Aryan superiority.

Hitler used a combination of political frame leadership behavior and symbolic behavior in pointing out that the National Socialist revolution was the most bloodless and disciplined revolution of all time. Unlike the bloody French Revolution and the American Revolution, Hitler was proud to declare that "no windows had been broken" during the German revolution (Redlich, 1998, 125).

In the late 1930s when the Western democracies and Russia protested Hitler's aggressive behavior but took no punitive action, the politically minded Hitler correctly interpreted it as a sign of weakness. He had an astute sense for identifying weakness in his enemies, and in the absence of any resistance, his use of political frame behavior proliferated.

Sometimes, however, his use of political frame behavior backfired. In a sarcastic 1939 speech about Franklin D. Roosevelt, Hitler neither considered nor cared that his words might offend Roosevelt and the American people, or that it might make it easier for the American president, in spite of stubborn U.S. isolationism, to reinforce ties between the United States and Great Britain. In a similar incident, Hitler miscalculated in thinking that Great Britain and France would not honor their treaty with Poland, when in 1939 Germany invaded Poland and France and England immediately declared war on Germany.

That same year, when the German-Polish conflict was acute, the ten-year Soviet-German nonaggression pact was signed. Hitler, the archenemy of the Bolshevists and Jews, and the antifascist Stalin, made for strange bedfellows. Of course, the pact was for political purposes only (i.e., to keep Russia from interfering in Poland), and Hitler had no intention of adhering to it. According to him, "It was a pact with Satan in order to drive out the devil" (Redlich, 1998, 147).

Hitler used more political frame behavior when, shortly before the outbreak of World War II, he signed major treaties with Japan and later Italy. The Tripartite Pact of 1940 carved the Eastern Hemisphere into spheres of influence controlled by Germany, Italy, and Japan. Ultimately, however, Hitler's use of political frame behavior became increasingly ineffective and helped lead to Germany's final humiliation and defeat.

THE MORAL FRAME

The moral frame is my own contribution to situational leadership theory. In my view, the moral frame completes situational leadership theory. Without it, leaders could just as easily use their leadership skills for promoting evil as for promoting good. Leaders operating out of the moral frame are concerned about their obligations and responsibilities to their followers. Moral frame leaders use some type of moral compass to direct their behavior. They practice what has been described as servant leadership and are concerned with those individuals and groups that are marginalized in their organizations and in society. In short, they are concerned about equality, fairness, and social justice. Adolph Hitler was the antithesis of a leader acting out of the moral frame.

Both during his life and after his death, Hitler was considered by many to be the devil incarnate. At the very least, he was an evil man. Because he was almost totally devoid of any well-intentioned human resource behavior, he became amoral at best and immoral at worst. This is what can happen when an otherwise great leader fails to operate out of the moral frame. Instead, Hitler drifted into a policy of amoral radical social Darwinism. He became what German psychiatrist Oswald Bumke described as a "hysterical sociopath" (Ridlich, 1998, 333).

CONCLUSION

As we have seen, Hitler was a highly intelligent man with a large store of knowledge—much of it half-knowledge, especially in critical areas. The centerpiece of his philosophy was social Darwinism and anti-Semitism. He was a fanatic but was an effective leader for much of his life. His defense mechanisms, especially his projections, could fill a psychiatry textbook. He was fixated on the paranoid belief of a Jewish world conspiracy against Germany.

When his military and political programs failed, he became rigid and extremely vindictive. His destructiveness far exceeded his constructive programs, which made him both one of the world's greatest leaders and one of its greatest criminals. No one who knew Hitler before 1919 would have predicted an extraordinary career but then a fundamental change occurred. He discovered that he could speak dramatically and convincingly.

But it would be naive to assume that Hitler had such an impact solely because he was an effective orator. He changed Germany and the world because he had a message and carried out a program that Germany at that time wanted to hear. As with great leaders before and after him, he was able to accurately gauge the readiness level of his followers to receive his message. He promised that he would make up for Germany's defeat and humiliation by making it the most powerful nation in Europe. He vowed to create a proud, patriotic Germany, to restore the German army to its former glory, and to create full employment and economic prosperity. He came dangerously close to fulfilling his promises.

There is no question that Hitler was an effective leader. His effective use of the structural, symbolic, and political leadership frames was exemplary. However, his deficiencies in the use of the human resource and moral frames rendered him a leader in the pursuit of evil rather than good and ultimately led to his demise. He is a tragic example of what can happen when an otherwise outstanding leader does not operate out of the moral frame and has no moral compass to direct his or her leadership behavior.

Chapter 9

Pope John Paul II

How many divisions has the pope?

—Joseph Stalin

BACKGROUND

John Paul II was born Karol Józef Wojtyła on May 18, 1920, in Wadowice, Poland. Growing up, John Paul II was athletic and enjoyed skiing and swimming. He went to Krakow's Jagiellonian University in 1938 where he showed an interest in theater and poetry. The next year Nazi troops occupied Poland. Wanting to become a priest, John Paul II began studying at a secret seminary. After World War II ended, he finished his religious studies at a Krakow seminary and was ordained a priest in 1946.

John Paul II served in several parishes in and around Krakow and became the bishop of Ombi in 1958 and then the archbishop of Krakow six years later. Considered one of the Catholic Church's leading thinkers, he participated in the Second Vatican Council, or Vatican II, in 1962. He was made a cardinal in 1967 by Pope Paul VI.

In 1976, John Paul II made history by becoming the first non-Italian pope in more than four hundred years. As pope, he traveled the world, visiting more than a hundred countries, scores more than any of his predecessors.

In 1981, an assassin shot John Paul twice in St. Peter's Square in Vatican City. Fortunately, he was able to recover from his injuries and later famously forgave his attacker.

John Paul II often spoke out as an advocate of human rights and strongly opposed capital punishment. A charismatic figure, John Paul II used his influence to bring about political change and is credited with the fall of communism in his native Poland.

In his later years, John Paul's health began to decline. He also visibly trembled at times and was rumored to have Parkinson's disease. He passed away on April 2, 2005, at his Vatican City residence. More than three million people passed his casket to bid farewell to their beloved Holy Father at St. Peter's Basilica. Church officials began the canonization process soon after his death, waving the usual five-year waiting period.

Many believe that Pope John Paul II's greatest accomplishment was his part in bringing about the demise of the Soviet Union. He and Ronald Reagan are considered by many to be the two external figures that most contributed to the ultimate defeat of atheistic and totalitarian communism as an effective form of government. John Paul II and Ronald Reagan worked very closely to bring about the final outcome. Thus I have interwoven the leadership behavior of Ronald Reagan with that of Pope John Paul II in this analysis. We will find that Pope John Paul II was the yin to Ronald Reagan's yang in this matter (Bernstein, 1996).

SITUATIONAL LEADERSHIP ANALYSIS

Situational models of leadership differ from earlier trait and behavioral models in asserting that no single way of leading works in all situations. Rather, appropriate behavior depends on the circumstances at a given time. Effective managers diagnose the situation, identify the leadership style or behavior that will be most effective, and then determine whether they can implement the required style. As we shall see, although he could be very rigid about Catholic dogma, it can easily be asserted that Pope John Paul II was a situational leader who was willing and able to vary his leadership behavior depending on the situation.

Even though he was more comfortable in certain of the five leadership frames, Pope John Paul II was able to appropriately alter his behavior when necessary. Normally apolitical in his outlook, once he decided that he would have to get involved in politics after all, he became a master at it. Jacek Woźniakowski, a leading spokesman for lay Catholics is Poland, said of John Paul II, "I was struck by what a quick study he was, how rapidly he assimilated information, how he reshaped it to his way of thinking, and how especially after following a long political discussion in silence, he had this extremely interesting way of summing things up" (Bernstein, 1996, 124).

After returning from a successful visit to Mexico, John Paul II found himself in a confrontation with Andrei Gromyko, the Soviet foreign minister. Gromyko was an aloof man used to masking his true thoughts with diplomatic legalese. Any observation or objection ran off of him like water running off the proverbial duck's back. The pope realized that his charm was useless here, but true to the situational nature of his leadership behavior, he bypassed human resource behavior and adopted a very formal structural frame manner in dealing with his soulless adversary.

John Paul II demonstrated his situational leadership nature on a visit to Poland, his homeland. His arrival at the national sanctuary at Czestochowa for a three-day stay coincided with a change of tone in his speeches. Religious themes now took over from political ones, though critical allusions to the communist system continued. In the wake of two recent labor strikes in Warsaw, John Paul II had chosen to intervene in a nonconfrontational way, turning his meetings and speeches from the previously inflammatory ones into a "living catechism."

Because of John Paul II's reliance on situational leadership behavior, his papacy can be seen as three distinct phases in which he varied his leadership behavior depending on the primary goal of each phase. The first phase was the reestablishment of the church as a universal influence for good in the world. His foreign visits and their symbolic implications were the primary vehicle for addressing this situation. The second phase was his battle against communism, in which he used mostly political leadership behavior. *Veritas Splendor*, published in the fifteenth year of his pontificate, is the encyclical that culminated his papacy. In it he confronts what he considered the greatest danger in modern times: moral relativism. Thus, in the third phase of his reign, the problem was the moral crisis in the Western world. In the later years of his papacy, issues such as materialism, secularism, abortion, and human rights were his focus, and he mainly used structural leadership in the form of using encyclicals to make his points.

THE STRUCTURAL FRAME

Structural frame leaders seek to develop a new model of the relationship of structure, strategy, and environment for their organizations. Strategic planning, extensive preparation, and effecting change are priorities for them. John Paul II was very astute at practicing structural leadership behavior under the proper circumstances.

When John Paul II was challenged theologically or philosophically, one could readily see his structural behavior come to the surface. He would firmly stand his ground, but in a loving way. In a somewhat paternalistic view, others had to be led by the hand, like children, onto the path of truth. On issues like contraception, abortion, women priests, gay marriage, and divorce, he would take a structural leadership approach and immediately go into his teaching mode, not allowing an objection, but with a human resource touch.

According to Cardinal Jean Villot, John Paul II's secretary of state, one's first impression of the pope was of his care for humanity. But there was an aspect of his personality that did not reveal itself initially, a hard, hidden core that sustained him, an iron will and the power of that will. "It is through the will that man is lord of his actions," Wojtyła noted in one of his essays, adding that self-control is the most fundamental manifestation of the value of a person (Bernstein, 1996, 121). Anyone who looked past his always abundant display of human resource behavior would have known that there were structural leadership leanings at his core.

One of the first things that John Paul II did as pope was to use structural behavior and expound on his policies and strategies: fidelity to the Vatican Council above all, and collegiality. And then, as requested by those who were frightened by the rapid changes of the post-council period, John Paul II insisted on obedience to the pope's teaching, respect for liturgical rules, and discipline. Finally, he stressed the need for ecumenism and for peace and justice in the world. He urged the clergy not to trade their priestly spiritualism for an exaggerated role in social problems and politics. He championed the case of celibacy as the best way to devote one's energies exclusively to the dissemination of Christ's teachings. At a conference with nuns, he insisted on the necessity of wearing the religious habit. He reminded members of the Vatican Secretariat for the Union of Christians that the ecumenical movement was not to compromise the truth. He lionized mothers who refused to have abortions when their lives were at risk. He warned of the dangers of divorce and forbade even the mention of the ordination of women.

In his negotiations with communist states, John Paul II utilized structural leadership behavior frequently, instructing his representatives that henceforth in their bargaining with the communist states, they should not minimize the repugnance of Marxism and its belief in a Godless society. Rather, they should highlight it.

The pope urged the recalcitrant clergy supporting liberation theology, mostly in Central and South America, not to make themselves available for political positions. "You are spiritual guides, not social leaders, not political executives or functionaries of a secular order," he said (Bernstein, 1996, 209). His Polish experience taught him not to align the church with any political party or ideology. "This notion," he proclaimed, "is not in harmony with the Church's teaching" (Bernstein, 1996, 209).

In true structural leadership style, he sent an unequivocal message to the Latin Americans and the rest of the world. John Paul II would never let Catholics align themselves with Marxist movements—or capitalist ones for that matter—in a battle for social justice and democracy. He would never approve of what the Italian pope Paul VI had declared in his encyclical *Populorum Progresso*—permission in extreme cases to revolt against deeply entrenched dictatorships. He imposed the peaceful methods that he used during the Nazi occupation of Poland on his Catholic flock.

Pope John Paul II used structural behavior in his efforts to overthrow the Communist Party in his native Poland. The labor strikes that occurred at the shipyards there were just the opening that the pope sought. His basic strategy for defeating communism was to take advantage of any weakness in communism's armor, so he publicly endorsed the strikes.

In a typical structural leadership move, John Paul II planned to use Zbigniew Brzezinski, the Polish-born national security advisor of Jimmy Carter and Ronald Reagan, in his assault on communism. After the initial stage was set through Brzezinski, John Paul II planned to use Reagan himself as his primary partner in the process. Reagan and the pope agreed with Brzezinski's assessment: "If you were able to shake and disrupt Poland, then the shock waves would radiate out in many directions, into the Ukraine, the Balkans, in Latvia, Lithuania and Estonia, and Czechoslovakia" (Bernstein, 1996, 262).

The pope's strategy to fight communism in Poland was to use the labor movement, Solidarity, to create unrest and to take further advantage of the situation when the time was right. The time was right in 1983 when the pope visited his native land, and soon after the visit the Communist Party's influence in Poland began to wane.

Pope John Paul II further exhibited structural behavior in his daily work schedule with seventeen-hour days. Unlike his predecessors, John Paul II took his responsibilities as bishop of Rome seriously. On Sundays he often visited one of the 323 Roman parish churches. The week before the visits, John Paul II would invite the pastors to the Vatican to hear about the problems of his parish and his parishioners.

As a practicing structural leader, Pope John Paul II always kept his primary goals in sight. Whether in the Vatican or on his travels, everything he did was aimed at building support for his leadership and his vision of a Catholic Church that was relevant. He demanded that the church's leaders, priests, nuns, bishops, prelates, and theologians obey papal teachings such as celibacy, staying out of politics, administering the sacraments, and wearing religious garb.

When John Paul II sensed that the church was moving away from traditional doctrine, he called the Great Synod in 1986. He made certain that the final report of the Synod reflected the traditional Roman Catholic ideals and practices.

During his papacy, some Vatican II reforms spread throughout the church and were actualized in the daily practices of the Catholic communities, including a modernized liturgy; improved relations with members of Protestant, Orthodox, and Jewish faiths; more frequent consultation between the Vatican and the bishops; increased roles for girls and women in the Mass and other religious ceremonies; and the church as a community, not a hierarchical, organization. However, as is oftentimes characteristic of a structural frame leader, the basic doctrine and practice remained very firmly intact.

THE HUMAN RESOURCE FRAME

Human resource leaders believe in people and communicate that belief. They are passionate about productivity through people. There are myriad instances of Pope John Paul II expressing his respect for human dignity through the practice of human resource frame leadership behavior.

John Paul II often expressed human resource behavior in an ecumenical way. For instance, Jurek Kluger, his Jewish boyhood friend, once ran into the parish church to get Karol to join him in a soccer game, to the amazement of the women who saw the son of the president of the Jewish community next to the altar. Wojtyła remarked, "Aren't we all God's children?" (Bernstein, 1996, 32).

He reinforced his position toward non-Christians after he become pope, when he declared that "the cause of Christ can also be furthered by the choice of a worldview diametrically opposed to Christianity. Everyone who makes this choice with the innermost conviction must have our respect" (Bernstein, 1996, 224).

As mentioned earlier, Pope John Paul II especially loved young people. They were his hope. For them he established World Youth Day in 1986, a biannual celebration attended by hundreds of thousands of young Catholics from around the world. He hosted each Youth Day and he expressed what he referred to as an "authentic fatherhood" toward the young people.

Perhaps the following incident best demonstrates John Paul II's reliance on human resource leadership behavior even in uncomfortable situations. A young student-body president at Louvain-la-Neuve, Veronique Yoruba, verbally attacked the pope about his stand on the sinfulness of contraception. Her question generated an audience outburst, with the pope's fans and Yoruba fans taunting one another. John Paul II's reaction was mild and paternal—he kissed the young student on the head.

THE SYMBOLIC FRAME

In the symbolic frame, the organization is seen as a stage, a theater in which every actor plays certain roles, and the symbolic leader attempts to communicate the right impressions to the right audiences. Considering John Paul II's experience on stage as a young actor, it is not surprising that as pope he was extremely active in the symbolic frame.

We begin the exploration of John Paul II's extensive use of symbolic leadership behavior in 1986 when the Polish Communist Party leaders refused permission for John Paul II's visit to Poland. After the decision was reversed, the pope finally made his triumphant journey to his homeland. The Communist Party proved correct in its resistance to the visit because John Paul II's presence resurrected the Polish nation's basic democratic leanings. As a result, immediately after the papal visit, the influences of communism in Poland began to wane.

During the nine days of his first visit to Poland as pope, the men, women, and especially the young people of Poland lived in a state of suspended animation and great excitement as if they were experiencing not just a visit of a hometown boy but the coming of a messiah. The experience was overwhelming.

What took place at Warsaw's Victory Square was a phenomenon. In true symbolic form, John Paul II never said anything that might lead directly to a confrontation between church and state; what he said brought about a new beginning for the Roman Catholic Church in Poland and the Soviet Union. Through him, the church was demanding respect for human rights as well as for Christian values. As intended, these demands represented a direct assault on Marxist ideology.

In the United States, Ronald Reagan was campaigning for the Republican presidential nomination. He was said to have been sitting in front of a television at his ranch near Santa Barbara with his friend Richard Allen, a Catholic, who would become one of his cabinet members. As the crowd became mesmerized by John Paul II, Reagan's eyes began to fill with tears. "What the two men were witnessing confirmed that there was metastasis in the body of communism" (Bernstein, 1996, 8).

"How many divisions has the pope?" Stalin asked contemptuously during World War II. To this question, an answer would soon be given in the form of the movement promoted by Solidarity, a noncommunist Polish workers union within the Soviet empire that, encouraged by John Paul II, would help free Poland from Russian domination.

John Paul II's challenge of communism was not based on some ideological principle. Rather, it was based on his belief in the morality of human rights. In an astute use of symbolic behavior, the pope was inserting the Vatican and Poland between the Washington and Moscow coordinates in order to help defeat communism.

John Paul II saw himself as a man called by God to change the face of his church and the world. He had been an actor, poet, playwright, and philosopher—and now a pontiff. So it was no surprise for him to be seen as a lightning rod for change. As pope, he became one of the most remarkable figures of the second half of the twentieth century. Through a magical display of symbolic leadership behavior, he energized and was energized during his many papal visits by perhaps the largest crowds in history ever assembled before a leader.

On a personal note, I had the opportunity to witness firsthand the characteristic charisma of John Paul II. In 1979, as co-chair of the Papal Visit Committee that organized the pope's visit to Philadelphia, and again a couple of years later when I attended the opening mass at the New Orleans Superdome when he visited there, I saw how the young people greeted the pontiff with the kind of mass hysteria usually reserved for rock superstars. His ability to effectively utilize symbolic leadership behavior was nonpareil.

Even as a young Polish cardinal, Wojtyła knew the impact of symbolic behavior. For example, from his earliest days as a bishop, he had tried to obtain a building permit for a long-promised church at the communist-built industrial park. So, in another symbolic gesture, he spent Christmas Eve celebrating midnight Mass outdoors in the snow and subzero cold at the site where the Polish communist regime had broken its promise.

John Paul II's use of symbolic leadership behavior began as early as his very first trip abroad as pope. He decided to make his first trip to countries outside of Europe that had a longstanding Roman Catholic tradition—Mexico and South America. However Cardinal Jean Villot, the pope's secretary of state, was afraid that the pope might be the object of assault in these anticlerical nations.

But John Paul II was not interested in the qualms of his secretary of state. What he had in mind was something unimagined by previous pontiffs, a reform similar to the Vatican Council —the remaking of the papacy—and thus he became the most traveled Holy Father in history.

As it happened, the Mexican people paid no attention to their government's anticlerical policies. Their faith swept away the memory of bygone days when the church favored the aristocracy over the poor. The pope was greeted with ringing church bells. Similar to his other papal visits, at the airport, a children's choir and small orchestra blasted out a papal welcome. Millions of Mexicans thronged the route to Mexico City's central square, waving thousands of little white-and-yellow papal flags.

Some comparative statistics dramatically demonstrate the extent to which John Paul II relied on symbolic leadership behavior. His predecessor, Paul VI, took only eight trips to foreign countries during his reign of fifteen years. In his first six years alone, John Paul II visited thirty-seven foreign countries. By the end of his papacy he had visited almost every continent in the world—some, including North America, more than once. In this symbolic way, he was asserting his global leadership.

He was the first pope to understand the power of television and master the medium. Liturgies celebrated by the pope became epic performances. Wherever he appeared in cities, a Super Bowl atmosphere prevailed.

John Paul II's visit to Auschwitz was particularly symbolic. He had with him a small bouquet of white and red carnations, which he placed on the grave of the Franciscan priest Father Maximilian Kolbe, who was martyred for having harbored hundreds of Jews, preventing them from being sent to the concentration camps. Of course some Jews were upset because he only honored a Catholic's martyrdom, but the pope's point was to apologize for past anti-Jewish sentiments by being the first pope to visit a site of the Holocaust.

In addition to political leadership behavior, Pope John Paul II utilized symbolic leadership behavior in his war on communism. While the pope worked in his study on plans to defeat communism, Lech Wałęsa's Solidarity movement, with the pope's encouragement, was wreaking havoc on the Polish shipyards.

On August 31, 1976, the historic Gdansk accords were signed, ratifying the establishment of the first independent labor union behind the Iron Curtain. It was the beginning of the end of communism in Poland and in the Soviet Union. And the symbolism of the Gdansk accords did not go unnoticed throughout the world. Sister Zofia Zdybicka, a philosopher friend of Karol Wojtyła, while watching the strikes on television news said, "This is a lesson for the whole world. Look at the contradiction: The *workers* are against communism" (Bernstein, 1996, 241).

Further use of symbolic leadership behavior is evident in John Paul II's relationship with Ronald Reagan, in their mutual efforts to defeat communism. Although they were intellectual opposites, the pope and Ronald Reagan did find common ground. Both had been actors. Both believed in the power of the symbolic act as well as in the role of divine providence, particularly after both had been shot by would-be assassins within six weeks of each other and had survived. In the first minutes of their first meeting, both agreed that they had been saved by God to play a special role in the destiny of Eastern Europe. "Look at the evil forces that were put in our way and how Providence intervened," Reagan said. The pope agreed (Bernstein, 1996, 357).

Visiting his would-be assassin, Mehmet Ali Agca, in prison served both a symbolic and a political purpose. It was symbolic because the pope was reflecting Christ's forgiveness, and political because the pope was sending a message to the Soviets, who many believed were responsible, that he was forgiving them for whatever complicity they may have had in the attempted assassination because not doing so would have branded the Soviets as the "bad guys" and seriously set back efforts toward world peace.

Pope John Paul II also had a symbolic purpose in creating so many new saints during his tenure. He was like a father proudly showing off his children. Among other things, saints are symbols of a healthy spiritual life, role models for communities, and a stimulus for priestly vocations. Sometimes John Paul II engaged in overtly political canonizations, like those members of religious orders killed in the Mexican and French Revolutions or the Spanish Civil War. He saw them as symbolic victims of the evil of bloody revolutions and atheistic, anticlerical Marxist regimes.

In 1986, John Paul II partook in yet another display of symbolic leadership behavior when he went to India to pray at the tomb of Mahatma Gandhi in New Delhi. Encouraged by his reception in India, he developed the idea of holding an international, interreligious assembly in Assisi, the birthplace of St. Francis, the most peace-loving of the Christian saints, to pray for world peace. His influence was such that at the first assembly on October 27, 1986, combatants momentarily held a ceasefire in many countries around the world.

Finally, in 1986, the Berlin Wall came down, and the communist influence began to wane. By 1989, the sidewalks leading to St. Peter's Square were filled with tens of thousands of pilgrims in a state of anticipation and excitement. The general secretary of the Communist Party of the Soviet Union and the supreme pontiff of the Roman Catholic Church were about to meet for the first time in history.

THE POLITICAL FRAME

Leaders operating out of the political frame clarify what they want and what they can get. Political leaders are realists above all. They never let what they want cloud their judgment about what is possible. They assess the distribution of power and interests. Although he dissuaded his priests from running for office or endorsing any particular political party, John Paul II himself heavily engaged in political frame leadership behavior.

Recognizing John Paul's potential for engaging in effective political leadership behavior, Soviet foreign minister Andrei Gromyko constantly warned his colleagues in the Kremlin not to underestimate Karol Wojtyła's ability to stir up the Polish masses the way Khomeini had incited the Iranian people. Gromyko proved to be prophetic when the pope collaborated with William Casey, a fervent Catholic and daily communicant and the director of the U.S. Central Intelligence Agency. Casey gave John Paul II a photograph taken by one of America's spy satellites. It was of John Paul II addressing his Polish followers in Victory Square in Warsaw in 1979. Casey used the photo to establish a secret alliance between John Paul II and Ronald Reagan. These two men met a half dozen times in an alliance that would see communism go asunder, first in the pope's homeland, Poland, then in Eastern Europe, and finally in the Soviet Union itself.

Even before becoming pope, Wojtyła became increasingly convinced that the Communist Party would not be able to maintain its dominance, so he began to exploit this fact to the church's advantage. He flooded the authorities with petitions and requests for new seminaries, churches, and religious processions. He resisted the attempt to prevent the teaching of the catechism to children; he demanded that the 1950 accord, which exempted seminaries from the draft, be honored; and he fought against religious discrimination.

But before utilizing political behavior to help defeat communism, the pope used it in the administration of his papal duties among Roman Catholics. After Vatican II, the Catholic bishops of the world wanted a greater share in the decision making within the church. John Paul II resolved the problem of power sharing by the tactical behavior of first suggesting a special committee to consider the question and then, before the committee even formed, establishing a new entity, the Synod of Bishops, as a consultative body. Thus he adopted alternating measures that placated the traditionalist minority and encouraged the reformist majority.

So John Paul II was well versed in the use of political leadership behavior by the time he took on the Soviet Union. For example, during a visit to Poland in the midst of the imposition of martial law in reaction to the labor strikes throughout the country, the pope decided to use political behavior to acknowledge that, although he disagreed with the communist ideology, he respected the Russian people. "Once again I choose to stop at another memorial stone [in a military cemetery], this one in Russia," he said. "I will not add any comments. We know what country it speaks of. We are aware of the past played by this country in the last terrible war for the freedom of the nations." The pope, however, was careful in his words, saying "Russians" not "Soviets" (Bernstein, 1996, 229).

The beginning of negotiations to end the strikes, in exchange for various concessions, turned into a dramatic use of political frame leadership behavior. Two close associates of John Paul II joined Lech Wałęsa in the negotiations. The firm stance in favor of Solidarity by John Paul II got the people of Poland on his side. So the pope's will became the national will of Poland. Now the communist government had little choice but to capitulate to the unions' demands.

Throughout the Polish crisis the pope sought a delicate balance—how to simultaneously support the workers and defeat communism, but avoid the bloodbath that would surely have occurred if the Soviets decided to use force to combat the unions.

As mentioned previously, John Paul II had a powerful ally in the process of overcoming communism, in the person of Ronald Reagan. Cardinal John Krol, the Polish Ordinary of Philadelphia, introduced Reagan to the pope and acted as an intermediary between the two. Being a friend of both, he convinced John Paul II that Reagan was sincere, even though he represented a capitalist and materialistic society of which the pope was suspicious. Thus Krol was in a position to do what no other prince of the church could do—convince Wojtyła that the interests of Poland, the Vatican, and the United States were in concert—and overcome whatever reservations the pope had about forming such a close relationship with the American politician.

Even though the pope was suspicious of the excesses of capitalism and materialism in the United States, he never once criticized the Reagan administration. In fact, when the Vatican Academy of Sciences prepared a report sharply critical of Reagan's Strategic Defense Initiative, dubbed "Star Wars" by the media, the pope used political leadership behavior and had it buried. His primary goal was to rid the world of communism, and he knew he had an ally in Reagan. Not until the Persian Gulf War in 1991, after the fall of communism in Eastern and Central Europe, did the pope publicly oppose an American policy—in this case, that of resolving a dispute with another country by taking up arms.

The advent of Mikhail Gorbachev brought rapid changes to church-state relations in Poland and created an atmosphere in which the pope could more effectively use political leadership behavior and be influential in Poland's cessation of martial law and communism. John Paul II and Gorbachev were both Slavs and could relate to one another. And as we have seen, the pope took full advantage of the circumstances.

THE MORAL FRAME

The moral frame is my own contribution to situational leadership theory. In my view, the moral frame completes situational leadership theory. Without it, leaders could just as easily use their leadership skills for promoting evil as for promoting good. Leaders operating out of the moral frame are concerned about their obligations and responsibilities to their followers. Moral frame leaders use some type of moral compass to direct their behavior. They practice what has been described as servant leadership and are concerned with those individuals and groups that are marginalized in their organizations and in society. In short, they are concerned about equality, fairness, and social justice.

It goes without saying that Pope John Paul II utilized the moral frame as an integral aspect of his overall leadership behavior. At his ordination to the Catholic priesthood, he took an oath to model his life after that of Jesus Christ and the Gospels. Thus, the life of Christ and the Gospels served as John Paul II's moral compass, giving direction to his leadership behavior.

CONCLUSION

There is no question that Pope John Paul II was a situational leader. We saw how he was active in all five frames of leadership behavior when appropriate. Most likely due to his experience as an actor, his forte seems to have been the symbolic frame. He had a charismatic personality that enabled him to attract huge and enthusiastic crowds. Leaders and potential leaders have much to learn by examining and internalizing his leadership principles.

Perhaps John Paul II's greatest achievement was his part in the defeat of communism. Along with his friend and collaborator Ronald Reagan, he is commonly credited with spearheading the ultimate victory. Of course Mikhail Gorbachev presented them with the opportunity because of his openness to change. We have seen how John Paul II utilized situational leadership principles in his contribution to the overthrow of communism.

Now let us look at Ronald Reagan's leadership behavior to determine whether he used these same principles in helping his colleague in this monumental endeavor.

Ronald Reagan believed that, for a statesman whose ultimate objectives are not in doubt and who moves resolutely to achieve them, adapting to the situation as it develops, including exhibiting inconsistency in words and even in actions, is not a vice. So, in effect, the situational nature of leadership was at his core.

Reagan had a reputation for operating out of the symbolic frame as the "Great Communicator" but was thought by some to be deficient in the structural frame of leadership. In examining his leadership behavior, however, a strong argument can be made to disarm these critics. For example, Reagan did not merely follow the path of public opinion. Like an effective structural leader, he worked hard to shape public opinion so that he could plan the best way for his country to achieve its ideals.

He defined leadership in a structural way: "to have the vision to dream of a better, safer world, and the courage, persistence and patience to turn that dream into a reality" (D'Souza, 1997, 230). Vision, action, and the ability to persuade one's followers is a combination of skills that are rare in one individual, but as was the case with Pope John Paul II, they were all present in Ronald Reagan. His structural leadership abilities, in particular, were tested in his first year as president in the strike by the Professional Air Traffic Controller Organization (PATCO). He took decisive action and ultimately fired the strikers and hired new air traffic controllers.

In contrast, Reagan utilized the human resource frame when appropriate. He was known to be a friendly man who had a "common man" persona, as witnessed by his humble demeanor and his ever-present jar of jelly beans at his White House meetings. He carefully cultivated his image as the nation's grandfather and, despite being a political conservative, was sincerely concerned about the plight of the poor.

Nonetheless, like John Paul II, Reagan was most comfortable using symbolic frame leadership behavior. He was an adept communicator with a common touch. For example, he declared that "There is no limit to what a man can do or where he can go if he doesn't mind who gets the credit." In his fight to defeat communism, he said, "We meant to change a nation, and instead we changed the world." And of course there was his famous demand: "Mr. Gorbachev, tear down this wall!" (D'Souza, 1997, 194).

He used symbolic behavior in developing the 1980 campaign question, "Are you better off today than you were four years ago?" (D'Souza, 1997, 45). Reagan "borrowed" that phrase from his Eureka College president's commencement address. Reagan understood the dramatic and theatrical demands of national leadership. Reagan once again utilized symbolic behavior when he described the liberals' approach to the economy in the following way: "If it moves, tax it. If it keeps moving, regulate it. And if it stops moving, subsidize it" (D'Souza, 1997, 53).

Reagan was famous for using symbolic leadership behavior in the form of homespun anecdotes. He loved to tell the story of two campers who were hiking and came upon a bear. One camper put on tennis shoes. The other said, "You can't possibly outrun a grizzly." The first camper replied, "I don't have to outrun the grizzly; I just have to outrun you." Another of his favorite stories was about an American and a Russian encountering each other. The American said, "I can go into the President's Oval Office and say, 'Mr. President, I don't like the way you're running the country.'" The Russian replied, "I can do the same thing. I can go into the Kremlin and say, 'I don't like the way President Reagan is running the country" (D'Souza, 1997, 188).

Reagan also used symbolic behavior in more serious situations. For example, in clarifying his position on abortion, he said, "If you don't know whether a body is alive or dead, you would never bury it. Until someone can prove the unborn child is not a life, shouldn't we give it the benefit of the doubt and assume that it is?" (D'Souza, 1997, 213).

Of course, being a politician by trade, Reagan was expert in using political leadership behavior. He would circumvent an uncooperative Congress by first winning the people over to his side on an issue, then he would urge them to pressure their congressional representatives, and then he would cut a deal that was very favorable to his policy priorities. His strategy in this respect was the classical one—he spoke in poetry and governed in prose.

Reagan believed that, after negotiating with the bosses of the Hollywood studios when he was president of the Screen Actors Guild, negotiating with Gorbachev was easy. But in true political frame style, he also believed that issuing ultimatums was not the way to go. Rather, the astute negotiator leaves room for compromise.

Using political frame behavior, Reagan established a close personal bond with Pope John Paul II beyond their mutual anticommunism ideology. The two men had the shared experience of having survived an assassination attempt. Reagan colluded with the Vatican to strengthen Polish churches as a base of resistance against communist tyranny, with the ultimate goal of defeating communism in all of the Soviet Union.

Although not as strong as that of John Paul II, Ronald Reagan had a significant sense of morality and used his personal moral code as a guide to his leadership behavior. His mother had taught him to see the best in people, not because she rejected the reality of sin, but because she accepted the more powerful reality of redemption. Reagan recalled that his mother's stories as well as his early reading left him "an abiding belief in the triumph of good over evil"—or the "Evil Empire," in the case of the Soviet Union (D'Souza, 1997, 41).

Reagan even rationalized his mediocre performance in school by adopting the conviction that the most important truths are moral, not intellectual. He also believed it was immoral for a nation to preserve its security by threatening the mass destruction of another nation's civilian population, thus the development of the Strategic Defense Initiative.

Reagan's moral sense was enhanced by an incident involving Mother Teresa. After his assassination attempt, Mother Teresa said to him, "You have suffered the passion of the cross and have received grace. There is a purpose to this. Because of your suffering and pain you will now understand the suffering and pain of the world. This has happened to you at this time because your country and the world need you" (D'Souza, 1997, 187). It has been said that Reagan was speechless and Nancy Reagan wept. Reagan used this incident as the inspiration to work with John Paul II in defeating atheistic communism.

We can readily see why these two leaders were able to work so well together in achieving a common goal. They were far more alike than would appear at first glance. They were both situational leaders who were comfortable operating in all five of the leadership frames and did so in pursuing a common cause, defeating communism in Poland and the Soviet Union. They were able to place situational leadership theory into effective practice in a way that can be an inspiration and a model for leaders and aspiring leaders in any field of endeavor.

Chapter 10

Martin Luther King Jr.

To succeed we need to get the Ph.D.'s, the M.D.'s, and the No.D.'s together in a common cause.

—Martin Luther King Jr.

BACKGROUND

Martin Luther King Jr. was born on January 15, 1929. Always a stellar student, he graduated from high school at the age of fifteen. He received his
B.A. degree in 1948 from Morehouse College. After three years of theological study at Crozer Theological Seminary in Chester, Pennsylvania,
where he was elected president of a predominantly white senior class,
he was awarded the bachelor of divinity degree in 1951. With a fellowship won at Crozer, he enrolled in graduate studies at Boston University,
completing his doctorate and receiving the degree in 1955. In Boston he
met and married Coretta Scott.

In 1954, King became pastor of the Dexter Avenue Baptist Church
in Montgomery, Alabama. Always a strong worker for civil rights for
members of his race, King was, by this time, a member of the executive
committee of the National Association for the Advancement of Colored
People. In December 1955, he conducted the first major Negro nonviolent
demonstration in the United States. The Montgomery, Alabama, bus
boycott lasted for over a year. On December 21, 1956, when the Supreme
Court of the United States declared unconstitutional the laws requiring
segregation on buses, King won his first great victory.

In 1957, King was elected president of the Southern Christian Leadership Conference, an organization formed to provide new leadership for
the now flourishing civil rights movement in the South. The ideologies
of the organization were inspired by Christianity, and its strategies by
Mahatma Gandhi.

King also led a massive protest in Birmingham, Alabama, that caught
the attention of the entire world, inspiring his "Letter from a Birmingham
Jail," a manifesto of the Negro revolution. He directed the peaceful march
on Washington, D.C., of 250,000 people to whom he delivered his "I Have
a Dream" speech.

At the age of thirty-five, King became the youngest man to receive the
Nobel Peace Prize. When notified of his selection, he announced that he
would turn over the prize money to the benefit of the civil rights movement. On the evening of April 4, 1968, while standing on the balcony of
his motel room in Memphis, Tennessee, where he was to lead a protest
march in sympathy with the striking garbage workers of that city, he was
assassinated. Two months after his death, James Earl Ray was arrested
and confessed to the killing (Oates, 1982).

SITUATIONAL LEADERSHIP ANALYSIS

Situational models of leadership differ from earlier trait and behavioral models in asserting that no single way of leading works in all situations. Rather, appropriate behavior depends on the circumstances at a given time. Effective managers diagnose the situation, identify the leadership style or behavior that will be most effective, and then determine whether they can implement the required style. Martin Luther King Jr. was an astute practitioner of situational leadership theory. As we shall see, he realized the need to adapt his leadership style to the situation and was very adept at doing so.

Dr. King recognized the need to be situational in applying his leadership behavior and proudly described himself as an "ambivert," which he defined as a cross between an extravert and an introvert. He liked to quote a French philosopher who once said, "No man is strong unless he bears within his character antitheses strongly marked" (Oates, 1982, 41). King also pointed out that Jesus, too, had recognized the need for being situational when he commanded his followers to be both tough-minded and tenderhearted. And although King could be tough-minded as an ideologue, he was tenderhearted in his treatment of people.

When King first began his ministry, his sermons tended to be as somber and intellectual as a classroom lecture. But he soon came to understand the emotional role of the Negro church, and to realize how much African Americans needed the sanctuary of the church to vent their pent up frustrations and really feel free. So he let himself go. The first *Amen!* from his congregation would inspire him to even more captivating oratory. For what was good preaching if not "a mixture of emotion and intellect?" he declared (Oates, 1982, 56). As we shall see, King did not restrict himself to one or two of the five leadership frames. Rather, in true situational leadership fashion, he utilized all five when appropriate.

THE STRUCTURAL FRAME

Structural frame leaders seek to develop a new model of the relationship of structure, strategy, and environment for their organizations. Strategic planning, extensive preparation, and effecting change are priorities for them. Martin Luther King Jr. was very active in this frame of leadership. His ideologies were well thought out and internalized, and he planned strategically to achieve the goals that he derived from them.

Most black preachers urged their congregations to expect their reward in heaven, but King, acting out of the structural frame, rejected that thought. He believed they should expect their reward in their temporal lives.

A class assignment in Thoreau's *Civil Disobedience* introduced King to the concept of peaceful resistance. The Congress of Racial Equality (CORE) had already conducted little-publicized "stand-ins" and "freedom rides." King was intrigued with Thoreau's argument that a creative minority could set in motion a moral revolution—and that is what he set about doing.

With 70 percent of its riders gone during the Montgomery bus boycott, the police commissioner ordered Negro taxi companies to charge the legal maximum rate per customer, thus ending cheap taxi fares for bus boycotters. In an assertive use of structural frame leadership behavior, King moved quickly to meet the crisis. The blacks countered by devising an ingenious carpool. Volunteer Negro drivers transported people to and from work, operating out of forty-eight dispatch and forty-two pickup stations established in key sections of the city. The carpool was so efficient that a local white judge later praised it as the best transportation system Montgomery had ever had.

King founded the Southern Christian Leadership Conference as a vehicle to facilitate the implementation of the activities of the civil rights movement. It would operate through the Southern Negro Church and function as a service agency to coordinate local civil rights activity—exactly what a structural leader would do. SCLC's main goal was to bring the Negro masses into the freedom struggle by expanding "the Montgomery way" across the South.

In this way it differed significantly from the NAACP (mostly legal), the National Urban League (focused on northern cities), and CORE (also mostly in the North and not too effective). SCLC's initial project was a southern-wide voter registration drive, called the Crusade for Citizenship, to commence on Lincoln's birthday—a symbolic gesture. Again demonstrating structural leadership behavior after the Montgomery bus boycott, King went on to outline what the Negro must struggle for in the near future. "We must seek the ballot," he said, "so that we will no longer be the convenient tool of unscrupulous politicians" (Oates, 1982, 123).

In another display of structural leadership behavior, King prepared for a full-scale assault on all forms of segregation by establishing an SCLC training program that would instruct youth and adult leaders in nonviolence and then send them into their communities to launch protests and demonstrations against segregated schools, eating establishments, and transportation facilities. So that he could devote himself full time to the SCLC, King resigned his position at Dexter Avenue Baptist Church and moved to Atlanta.

In the rare instances where his strategies did not work—like the failed Albany movement, a Georgia civil rights protest—King used structural behavior to conduct a postmortem analysis to determine where he and his followers went wrong. King and his staff conceded that they should not have obeyed the federal court injunction, with the assessment that it had "broken [their] backs." King's inability to stay in jail had also hurt the movement, and so had Chief Pritchett's clever tactics. "We were naive enough to think we could fill up the jails," but Pritchett was smart enough to bus the prisoners to surrounding jails. Worse still, the SCLC had charged into Albany without proper planning and preparation. "We didn't know then how to mobilize people in masses and our protest was so vague," King concluded (Oates, 1982, 199).

But in the true structural mode, King learned from his mistakes. He and his followers had no intention of proceeding naively into Birmingham as they had in Albany. At a three-day retreat held at SCLC's training center in Dorchester, Georgia, King and his aides and advisors developed a detailed plan called Project C, for *Confrontation*. They would increase the number of marches, streamline the boycotts, and fill up even the surrounding area's jails until they brought about a moment of recognition when the evils of segregation would be revealed and white merchants would have to capitulate.

In 1964, King and his staff completed their final plans for Project Alabama, the action plan in Selma designed to gain southern Negroes the unencumbered right to vote. In structural frame style, another organizing retreat was held. King intended to reach his goals by applying all the skill and experience he had gathered in the battles at Albany, Georgia; Birmingham, Alabama; and St. Augustine, Florida. Selma had all the ingredients for King to make his point: a black ghetto, the birthplace of the notorious segregationist policeman Bull Connor, and Selma's sheriff, Jim Clark, who in Bull Connor's image used salty language and had a military swagger and a no-nonsense approach to civil rights.

After a number of successes in the South, King decided to move North with the campaign because ghetto blacks were not able to reduce racial discrimination there even with the right to vote. The question was where to start. After much deliberation, King chose Chicago and developed a plan to convince the politicians to address the plight of the ghetto. "Egypt still exists in Chicago," he declared, "but the Pharaohs are more sophisticated and subtle" (Oates, 1982, 380).

In yet another example of King's use of structural leadership behavior, he established the "Poor Peoples' Army" in Washington, D.C., to highlight the plight of Negroes in the slums. He and his staff completed a master plan for the Washington campaign that involved recruiting blacks from all over to march on Washington and encamp in a very public and visible shantytown. He even thought of having a mule train travel from Mississippi to D.C. to dramatize the pilgrimage—combining symbolic behavior with structural behavior.

THE HUMAN RESOURCE FRAME

Human resource leaders believe in people and communicate that belief. They are passionate about productivity through people. Martin Luther King Jr. had a great capacity for practicing human resource leadership frame behavior. His entire life was dedicated to helping people, especially those marginalized in and by society.

King was very fond of Bayard Rustin, an intellectual who helped shape King's ideologies. Rustin had once been a member of the Communist Party and cautioned King about being too closely tied to him and what it could do to King's reputation. However, using human resource frame behavior, King said to him, "Look, we need everybody who can come to help us" (Oates, 1982, 94).

When a deranged woman tried to kill King by stabbing him within a quarter-inch of his heart, in typical human resource manner, King harbored no malice toward her. "Don't do anything to her," he counseled the authorities. "Don't prosecute her; get her healed," he said (Oates, 1982, 140).

Ralph Abernathy, King's second in command, who historians say had some intellectual and personality deficiencies, was particularly admired by King, who dwelled on his good points. In King's eyes, Abernathy was a savvy, loyal friend who was always there when King needed him. "I want you to know how much I appreciate your loyalty," he once told Abernathy. "I get all the attention from the press, but you're just as important to the movement as I am" (Oates, 1982, 183).

In a true test of his devotion to human resource behavior, King even applied it to his enemies. Police Chief Laurie Pritchett, who was King's nemesis during the Albany movement, but was conscientious enough to place King under round-the-clock police protection, was well thought of by King. As the campaign progressed, King developed a grudging respect for him. Once, King even canceled a demonstration so that Pritchett could spend the day with his wife. It was their wedding anniversary.

King's use of human resource behavior was recognized by his friends and colleagues. Andrew Young, one of his aides, said this of King: "He was able to find that common bond of love and worth in each of us that would make us produce our best. We were strong-willed and it took a terrible amount of love to handle us. I would lose my temper, and Dr. King would caution 'Hosea.' Just like that. Where others would get angry with me around the table, he had the capacity to love me instead" (Oates, 1982, 285).

THE SYMBOLIC FRAME

In the symbolic frame, the organization is seen as a stage, a theater in which every actor plays certain roles, and the symbolic leader attempts to communicate the right impressions to the right audiences. Many consider the symbolic frame to be Martin Luther King Jr.'s strongest. King's facility with the symbolic frame became evident at an early age. In the eleventh grade, he entered an oratorical contest sponsored by the Negro Elks in Washington, D.C. Speaking on "The Negro and the Constitution," King captured a prize for the strength of his presentation.

That night, on the way back to Atlanta on a crowded bus, the bus stopped and some whites got on. There were no empty seats. The white driver came back and ordered King to give up his seat, but King refused to budge. The driver threatened him and called him a black son of a bitch. He finally capitulated and stood in the aisle for the remainder of the long trip. "That night will never leave my mind," King said later. "It was the angriest I have ever been in my life" (Oates, 1982, 16).

In a similar incident, this time on a train, King was traveling back to Atlanta from New York. As the train reached Virginia, King made his way to the dining car. But the train was below the Mason-Dixon Line now, and the waiter led him to a rear table and pulled a curtain down to shield the white passengers from his presence. "I felt," he said, "as though the curtain had dropped on my selfhood" (Oates, 1982, 17).

In 1949, King spent his time reading Karl Marx. He carefully scrutinized *Das Kapital, The Communist Manifesto*, and several interpretive studies of Marx and Lenin. He came away from this experience with deep concern. Communism, he believed, was profoundly and fundamentally evil. The communists contemptuously dismissed God as a figure of man's imagination and religion as a product of fear, ignorance, and superstition. King engaged in symbolic leadership behavior and publically dismissed communism as a viable ideology.

Additionally, King could not accept the communist tenet that the ends justify the means. He could not agree with Lenin that to achieve a classless society, we must be ready to employ deceit, and trickery. King also distained communism's debilitating totalitarianism, which he felt denied individuals their inalienable rights and bound them to the mercy of the state.

At Crozer Seminary in Chester, Pennsylvania, King graduated at the top of his class in 1951 with a B.A. in divinity. He displayed his penchant for symbolic behavior once again by qualifying to give the valedictory address and by earning a scholarship to Boston University's prestigious School of Theology, where he obtained his Ph.D. As part of his dissertation, he made a statement regarding humility: "Keep Martin Luther King in the background and God in the foreground and everything will be all right. Remember you're the channel of the gospel, not the source" (Oates, 1982, 48).

King was prompted once again to engage in symbolic behavior at a Sunday church service in Philadelphia. He had attended a lecture by Dr. Mordecai A. Johnson, president of Harvard University. Dr. Johnson had just spent fifty days in India, and his lecture was a stirring presentation of the life and teachings of Mahatma Gandhi. Johnson explained how Gandhi had fused the power of love, truth, and peace into a viable vehicle for social change.

Johnson argued that nonviolent protest could also improve race relations in America. This was a revelation to King, who had felt hatred for whites. So King took Thoreau's theory and gave it practical application in the form of nonviolent activities like strikes, boycotts, and protest marches in the South, much as Gandhi had done in India and South Africa. Further, King espoused love of one's neighbor, not in the commonly understood form of love, but as agape, an unconditional and uncompromising love.

King was determined to practice what he preached. So in symbolic leadership fashion, he launched an ambitious social action program at Dexter Avenue Baptist Church. He established action groups to tend to the sick and needy, and administer scholarship funds. At the same time, a political action committee scheduled a speaker's series to keep his followers abreast of the latest developments in the civil rights movement.

Looking for any occasion to further his cause symbolically, King received great news in 1955 from his friends in the NAACP. They had come upon a perfect case. Rosa Parks, a tailor's assistant in a downtown Montgomery, Alabama, shop had taken a seat behind the white section of the bus. When the bus filled up, the driver ordered Mrs. Parks to stand and give up her seat to a white man. She refused to move. She was arrested for violating the city bus ordinance.

Unwittingly, the Montgomery officials had played right into King's hands and their actions made them vulnerable to a federal court test of the Jim Crow laws. The local courts found against Mrs. Parks. This precipitated the so-called "Miracle of Montgomery," the bus boycott that ultimately changed the law requiring blacks to sit in the back of the bus and made Martin Luther King Jr. a household name.

King's arrest and trial made the Montgomery bus boycott national front-page news and brought reporters from all over the world to cover the civil rights movement and the challenge to the South's way of life. The jailed King now served as the role model for nonviolent protest against racial injustice.

In establishing respect for the civil rights and dignity of the black race, King preached the cleansing of one's own house first. "They say we smell. No one is too poor to buy a bar of soap. They say we kill and cut each other," he said. In New York, Negroes constituted 10 percent of the population and 35 percent of perpetrators of crime at that time. The blacks needed to correct this, King declared. "They say we speak poorly," he said. "You don't need to speak good English in order to be good," he asserted (Oates, 1982, 126). He also disdained the use of Cadillacs and other big cars as a symbol to his followers that they, too, should not feed the stereotype.

King did not see himself as the messiah that some claimed him to be, but he did have a sense of destiny. He saw himself as an instrument of God. Like Christ, he went about spreading the word in a mostly symbolic way. His first book, *Stride toward Freedom: The Montgomery Story*, was part the story of the bus boycott, part an autobiography, and part an argument for nonviolence and racial change.

King was determined to carry out his mission using as much symbolism as he could muster. He preached that the time had come when he should no longer accept bail. If he committed a crime in the name of civil rights, he would go to jail and serve his time—in effect be a martyr for the cause. He was determined to give himself entirely to setting an example to his followers. So, he used his trials as a forum to proudly state his position and beliefs regarding the civil rights movement. King would hand his policy statements to the surprised judges and had his staff distribute copies to the newsmen. It was brilliant theater reminiscent of the great abolitionist protests of the past.

In yet another display of symbolic leadership behavior, King professed indifference to material things and tried to emulate Gandhi. He drove around in a dusty three-year-old Chevrolet and only accepted a dollar a year as SCLC president. One year, he donated almost $230,000, earned from speaking fees, to SCLC.

King deplored his father's deliberate approach toward desegregation. He once scolded his father for not doing more to challenge Atlanta's segregated facilities and other Jim Crow laws. He was different from his father in that he wanted to be free *now*.

Always cognizant of the effect of symbolic behavior, he chose "We Shall Overcome," an old labor union song, to become the hymn of the Negro movement. He implored his followers to follow the "Montgomery way" and not strike back at whites who attacked and humiliated them, but to be persistent nonetheless.

However, King was not always successful with his expressions of symbolic behavior. An example was the unsuccessful Albany movement in Georgia in 1961 and 1962, where divisions within the black community and the shrewd, subdued response by the local police stymied his efforts. But even in defeat he learned what not to do the next time.

In reality, King conducted the Birmingham campaign to make up for the debacle in Albany and to show the nation that SCLC was still effective and that nonviolence was still viable. Birmingham, Alabama, was chosen because it was known to be the cradle of the Confederacy—the most segregated city in the South. Through the campaign and through his famous

Letter from Birmingham Jail, written in 1963, he was able to get the civil rights movement back on track.

King often observed that the nonviolent approach would force his oppressors to commit their brutality openly, with the rest of the world watching. Thus, along with being chosen because it was the most segregated city in the South, Birmingham was a good choice because of the inflammatory personalities of both Police Chief Bull Connor and Governor George Wallace. One or both could be counted on to make a tactical mistake in judgment, with virtually the whole nation watching on television or reading about it on the front pages of newspapers.

These strategies paid off when Bull Connor made his predictable mistake. He stood in the midst of a protest march, a cigar in his mouth and a sweat-stained hat on his head, leading his charges. Several policemen had German shepherd police dogs, which growled in attack mode. When the peaceful demonstrators refused to disperse, Connor bellowed, "Let 'em have it" (Oates, 1986, 237).

With scores of reporters and television cameras from all over the world recording what happened, the firemen turned their hoses on the protesters, knocking them down and ripping off their clothes. Of course, all of this ended up on the six o'clock evening news and became Birmingham's national day of shame. A few days later, Connor ordered his men to do the same thing again. This time they flatly refused to obey his orders. Two weeks later, Birmingham gave in to King's demands—mission accomplished. Looking back on it, one Birmingham police official asked, "How stupid could we be?" (Oates, 1986, 233).

King's Letter from Birmingham Jail became a classic in protest literature and is viewed by many historians as the most eloquent and learned expression of the goals and philosophy of the nonviolent movement ever written. Among other things, it urged white clergymen to join the cause on moral grounds and made it virtually impossible for them to refuse their support and still maintain their integrity as men of the cloth.

King continued to make frequent use of symbolic leadership behavior throughout his career. To get the civil rights legislation moving in Congress in the 1960s during the Kennedy administration, King organized a march on Washington, which drew more than 250,000 people. It was at this march that he gave his famous "I have a dream" speech. He ended it with the memorable words: "We will be able to speed up that day when all of God's children, black men and white men, Jews and Gentiles, Protestants and Catholics, will be able to join hands and sing in the words of the old Negro spiritual, 'Free at last! Free at last! Thank God almighty, we are free at last!'"

King continued to build his reputation when in 1964 he won the Nobel Peace Prize. And after Kennedy's assassination, King symbolically declared, "No memorial oration or eulogy could more eloquently honor President Kennedy's memory than the earliest possible passage of the civil rights bill for which he fought so long" (Oates, 1986, 274). In 1964, King became the first American Negro to be named *Time*'s Man of the Year.

After the Civil Rights Act was passed, King heard the same questions repeatedly: "What more will the Negro want? What will make these demonstrations end?" In *Why We Can't Wait*, which came out during the St. Augustine campaign, King answered the question in symbolic terms: "The Negro wants absolute freedom and equality, not in Africa or in some imaginary state, but right here in this land today" (Oates, 1986, 303).

King used symbolic leadership behavior in protesting over another of his causes—the Vietnam War. He dramatically pointed out the disproportionate number of Negroes among the troops and the violation of the civil rights of the Vietnamese. He was also in favor of China being admitted into the United Nations.

The use of symbolic leadership behavior by King occurred once again in 1966, at the Palmer House in Chicago, when Mayor Richard Daly and King reached what became known as the Summit Agreement. According to its terms, real estate brokers would be required to post a summary of the city's open housing policy in their offices and there was a ban on any further "redlining" (a real estate tactic to indicate neighborhoods wherein there is an understanding that African Americans are not permitted to purchase property).

King continued to use symbolic leadership behavior until he drew his last breath. The Memphis sanitation workers' strike, with protesters carrying signs reading "I AM A MAN," was King's last significant campaign. The Memphis strikers asked a racist city government for decent pay and a place in the union movement for blacks. Historically, the unions had improved the lot of millions of whites but, until that time, was closed to blacks.

In conjunction with the Memphis campaign, King gave his last great speech, the "I have been to the mountaintop" speech, on April 3, 1968. In the speech, he virtually predicted his death a day before it happened. "I don't know what will happen now. . . . But it really doesn't matter with me now, because I have been to the mountaintop. Like anybody, I would like to live a long life. . . . So I'm happy tonight. I'm not worried about anything. I'm not fearing any man. . . . I have a dream this afternoon that the brotherhood of man will become a reality. . . . Free at last, free at last, thank God almighty, we are free at last" (Oates, 1986, 470). King was assassinated the next day.

THE POLITICAL FRAME

Leaders operating out of the political frame clarify what they want and what they can get. Political leaders are realists above all. They never let what they want cloud their judgment about what is possible. They assess the distribution of power and interests. Needless to say, Martin Luther King Jr. made it a point to effectively utilize political frame leadership behavior.

In his very first position as pastor of Dexter Avenue Baptist Church in Montgomery, Alabama, King practiced political leadership behavior. He served as his parishioners' character witness in court and negotiated on their behalf with whites. To keep harmony within civil rights ranks, King often went to the New York headquarters and had long talks with Roy Wilkins of the NAACP, assuring him that SCLC's approach supported and complemented theirs. He did the same with the leadership of CORE and the Urban League.

Inevitably, SCLC's growth and success brought about jealousies with the NAACP, and competitive staffers started to demean one another. The SCLC called the NAACP a "black bourgeoisie club," and the NAACP staffers responded in kind. When former baseball star Jackie Robinson wrote him about the infighting, King replied in typical political frame fashion, indicating that he had always stressed the need for cooperation between the two organizations and complimented the NAACP as "our chief civil rights organization." He continued, "The job ahead is too great, and the days ahead too bright to be bickering in the darkness of jealousy, deadening competition and internal ego struggles" (Oates, 1986, 158).

King was political by not being political. He refused to endorse any political candidate, even Kennedy or Johnson, as he repeatedly said that no white leader except Lincoln had ever given enough support to the Negroes' struggle to warrant their confidence. Moreover, "I feel that someone must remain in the position of nonalignment, so that he can look objectively at both parties and be the conscience of both—not the servant or master of either" (Oates, 1986, 159). But when he thought it was in the best interest of the cause, King took a political stand. Though he never publicly endorsed Kennedy, for example, he did about everything short of it. He let it be known that his constituents should vote for Democrats.

King never limited himself to civil rights in using the political clout he had accumulated. For example, he felt so strongly about the Bay of Pigs invasion that he signed a major newspaper advertisement denouncing it. "I did it," he said, "because I am as concerned about international affairs as I am about the civil rights struggle" (Oates, 1986, 173).

In another political maneuver, King sought to strengthen SCLC's ties with organized labor. George Meany's AFL-CIO, the nation's most powerful labor union, became one of his greatest supporters. "Negroes,"

King said, "found that the history of labor mirrors their own experience" (Oates, 1986, 186).

At times, however, King used political frame behavior reluctantly. For example, two months after the Birmingham campaign that inspired the Kennedys to introduce a new civil rights bill to Congress, the word was spread by J. Edgar Hoover that King was a communist and that there were many more in the SCLC. Kennedy informed King that the charge of communism could derail the civil rights bill, so against his better judgment, King decided to release suspected communist Jack O'Dell from the SCLC and curtail the activities of another suspected party member, Stanley Levison. Thus King used political frame leadership behavior to further his goals even when the use of it was personally repugnant.

THE MORAL FRAME

The moral frame is my own contribution to situational leadership theory. It my view, the moral frame completes situational leadership theory. Without it, leaders could just as easily use their leadership skills for promoting evil as for promoting good. Leaders operating out of the moral frame are concerned about their obligations and responsibilities to their followers. Moral frame leaders use some type of moral compass to direct their behavior. They practice what has been described as servant leadership and are concerned with those individuals and groups that are marginalized in their organizations and in society. In short, they are concerned about equality, fairness, and social justice.

As an ordained minister, King's life was dedicated to a moral cause—the teachings of Jesus Christ. His concern for civil rights was rooted in Christ's command to "love one another as I have loved you." He opposed the Vietnam War and world poverty, not on a political basis but on a moral one. He was also a disciple of Mahatma Gandhi, whose policy of nonviolence in pursuit of human rights was based on moral law. King clearly relied on a moral compass to direct his leadership behavior (Oates, 1982).

CONCLUSION

Martin Luther King Jr. was definitely a disciple of situational leadership theory. He effectively modeled all five frames of leadership behavior. For example, he used the structural frame in establishing the SCLC as the vehicle through which he pursued his civil rights agenda. He used the human resource frame in dedicating his life to obtaining human rights and promoting peace for all, especially the most disadvantaged. His numerous inspirational speeches are an indication of his use of the symbolic frame of leadership, and his political maneuvering with presidents Kennedy and Johnson enabled him to create a positive political climate for the passage of civil rights legislation.

Finally, we saw above how he engaged in the moral frame by basing his leadership behavior on a moral code, namely, the teachings of Jesus Christ. Internalizing the leadership principles that Martin Luther King Jr. espoused and practiced would be a wise and prudent approach for leaders and aspiring leaders to consider.

Chapter 11

Vladimir Lenin

Library of Congress, Prints & Photographs Division, LC-USZ62-101877.

We must put down the resistance with such brutality that they will not forget it for several decades. The greater the number of representatives of the reactionary clergy and reactionary bourgeoisie we succeed in executing the better.

—Vladimir Lenin

BACKGROUND

Vladimir Lenin was born in 1870 in Simbirsk, Russia, and was the Russian revolutionary who founded the Bolshevik political party. He was a statesman who presided over Russia's transformation from a country ruled for centuries by czars to the Union of Soviet Socialist Republics (U.S.S.R.). He led the so-called October Revolution, which was the movement that spawned the Union of Soviet Socialist Republics (U.S.S.R.).

Because Lenin's father had risen into the ranks of the Russian nobility, Lenin grew up in relatively privileged circumstances. But he shifted to his radical anti-imperial views with the execution by hanging of his older brother, Alexander, in 1887 after Alexander and others had plotted to kill the czar. What further rankled Lenin was that his sister, who had nothing to do with the plot, was exiled.

Lenin graduated from secondary school with high honors and enrolled at Kazan University, but he was expelled after participating in a communist demonstration. He retired to the family estate but was permitted to continue his studies away from the university. He obtained a law degree in 1891.

In 1893 Lenin moved to St. Petersburg, Russia. By this time he was already a committed Marxist. In 1897 Lenin was arrested, spent some months in jail, and was finally sentenced to three years of exile in the remote area of Siberia. He was joined there by a fellow Marxist, Nadezhda Kostantinovna Krupskaya, whom he married in 1898. During his Siberian exile he produced a major study of the Russian economy, *The Development of Capitalism in Russia*.

Lenin further expressed his ideologies in his important book, *What's to Be Done?*, in 1902. Russian Marxism eventually split into two factions. The one led by Lenin called itself the majority faction (Bolsheviks), while the other took the name of minority faction (Mensheviks). The Bolsheviks and the Mensheviks disagreed not only over how to organize the movement but also over many other political and ideological questions.

During World War I Lenin lived in Switzerland. He wrote another important book, *Imperialism: The Highest Stage of Capitalism*, in 1916. The influence of this book led to the overthrow of the Russian czar in the winter of 1917, marking the beginning of the Russian Revolution.

As a result of the October Revolution, Lenin found himself not only the leader of his party but also the chairman of the Council of People's Commissars of the newly proclaimed Russian Socialist Federation Soviet Republic, which was the genesis of the U.S.S.R.

From 1918 to 1921 a fierce civil war raged, which the Bolsheviks finally won, defeating the Mensheviks against seemingly overwhelming odds. During the civil war Lenin tightened his party's reigns and eventually eliminated all rival political parties. When the civil war had been won and the regime firmly established, the economy was in ruins, and much of the population was bitterly opposed to the Bolsheviks. At this point Lenin reversed many of his policies and instituted a reform called the New Economic Policy (NEP). It was a temporary retreat from the goal of establishing radical socialism. Instead, the stress of the party's policies would be on economic rebuilding and on the education of the peasant population for a life of socialism in the twentieth century.

But on May 26, 1922, Lenin suffered a series of strokes. He was so seriously ill that he could participate in political matters only occasionally. He moved to a country home at Gorki, Russia, near Moscow, where he died on January 21, 1924, at age fifty-three. Almost a million mourners passed through the Hall of Columns during the four days and nights that his body lay in state (Service, 2000).

SITUATIONAL LEADERSHIP ANALYSIS

Situational models of leadership differ from earlier trait and behavioral models in asserting that no single way of leading works in all situations. Rather, appropriate behavior depends on the circumstances at a given time. Effective managers diagnose the situation, identify the leadership style or behavior that will be most effective, and then determine whether they can implement the required style.

Although we will find that Vladimir Lenin was less flexible that many of the leaders profiled in this book, he had definite situational leadership tendencies. On most occasions he altered his leadership behavior depending on the situation. He was willing, for example, to modify his policies in light of popular demands. In what became known as his *April Theses*, he had called for land nationalization. But after a poll of the peasants indicated a rejection of such nationalization, Lenin dropped the idea.

Another change in policy occurred when he learned that employers in Petrograd were beginning to encourage participative decision making in their factories. Just as he had previously objected to allowing peasant communes to control the villages, so he had never liked the idea of workers having too much power in their factories without direction from the party. But this was a revolutionary situation, and workers had to be encouraged to join the cause. Thus their creativity and initiative had to be fostered, so he allowed employee empowerment to continue.

In another indication of his situational nature, although no one would accuse Lenin of not being a Marxist hard-liner, the reality was that Lenin treated the Marxist ideal ambivalently whenever pragmatism was a better way to reach a party goal. Although he thought seriously about Marxist social and economic theory and liked to remain within its basic tenets, his adherence was not absolute by any means. In the mid-1920s, the priority for him was the global release of revolutionary energy. Ideas about the formal, protracted stages of social development were pushed to his subconscious. Better to conduct a successful revolution, however inefficiently, than to create a sophisticated but impractical theory.

THE STRUCTURAL FRAME

Structural frame leaders seek to develop a new model of the relationship of structure, strategy, and environment for their organizations. Strategic planning, extensive preparation, and effecting change are priorities for them. This was one of Lenin's strongest frames.

In Lenin's era, there was a great emphasis in Russia on the part of parents to encourage their sons to obtain a quality education. Lenin's parents were no exception, and Lenin became not only an outstanding student but also a well-recognized scholar. His obsession to thoroughly research problems, plan and strategize, and adhere strictly to timelines—all structural frame traits—remained with him for his entire life.

In true structural leadership form, he became a party boss who was almost a one-man court of appeal. Lenin alone was to be respected as the great and glorious leader by all members of the Bolshevik party, and his patriarchal style strengthened his dominance. He also had a way of handling the party officials with finesse, managing to sound radical even when he was making compromises.

Being the structural leader that he was, he adhered closely to his ideological plan, and as a result, Lenin made history. In the *April Theses* of 1917, he drafted a strategy for the party to seize power. In March 1918, he headed off a German invasion of Russia by negotiating a separate treaty signed at Brest-Litovsk. In 1921, he introduced the New Economic Policy and saved the Soviet Bloc from being overthrown by a popular rebellion. If Lenin had not initiated these strategies, the U.S.S.R. would have gone asunder before it had any real chance of succeeding.

But Lenin was sometimes a structural leader to a fault. He had no concern for morality and ethics. To him, the goal justified the means. He justified dictatorship and terror and encouraged the need for firm leadership that often condoned violence and murder. He convinced his party that his Marxism was pure and that it embodied the only correct interpretation.

In strategy, organization, and planning, however, Lenin had a lasting impact on how to operationalize radical socialism for his country and the world. He was so obsessed with his cause that in his adult years he gave up his leisure-time interests in chess, classical music, and ice- skating to concentrate on his revolutionary tasks.

Many of Lenin's party colleagues wanted the right to have at least some independent thought, but in true radical structural frame fashion, Lenin was in favor of leadership, leadership, and more leadership. Everything else was to be subordinate to this end.

Lenin, therefore, lived life on his own terms. His bookishness, his demands on other peoples' time, his dedication to regular physical exercise, and his willingness to give advice on virtually every topic were all structural frame traits. These characteristics were treated as evidence of his great genius.

Another of Lenin's obsessive-compulsive tendencies was his insistence on absolute silence when he was working. His staff moved around on tiptoe so as not to interrupt his train of thought. A slave to detail, everything had to be in its place, from his pencils to his political and economic policy files.

During the wartime years, Lenin used structural behavior to develop strategies to compress the schedule of the revolution. Conventional Marxism held that there would be two stages to the revolution. First, a bourgeois-democratic revolution would occur to bring down the monarchy and to consolidate power between democracy and capitalism. Then, the socialist revolution would take place, putting the working class into power. Lenin hastened the process by abandoning the consolidation step and proceeding directly to socialism, which, in effect, he accomplished with the Bolshevik Revolution of 1917.

Once, on a train ride back to Russia, Lenin showed his structural frame compulsions by sketching his proposed strategy for the revolution in the form of his *April Theses*, which consisted of ten theses on how to operationalize and institutionalize the revolution. After he convinced the party members of his strategy, he next went about developing a propaganda campaign to convince the workers and peasants.

Lenin's vision of world communism evolved in a very structural frame way. His view was that capitalism would be overthrown by a violent revolution that would be consummated by the "dictatorship of the proletariat." The dictatorship would initially be benign but would steadily institutionalize the practices and ideals of socialism. Under communism, the ultimate goal of a fair and compassionate society would be realized.

"From each according to his abilities, to each according to his needs," Lenin declared (Service, 2000, 296).

Sometimes, however, Lenin was slow to apply structural leadership behavior when it was needed. For instance, no great skill was required of Lenin to create his New Economic Policy when Russia had experienced a devastating famine, but Lenin put off the decision until it was too late. It was a no-brainer that farmers should be allowed to more freely decide what they wanted to grow and to exchange their goods more readily.

The NEP was an obvious way to restore the easy exchange of products between village and town. This policy was also a remedy for famine, disease, industrial ruin, and popular rebellion. Even though he was late in implementing it, along with the Brest-Litovsk Treaty, the NEP was Lenin's most significant accomplishment—except for the Bolshevik Revolution, of course.

THE HUMAN RESOURCE FRAME

Human resource leaders believe in people and communicate that belief. They are passionate about productivity through people. Despite giving lip service to this leadership frame, instances of Lenin's use of human resource leadership behavior are few and far between. Ironically, even though the ultimate goal of communism is giving power to the workers, the reality was that the power was concentrated in the hands of Lenin and a few influential party members. So, in effect, even though communism as an ideology is humanistic, Lenin's interpretation of it was not so.

Lenin would never be characterized as gregarious or sensitive, but when his brother Alexander was in prison and later executed, he became very depressed and maudlin, showing that he did have a human side. As a rule, however, Lenin did not let human affairs or affairs of the heart get in the way of public affairs, and this was to remain the case even during his involvement with Inessa Armand before World War I.

Still, the death of his comrade and soul mate Inessa Armand left Lenin noticeably overcome with grief. At her funeral, he had to be supported by a couple of the mourners so that he did not collapse. No one present could forget his pitiful countenance. The testimony of many of his friends and associates who were by his side that day indicated that he was deeply moved by her death.

There were other rare instances in which Lenin did demonstrate a human touch. For example, when Nikolai Valentinov, a young Bolshevik recruit, arrived penniless from Geneva, Lenin helped him obtain a part-time job as a barrow pusher. Valentinov once had a delivery that he could not fulfill by himself. Lenin leaned a shoulder to the barrow to help, and Valentinov never forgot the favor. But Lenin's family had instilled in him the idea that pride in oneself was abhorrent, and that good deeds had to be done without recognition or fuss. This reserve stayed with him throughout his life and precluded any significant use of the human resource frame.

Similar to Adolph Hitler, Lenin's saving grace regarding human resource behavior was his genuine love of children. His greatest pleasure came not from his political achievements but from the presence of children. It was clear that Lenin and his wife would have loved to have children of their own, and the visits of their young relatives and friends brought them great joy. They took responsibility for the Armand children after his friend Inessa's death, and there is much evidence to indicate that Lenin and his wife made provisions for their future welfare and treated them well. Nevertheless, in his professional life, there is a paucity of evidence that Lenin practiced a great deal of human resource leadership behavior.

THE SYMBOLIC FRAME

In the symbolic frame, the organization is seen as a stage, a theater in which every actor plays certain roles, and the symbolic leader attempts to communicate the right impressions to the right audiences. As with many of his dictator counterparts, Vladimir Lenin was adept at the effective use of the symbolic frame.

Lenin's austere personality and inadequacies as a public speaker were more than compensated for by his considerable abilities as an intellectual and author. He was one of the literati, a man of the printed word, an ardent reader, and an excellent writer. His many books and publications were the primary vehicle through which he expressed symbolic leadership behavior.

Lenin's favorite book as a young man was *Uncle Tom's Cabin*. Its focus on human rights and racial equality appealed to him. Thus Harriet Beecher Stowe was among his early influences, even predating Karl Marx. Promulgating his ideals through the written word became his passion.

Another of Lenin's early influences was Nikolai Chernyshevski, a revolutionary agrarian socialist who demanded a democratic political system based upon universal suffrage elections. He advocated a classless society and depicted the imperial monarchies as mostly barbaric, hypocritical, and outdated. Lenin adopted these ideals and often spread them through symbolic leadership behavior.

Lenin was attracted to Chernyshevski emotionally as well as rationally. He was profoundly affected by the heroic example of a man who endured imprisonment in Siberia for the sake of his political ideals. Lenin even carried a photo of his Chernyshevski in his wallet. Thus, when Lenin was arrested and served time in jail, he looked upon the experience as symbolically honoring his hero.

By the early 1900s, Marxism had become Lenin's preoccupation. It so dominated his life that he began to translate *The Communist Manifesto* into Russian. As students, he and his companions wanted to change the world for the benefit of the lower social classes. However, Lenin and his followers rejected concepts such as conscience, compassion, and charity. He perceived the mercantile middle class as parasites on society, and he expressed these views symbolically in his book *The State and Revolution*.

Lenin's book *The Development of Capitalism in Russia* demonstrated that Russia was already a capitalist country and, as such, should not be ruled by a monarchy. He claimed that a capitalist country needed political democracy and a guarantee of human rights. Ultimately, he argued, after the monarchy had been overthrown for democracy and capitalism, democracy and capitalism would then be overthrown by Marxist socialism.

In another display of symbolic behavior, his book *What Is to Be Done?* thrust him further into the limelight. It ultimately led to the October Revolution of 1917 and became a political classic. In it, he called for a disciplined and centralized party that would persuade the working class, but not the peasants, to lead the revolution against the czars.

Quick to exploit an opportunity to identify himself with a dramatic and symbolic event, on January 9, 1905, known as Bloody Sunday, when demonstrators in a peaceful anti-czarist march in St. Petersburg were fired upon by the army, Lenin used the incident to signify the beginning of the symbolic downfall of the throne of the once great czars.

After being forced to spend ten years abroad in exile in Finland, Lenin made his triumphant and symbolic return to Russia to take charge of the Bolshevik Revolution. As his train arrived at the station, Lenin made certain that when he stepped down from the train platform he would have a throng of disciples and the press waiting for him. In his opening speech he declared in typically dramatic fashion that he was leading not just a Russian revolution but a "world socialist revolution" (Service, 2000, 261).

As mentioned earlier, Lenin was not a brilliant orator, but his countenance conveyed passion and willpower, and he was able to give the impression that he was a man of the people, one with the workers. In typical symbolic frame mode, he cultivated and promoted that image.

Again in symbolic terms, in the October Revolution of 1917, Lenin declared, "Comrades! The workers' and peasants' revolution, which the Bolsheviks have all this time been talking about the need for, has been accomplished" (Service, 2000, 313). Films were made of the event, novels written, songs sung, and even ballets performed. The familiar image of Lenin with his fist raised, mouth tensed, and bearded chin was seen everywhere.

Despite writing about the incompatibility of democracy and dictatorship, he could not wait to impose absolute authority and would let nothing get in his way. Coercion was used instead of persuasion. He sanctioned violence, including outright terrorism. The quote with which we began this chapter was a symbolic indication of Lenin's true beliefs: "We must put down the resistance with such brutality that they will not forget it for several decades. The greater the number of representatives of the reactionary clergy and reactionary bourgeoisie we succeed in executing the better" (Service, 2000, 321).

Even in death, his flair for the dramatic was evident. The Lenin Mausoleum was to be favorably compared to that of the ancient pharaohs. However, the Soviets did the Egyptians one better. A giant statue and picture of Lenin were to be visible to all visitors to Red Square. Simultaneously, Lenin's writings acquired the status of the Bible. An Institute of the Brain was established in his honor; thirty thousand slices of his cerebral tissue were collected so that research might be done on the secrets of his great genius. Of course, all of this changed with the dissolution of the Soviet Union, but not until then.

THE POLITICAL FRAME

Leaders operating out of the political frame clarify what they want and what they can get. Political leaders are realists above all. They never let what they want cloud their judgment about what is possible. They assess the distribution of power and interests. Along with the symbolic and structural frames, the political frame was among Lenin's strongest.

We saw earlier that Lenin could be somewhat inflexible in the application of his leadership behavior. However, we also saw that even though he remained steadfast to certain principles, he was a man who saw the advantage of temporary and partial compromise. He modified his policies when his power was threatened. Thus Lenin was a political animal and was not beyond exploiting people and events to his own advantage. By his own admission, he was a devotee of Machiavelli.

For example, even though the working class was his primary focus, Lenin altered his plan and utilized political frame leadership behavior to also attract the peasants by campaigning for the restoration of some of the land they had lost under the 1861 Emancipation Edict. He was keenly aware of the fact that 85 percent of the Russian population were peasants.

Lenin was adept in the use of political behavior in making friends and influencing people. When he decided that a friendly relationship with Alexander Bogdanov, a brilliant young Marxist writer, was necessary if he was to have access to the money and personal support he would need in order to resurrect his party career, he befriended him, even though Bogdanov could have been an ideological threat to him.

As with most leaders operating out of the political frame, he enjoyed and relished power and yearned to keep his party in the ascendancy. But he wanted power with a purpose and that purpose was worldwide communism. For example, in 1917 while his party received money from Germany, he did not regard himself as a sympathizer with the German cause of world domination any more than the Germans felt that they had bought into communism. Each side was exhibiting political leadership behavior, confident that it had outmaneuvered the other.

In another display of political frame behavior, once World War I was over, Lenin took the opportunity to invade the western border of Russia. The Red Army gained a number of victories and Lenin was able to form independent soviets in Estonia, Lithuania, Belorussia, Latvia, and the Ukraine. Of course, the alleged independence was only a facade. In time, those countries became Soviet satellites, solidly under Moscow's control.

Lenin said to his aides, "Let us, the Great Russians, display caution, patience, etc., and gradually we'll get back into our hands all these Ukrainians, Latvians" (Service, 2000, 403). In true political frame fashion, he pretended that the Ukrainian Soviet Republic was truly independent of Russia. Of course, in reality the Ukrainian government would remain strictly under the control of the Soviet Union.

In Lenin's view, extreme circumstances called for desperate measures. And desperate measures usually involved political leadership behavior. Toward the end of his life, no longer having an ally in Joseph Stalin, Lenin turned to the very person against whom he had formed the alliance with Stalin, namely, Leon Trotsky. Since Trotsky supported the state foreign trade monopoly that Stalin opposed, Lenin and Trotsky again became bedfellows.

Once Trotsky threw his support to Lenin, Lenin returned the favor and spoke on Trotsky's behalf. "Comrade Stalin, having become General Secretary, has concentrated unlimited power in his hands, and I am not convinced that he will always manage to use this power with sufficient care," he said. "On the other hand, comrade Trotsky, as is shown by his struggle against the Central Committee in connection with the People's Commissariat of the Means of Communication, is characterized not only by outstanding talents. To be sure, he is personally the most capable person in the present Central Committee" (Service, 2000, 465). However, despite this display of political leadership behavior, Lenin was unable to prevent Joseph Stalin from succeeding him as leader of the Soviet Union (Service, 2000).

THE MORAL FAME

The moral frame is my own contribution to situational leadership theory. In my view, the moral frame completes situational leadership theory. Without it, leaders could just as easily use their leadership skills for promoting evil as for promoting good. Leaders operating out of the moral frame are concerned about their obligations and responsibilities to their followers. Moral frame leaders use some type of moral compass to direct their behavior. They practice what has been described as servant leadership and are concerned with those individuals and groups that are marginalized in their organizations and in society. In short, they are concerned about equality, fairness, and social justice.

Vladimir Lenin is typical of a leader who fails to operate out of the moral frame of leadership. The human atrocities that occurred during and after his regime are a direct result of his abhorrence of God and religion and their accompanying moral and ethical codes. Much of the violence and denial of human rights that occurred during the atheistic communist regimes could have been prevented if the leaders were filtering their behavior through a moral or ethical lens. Even if their moral compass was that of a secular humanist, many of the atrocities would not have taken place. Vladimir Lenin is an example of a great leader who was not a good leader—defining the word *good* in the moral/ethical sense. The opening quote in this chapter gives evidence of Lenin's disregard for moral philosophy. Suffice it to say, Lenin had little time for moral frame leadership behavior (Service, 2000).

CONCLUSION

There is no question that Vladimir Lenin was one of the greatest leaders in history. He had a worldwide impact that still exists today, although the spread of communism appears to be on the decline. There is also no question that Lenin, whether consciously or not, practiced situational leadership theory. We saw how he selectively used leadership behavior from the various frames, with the possible exception of the moral frame. He operated out of the structural frame in carefully planning the Russian Revolution. Although not one of his strongest frames, to say the least, he did show evidence of acting out of the human resource frame on occasion.

The symbolic and political frames were Lenin's forte. He practiced symbolic leadership in building his image as a revolutionary and agent of social and political change by his prolific publications, including the *April Theses, The Development of Capitalism in Russia, What Is to Be Done?,* and *The State and Revolution.* In these and other writings, he established the need and outlined his plans for a worldwide communist revolution. We then saw how he used political frame leadership behavior to further his plans and finally implement and sustain the Bolshevik Revolution.

So, by most traditional standards, Lenin would be considered to be among the great leaders in world history. Both *Life* and *Time* magazines named him one of the one hundred most influential people of the second millennium. Although he is acknowledged to have been a great leader, the question arises as to whether he was a *good* leader, in the moral/ethical sense of the term. As pointed out earlier, there is a dearth of evidence of him operating out of the moral frame. As a result, like Adolph Hitler and Mao Zedong, Lenin does not meet the definition of a complete and heroic leader. He failed to filter his behavior through a moral lens and, as a result, a number of human atrocities occurred during his tenure. In examining Lenin's leadership behavior, the clear message for leaders and aspiring leaders is the need to engage oneself in all five leadership frames, including the moral frame, if one wishes to be a complete and maximally effective leader.

Chapter 12
Mao Zedong

> People who try to commit suicide—don't attempt to save them! . . .
> China is such a populous nation, it is not as if we cannot do without a
> few people.
>
> —Mao Zedong

BACKGROUND

Mao Zedong was born in 1893 and was a Chinese statesman whose status as a revolutionary in world history is second only to that of Vladimir Lenin. Mao was born in Shaoshan, Hunan, China. By 1918, Mao was already committed to communism. With the rise of the Chinese Communist Party (CCP) in 1921, of which Mao was one of fifty founding members, he pursued his political agenda.

Meanwhile, the major political party, the Kuomintang (KMT), was reorganized, and a coalition was formed between the KMT and CCP. Mao remained a minor figure in the coalition until he discovered the revolutionary potential of the peasants who had been treated poorly by the Chinese warlords.

Eventually, the communists took up arms against the government and established rural soviets in central and northern China. One of these soviets served as Mao's home base. Years of struggle occurred between the Communist Party and Chiang Kai-shek's anticommunist party. Eventually Chiang was able to drive the communists out of their base areas, and they were forced to retreat on what was called the Long March, a year-long, six-thousand-mile journey through the hills of Shensi.

The various communist parties were searching for a communist leader who could rival Chiang in case a civil war broke out. Mao filled this role and his popularity soon soared. The personality cult of Mao grew until his concepts were written into the party's constitution of 1945. Under Mao's leadership, the party won one military victory after another.

On January 21, 1949, in a decisive battle, Chiang's forces suffered massive losses against Mao's Red Army. Red Army troops then laid siege to Chengdu, the last Kuomintang-occupied city in mainland China, and Chiang Kai-shek evacuated from the mainland to the island of Formosa (Taiwan).

The People's Republic of China was officially established on October 1, 1949, after two decades of civil and international war. In 1954, Mao took control of the national Communist Party and became known as Chairman Mao. Following the consolidation of power, Mao launched the First Five-Year Plan. The success of the First Five-Year Plan encouraged Mao to instigate the Second Five-Year Plan, called the Great Leap Forward, in 1958. Under this program, land was taken from landlords and wealthier peasants and given to poorer peasants. The program was a colossal failure.

Facing the prospect of losing his place on the world stage, Mao responded by launching the Cultural Revolution in 1966. As part of the revolution, Mao organized the army and young students into the Red Guards. With their help, Mao began to consolidate his power. Soon there was no official Chinese thought beyond the extent of Mao's thought, which was compiled in the ubiquitous *Little Red Book.*

During the Cultural Revolution, Mao closed the schools in China, and the young intellectuals and many university professors living in the urban areas were ordered to the countryside. For example, one of my Chinese friends was the esteemed chair of the geology department at Nanjing University. He ended up being sent to a farm to perform manual labor. His daughter told me that this humiliation almost led him to commit suicide. The Cultural Revolution led to the destruction of much of China's cultural heritage.

In 1969, after three years of national misery, Mao declared the Cultural Revolution to be over. In the last years of his life, Mao was faced with declining health due to Parkinson's disease. He died on September 9, 1976 (Halliday, 2005).

SITUATIONAL LEADERSHIP ANALYSIS

Situational models of leadership differ from earlier trait and behavioral models in asserting that no single way of leading works in all situations. Rather, appropriate behavior depends on the circumstances at a given time. Effective managers diagnose the situation, identify the leadership style or behavior that will be most effective, and then determine whether they can implement the required style. Although Chairman Mao had a reputation for being a rigid demagogue, there were times when he realized that being more situational in his leadership behavior would be beneficial to the attainment of his long-range goals.

Initially, Mao's philosophy toward communism varied somewhat from that of the Russians. Whereas Lenin and Stalin saw the urban workers as the leaders of the communist revolution, Mao believed the farmers and peasants should serve in that role. But being the situational leader that he was, Mao shifted with the prevailing winds. He was not stubbornly attached to his views. "On the peasant question," he said, "the class line must be abandoned, there is nothing to be done among the poor peasants and it is necessary to establish ties with landowners, and gentry" (Halliday, 2005, 39).

By nature, Mao was an impulsive man, but as a situational leader, he usually was able to control his impulses. Staff who had commented on his "unruffled calm" and "impeccable self-control" were told by Mao:

"It's not that I am not angry. Sometimes I am so angry I feel my lungs are bursting, but I know I must control myself, and not show anything" (Halliday, 2005, 260). In this instance, he was alluding to the kidnapping of his son by Joseph Stalin. His impulse was to strike back in some way, but upon reflection, he decided to display political frame behavior, and as we will see, it paid dividends.

Mao used terror as a tool whenever he wanted to achieve something or was challenged in any way. But in 1956, after Khrushchev condemned Stalin's use of terror, Mao decided to curb arrests and executions. So, in situational leadership fashion, Mao gave orders to his police chief: "This year the number of arrests must be greatly reduced from last year. The number of executions especially must be fewer" (Halliday, 2005, 416).

Another indication of his reliance on situational leadership behavior was when the Great Famine occurred during the Great Leap Forward and the Chinese were struggling mightily. Mao decided that the purges should be decreased. As soon as the famine passed, however, the Great Purge and the Cultural Revolution took place, and the Red Guard was revitalized.

THE STRUCTURAL FRAME

Structural frame leaders seek to develop a new model of the relationship of structure, strategy, and environment for their organizations. Strategic planning, extensive preparation, and effecting change are priorities for them. It is fair to assert that the structural frame was one of Mao's strongest. In an effort typical of a structural leader, he was one of the first world leaders to devise a national long-range plan built upon successive five-year strategic plans.

Even as a youth, Mao practiced a combination of structural and political leadership behavior. He was in charge of a bookshop, but he got a friend to run it. An important trait emerged at this time. He had a gift for delegating chores, and identifying and convincing people to perform them. He also had an excellent work ethic. He would work himself to exhaustion but with the adrenalin continuing to flow, he had to rely on sleeping pills to fall asleep. Later in his life, he almost comically ranked the inventor of sleeping pills alongside Marx as the greatest men in history.

Mao was partial to the highly structured and hierarchical military approach to management. In 1927, he told an emergency Communist Party meeting, "Power comes out of the barrel of the gun" (Halliday, 2005, 50).

Like a prototypical structural leader, he had a well-thought-out plan that included the building of his own army, staking claim to his own territory, and dealing with Moscow and Washington, D.C., from a position of strength. During World War II, for example, Mao opted not to fight the Japanese or the Chinese Nationalists. With Russia preoccupied with Germany and in no position to intervene, Mao seized the opportunity to consolidate his party and prepare his army for the forthcoming civil war against the forces of Chiang Kai-shek.

In true, albeit extreme, structural leadership style, the Chinese people were pounded into submission at indoctrination meetings, rallies, and interrogations. Consumed in writing "thought examinations," the Chinese people had no time to think of rebellion. "Get everybody to write their thought examination and write three times, five times, again and again," Mao said. "Tell everyone to spill out every single thing they have ever harbored that is not so good for the Party" (Halliday, 2005, 245).

Mao succeeded in getting people to inform on each other. After two years of indoctrination and terror, the young volunteers were transformed from passionate champions of justice and equality into robots at the service of Mao. By forcefully operating out of the structural frame, he was able to attain this influence over his followers. Every day, at the interminable party meetings, Mao's simplistic modus operandi was made know to his disciples: "For everything wrong in the party, blame others; for every success, himself" (Halliday, 2005, 268).

The use of structural behavior such as this served Mao well in his preparation for successfully managing the Chinese civil war. His nonmilitary intelligence networks provided Mao with precise information about the movements of Chiang Kai-shek's army, which placed Chiang at a huge disadvantage.

Mao used structural frame behavior in seamlessly transitioning China from nationalist rule to communist rule. The plan called for the conquering army to replace government workers with young communist recruits. Another part of the plan was to co-opt the legal system and the news media. Once the state was secure, Mao began systematic terrorization of the population to induce long-term conformity and obedience.

In a combination of structural and symbolic frame behavior, Mao became famous for launching his five-year plans, with various goals like ending poverty and building worldwide domination. However, the breakneck speed he imposed in the Great Leap Forward, whereby China would have the atomic bomb and become a world leader, spawned a long-term quality- control problem that plagued arms and industrial production throughout his time in power.

Beginning in 1960, the national goal was to propagate Mao Zedong's beliefs around the world in the form of Maoism. Mao used structural leadership behavior to formulate the goal and in bringing it to fruition. Thus, as we have seen, Mao utilized structural leadership behavior, albeit very often to an extreme, as an integral part of his overall leadership style.

THE HUMAN RESOURCE FRAME

Human resource leaders believe in people and communicate that belief. They are passionate about productivity through people. Although he gave lip service to his concern for his countrymen, there was little evidence that Mao thought seriously about employing human resource leadership behavior. Nevertheless, when it served his purposes, Mao was capable of utilizing human resource behavior.

For example, as a means of currying favor with his troops, Mao set up "soldiers committees" to satisfy their desire for input into how to distribute the proceeds of their looting. Still, Mao's relationship with his army was in many ways a remote one. He never tried to inspire his troops in person, never visited the front, and never went to meet the troops in the field. He did not care about them as individuals, just as a war machine to achieve his goals. Other than this one diluted example of Mao's use of human resource behavior, it is difficult to find any substantial evidence that he utilized the human resource frame to any great extent.

THE SYMBOLIC FRAME

In the symbolic frame, the organization is seen as a stage, a theater in which every actor plays certain roles, and the symbolic leader attempts to communicate the right impressions to the right audiences. One could argue that, along with the political frame, the ability to exploit the symbolic frame was one of Mao's greatest strengths.

Even at a young age, Mao went about cultivating his public image as a great scholar and thinker. He spent many hours in the library reading books, including translations of Western writings. In the process, he scorned his fellow Chinese writers. "The nature of the people of the country is inertia," he said. "They worship hypocrisy, are content with being slaves, and narrow-minded" (Halliday, 2005, 12). He took part in book burning. This was an early indication of a theme that was to typify his rule—the destruction of Chinese culture.

Unlike most founding dictators like Lenin, Mussolini, and Hitler, Mao did not inspire a passionate following through his oratory or writings. He simply sought willing recruits who were ready to blindly follow his orders.

Mao's use of symbolic leadership behavior was so effective that despite his disdain for the peasants and working class, his image as the champion of the workers survives to this day. Writing to a friend in 1920, in which he complained about his own conditions as an intellectual, he remarked, "I think laborers in China do not really suffer poor physical conditions.

Only scholars suffer" (Halliday, 2005, 30). Nevertheless, as a testament to his ability to effectively employ symbolic leadership behavior, he retained the image of the working man's hero.

To help develop his image as a godlike figure, Mao had one of his poems widely circulated:

> Eagles soar up the long vault,
> Fish fly down the shallow riverbed,
> Under a sky of frost, ten thousand creatures vie to impose their will.
> Touched by this vastness,
> I ask the boundless earth:
> Who after all will be your master? (Halliday, 2005, 38)

Mao was famous for taking advantage of every opportunity to create and propagate his image. He did so in dramatic fashion when Chiang Kai-shek decided to purge his National Party of any communist influence. Mao immediately went public in his opposition, once again casting himself as the champion of the common man. In typical symbolic frame fashion, he labeled his opposition to Chiang's army as the Autumn Harvest Uprising.

After one of his early victories over Chiang in the Autumn Harvest Uprising, one of his officers came to offer congratulations: "Mao Zhuxi!" (Chairman Mao), he called out. "You learn really fast," Mao replied. "You are the first person." This officer was the first person to use the title that was to become part of the world's vocabulary: Chairman Mao (Halliday, 2005, 100).

In another example of his use of symbolic behavior, Mao was a devotee of public executions. He organized large rallies to view the executions as a way of intimidating the populace into obeying him. In time, he made these viewings mandatory.

In 1934, Mao led some eighty thousand soldiers on what came to be called the Long March. The ten-day-long retreat across hundreds of miles of terrain and rivers created one of the most enduring images of Mao's legend. It was yet another chapter in his becoming the peoples' hero.

In 1937, Mao once again used symbolic behavior by publishing the political pamphlet *Red Star* in a number of languages. In what was now a grand tradition, it painted a favorable picture of Mao as the champion of the workers and had a tremendous influence on his image in the West, including the United States.

Public opinion was further influenced by the publication *Stories of a Journey to the West*. In addition to this book and the Mao Zedong autobiography, a third book was produced from Edgar Snow's material, *Impressions of Mao Tse-tung*. Edgar Snow was a British news reporter and Mao's pawn. These publications helped shape Mao's positive image both at home and abroad.

Mao adroitly exploited his followers' idealism, somehow convincing them that his harsh treatment of them worked to their advantage and was part of "serving the people," an expression he coined. "We were fighting the enemy in the dark," he said, "and so wounded our own people." Or, "It was like a father beating his sons. So please don't bear grudges. Please just get up, dust the mud off your clothes and fight on" (Halliday, 2005, 248). These declarations, of course, were all rationalizations, but nonetheless believable to the Chinese people.

Mao was jealous of Chiang Kai-shek's lingering reputation as the nation builder of modern China. Thus, he set out to debunk that image. In 1944 he ordered the party to be reeducated on the question, "Who is the nation-builder of China, the Nationalists or the CCP?" (Halliday, 2005, 251). He developed a strategy whereby the answer would be Chairman Mao. This strategy led to what was to become known as "Mao Zedong Thought."

Eventually, Mao was successful in developing his own personality cult. The turning point occurred when the Chinese people "firmly established in their minds that Chairman Mao is our *only* wise leader" (Halliday, 2005, 268). It was at that time that the deification of Mao had begun.

On October 1, 1949, the symbolic behavior continued as Mao appeared standing on top of Tiananmen Gate, in front of the imperial Forbidden City, and formally established the People's Republic of China (PRC). From then on, Mao would make these appearances on special occasions, a practice modeled after Soviet leaders ascending Lenin's Tomb in Red Square to make their political speeches.

In typical symbolic leadership fashion, Mao became famous for coining terms for many of his programs. The *Three-Antis* targeted embezzlement, waste, and bureaucratism or laziness. This campaign was followed shortly by the *Five-Antis*: bribery, tax evasion, pilfering state property, cheating, and stealing economic information. Of course, he also coined the terms *Five-Year Plan*, *The Great Leap Forward*, and the *Cultural Revolution* (Halliday, 2005).

The campaign to spread Maoism embraced a great reliance on symbolic behavior, including the carrying of the *Little Red Book*, which contained many of Mao's ideals. Mao's face dominated the front pages of the *Peoples' Daily*, which was required to run a column of his quotes every day.

The Cultural Revolution, which sought to eliminate the remains of past Chinese cultures, was characterized by such symbolic behavior as book burnings, condemnation of the intelligentsia, and confiscations of land. Mao wanted to create a society of robots that, devoid of any independent thought, would mindlessly obey his orders. Through the prolific use of symbolic and political behavior, he was able to achieve this goal—at least temporarily.

THE POLITICAL FRAME

Leaders operating out of the political frame clarify what they want and what they can get. Political leaders are realists above all. They never let what they want cloud their judgment about what is possible. They assess the distribution of power and interests. Mao's capacity to operate out of the political leadership frame effectively was also one of his strengths.

Mao learned at an early age the effectiveness of astutely applied political behavior. He was fond of telling the story of having an argument with his father over his laziness. He ran out of the house, and his father pursued. He told his father that he would jump into the pond in the backyard if he came closer. "My father backed down," he said. "Old men like him didn't want to lose their sons. This is their weakness. I attacked at their weak point and I won" (Halliday, 2005, 6).

One of his first significant uses of political frame behavior came when he was not invited to a communist congress while he was serving as party boss in his hometown area, Hunan. Not being invited meant that he might lose his job as the head communist in Hunan province. So he decided to be proactive and schedule very visible visits to the lead and zinc mine and the coal-mining center. He also led a number of demonstrations and strikes in support of the Communist Party. Mao also infiltrated the Nationalist Party and undermined Sun Yat-sen's leadership.

This success lead to Mao's power struggles with Sun's successor, Chiang Kai-shek, the new commander of the Nationalist Party army. As mentioned earlier, when Chiang gave orders to cleanse the Nationalist Party of communist influence, Mao saw a chance to make a name for himself by keeping the communist influence alive. It marked his political coming of age.

By 1944, Mao had anticipated that Russia would soon join the Chinese and the United States and enter the war against Japan. After Japan was defeated, Mao would need "friends" in his fight to unseat Chiang Kai-shek, so he engaged in political behavior once again in beginning to tone down the terror so that he would be perceived in a better light by Russia and the United States. He would also recognize the Nationalist Party as the legitimate government and place the Red Army and its territory under Chiang Kai-shek.

Mao's basic plan for the Sino-Japanese War, therefore, was to preserve his forces and expand the sphere of the Communist Party. So, when the Japanese pushed deeper into China, in exchange for relinquishing Red-held territory, Mao got Chiang to agree that the Red Army would not be put into any battles and would operate only as auxiliaries to the government troops. This way, Mao could preserve his army for the civil war that would come *after* the Sino-Japanese War.

Thus, Mao played both the United States and Soviet Russia like a proverbial fiddle. He convinced Stalin to invade China in 1945, thus creating the conditions to seize power. At the same time, Mao carefully exploited the fact that United States officials were becoming increasingly disenchanted with Chiang. Mao carefully fostered the delusion that the CCP was a moderate agrarian reform party that would be a friendly ally of the United States. After the war, Mao continued to use political behavior to enhance his power and influence. While an armistice was being negotiated to end the Korean War in 1953, Mao once again used political behavior to further his agenda. President Eisenhower mentioned the possibility of using the atom bomb to hasten the talks toward a peaceful conclusion. Mao immediately exploited Eisenhower's threat by pushing Russia to give him nuclear weapons and information on how to build an atomic bomb.

In the era of de-Stalinization that followed Stalin's death, Mao once again engaged in political frame leadership behavior. In what he called the Hundred Flowers Campaign, he invited people to speak out against the evils of communism so that it could be reformed. Once the reform fad had passed, he arrested and in some cases executed those who had spoken out. In effect, he used the occasion to identify his political enemies.

By 1970, Maoism had waned. Ever resourceful, Mao came up with yet another political strategy that would get him back on the world stage. He decided that he would convince the president of the United States to visit China—enter Richard Nixon. After Nixon's historic visit, Mao had a rebirth, and world leaders from every country around the world were anxious to get an audience with the great and powerful Chairman Mao.

THE MORAL FRAME

The moral frame is my own contribution to situational leadership theory. In my view, the moral frame completes situational leadership theory. Without it, leaders could just as easily use their leadership skills for promoting evil as for promoting good. Leaders operating out of the moral frame are concerned about their obligations and responsibilities to their followers. Moral frame leaders use some type of moral compass to direct their behavior. They practice what has been described as servant leadership and are concerned with those individuals and groups that are marginalized in their organizations and in society. In short, they are concerned about equality, fairness, and social justice. Chairman Mao is another of example of a great leader who was not a *good* one. There is little in his leadership behavior to indicate that he gave even one iota of consideration to acting out of the moral frame.

Mao's attitude toward morality consisted of one core value, the self. "I do not agree with the view that to be moral, the motive of one's action has to be benefiting others. People like me want to satisfy ourselves to the full, and in doing so automatically have the most valuable moral codes. Of course there are people and objects in the world, but they are only there for me," he declared (Halliday, 2005, 13). As a result of this credo, Mao will be remembered in history primarily as a leader who was responsible for the deaths of millions of his own people.

CONCLUSION

There is an abundance of evidence that Mao Zedong was a situational leader. We saw how he utilized structural frame leadership behavior and developed a strategic plan to achieve his goals, and he was the first to popularize the term *five-year plan*. Once his plans were set in motion, he made good use of symbolic and political frame leadership behavior. For example, he labeled many of his movements in creative ways so as to gain attention. *Great Leap Forward, Cultural Revolution*, and the *Hundred Flowers Campaign* are but a few of the catchy terms that he used to derive maximum impact.

We saw that he was a master at utilizing the political frame, especially in his dealings with the United States, Nationalist China, and the Soviet Union. He convinced the Soviet Union to support him in his efforts to displace the Nationalist government of Chiang with his Chinese Communist Party, and when his reputation was flagging, he enticed Richard Nixon to visit China, thereby resurrecting his image as a world leader.

However, there were two frames, human resource and moral, in which Mao displayed little or no activity. The lack of practicing any significant leadership behavior in these two frames led to Mao's place in history as a notorious leader who caused more evil than good. He is often mentioned in the same breath as Adolph Hitler, Joseph Stalin, Vladimir Lenin, and Benito Mussolini—not the best of company, indeed!

Chapter 13

John D. Rockefeller

God gave me my money.

—John D. Rockefeller

BACKGROUND

John D. Rockefeller, an American industrialist and philanthropist, was born in 1839 in Richford, New York. He is most famous for having founded the Standard Oil Company and the Rockefeller Foundation. The Rockefeller family moved to Cleveland, Ohio, in 1853, when it was beginning to grow into a major industrial center.

Rockefeller found his first job at the age of sixteen as a produce clerk. In 1859, at the tender age of nineteen, he started his first company, the Clark and Rockefeller stock-trading company. From the start, Rockefeller showed a genius for organization. With the Pennsylvania oil find in 1859 and the building of a railroad to Cleveland, it was an ideal time to branch out into the oil-refining business. Within two years, Rockefeller became senior partner and the company became Cleveland's largest refinery.

Rockefeller's Standard Oil Company was begun in Ohio in 1870. At the time, Standard Oil already controlled 10 percent of America's oil refining. However, Rockefeller still hoped to monopolize the entire oil-refining industry. He bought out most of the Cleveland refineries as well as others in New York, Pittsburgh, and Philadelphia. By 1879 he was refining 90 percent of America's oil, and Standard Oil owned its own tank cars, fleet of ships, docking facilities, barrel-making plants, depots, and warehouses.

In 1883, after gaining control over the pipeline industry, Standard Oil's monopoly was at a peak. Rockefeller had created America's first great trust, a kind of corporation of corporations. But the firm was attacked for its monopolistic practices, and these attacks ultimately gave momentum to the antitrust movement. In 1892 the state of Ohio finally forced a separation of Standard Oil of Ohio from the rest of the company. However, in 1899 Standard Oil was recreated legally under a new structure known as a "holding company."

Later in life Rockefeller became famous for his philanthropy. From the start of his career, Rockefeller had tithed 10 percent of his earnings to the Baptist Church. As his wealth grew, he increased his giving, and in the process, revolutionized the planned-giving process. Many of the strategies used in the systemized approach of current-day philanthropy were garnered from Rockefeller's methods. In May 1937, the great industrialist and philanthropist died of arteriosclerosis, two months before his ninety-eighth birthday (Chernow, 1998).

SITUATIONAL LEADERSHIP ANALYSIS

Situational models of leadership differ from earlier trait and behavioral models in asserting that no single way of leading works in all situations. Rather, appropriate behavior depends on the circumstances at a given time. Effective managers diagnose the situation, identify the leadership style or behavior that will be most effective, and then determine whether they can implement the required style. John D. Rockefeller gave every indication that he was a leader in the situational leadership tradition.

As we shall see, Rockefeller was not dedicated exclusively to one type of leadership behavior. Rather, he was active in all the frames of leadership, depending on the situation. Illustrative of this flexibility was the seeming contradiction between how he acted as an industrialist versus how he behaved as a philanthropist. One of the things that makes Rockefeller's historical image so enigmatic is that his good side, as expressed mainly through his philanthropy, was every bit as good as his bad side, expressed through his monopolization of the petroleum business and the demolishing of his competitors, was bad.

Seldom has history produced such a contradictory figure. But he was only being situational. The leadership behavior he exhibited to be successful in business was not necessarily the behavior he practiced to be an effective philanthropist. Nevertheless, he was insistent that his philanthropy paled in importance with the good he had done in creating jobs and furnishing affordable kerosene through the success of Standard Oil.

Another indication of Rockefeller's situational leadership tendencies was his behavior in his later years. Then, Rockefeller's metamorphosis into a master of public relations after a lifetime of avoiding publicity was another apparent contradiction. But in his view, the situation had changed, and different behavior was required.

For example, toward the latter part of his career he met with a delegation from the American Press Humorists Society, who were so impressed by his sense of humor that they elected him an honorary member and jokingly bragged that they now had the highest per-capita income of any such society in the world.

THE STRUCTURAL FRAME

Structural frame leaders seek to develop a new model of the relationship of structure, strategy, and environment for their organizations. Strategic planning, extensive preparation, and effecting change are priorities for them. A compelling argument could be made that the structural frame was Rockefeller's strongest.

From the start, Rockefeller was supremely confident in his abilities to plan, strategize, and bring ideas to fruition. Having an internal locus of control and being indifferent to the approval of others, he was always able to focus on what he thought was important. He was mature beyond his years. "I'll move just as soon as I get it figured out," he told his classmates and teachers who tried to rush him. "You don't think I'm playing to get beaten, do you?" (Chernow, 1998, 18).

From his mother, he learned economy, order, thrift, and other structural frame virtues that led to the success of his business and philanthropic ventures. Her frequent admonition, "We will let it simmer," was a notion that Rockefeller employed throughout his business career (Chernow, 1998, 22). From his father, Rockefeller got the message that big business was a difficult profession in which ethics were oftentimes an afterthought.

The result of these influences was that Rockefeller displayed the structural frame habits of thriftiness, punctuality, and industriousness. For example, refusing to deviate from his routine, he worked the morning of his wedding day.

Although he ultimately made his fortune in oil, Rockefeller did not instantly see its potential. Rather, in a structural frame way, he chose the oil business only after much deliberation over possible alternatives. Finally, in 1863, he and his partner invested $4,000, a huge amount of money at that time, to buy into the oil business.

Rockefeller's structural frame tendencies came to the fore in his choice of oil refining as opposed to oil exploration. Whereas searching for oil was wildly unpredictable, refining was more methodical, so he chose the more predictable business.

Never one to let any grass grow under his feet, Rockefeller no sooner acquired a new company than he would be thinking of ways to expand it. For example, he had first paid small coopers up to $2.50 a piece for white-oak barrels before he showed, in an early demonstration of economies of scale, that he could manufacture them more cheaply himself. Soon, his company made thousands of barrels daily for less than a dollar each. He also extended the market for petroleum by-products, selling benzene, paraffin, and petroleum jelly in addition to his staple, kerosene. This was all before the advent of the automobile, which of course increased his profits exponentially.

Displaying structural behavior once again, Rockefeller was fond of saying, "I hate frills. Used things, beautiful things, are admirable: but frills, affectations, mere pretences of being something very fine, bore me very much" (Chernow, 1998, 120). In his rigidly compartmentalized life, he accounted for every hour. There was no time to waste on frills.

Rockefeller was not one to let obstacles stand in the way of achieving success. In the late 1800s, states would not let corporations own property outside their state of incorporation. To circumvent this obstacle, the partnership of Rockefeller, Andres, and Flagler was abolished and replaced by the joint-stock firm named the Standard Oil Company of Ohio, with Rockefeller as president—the first holding company in history.

Rockefeller's use of the structural frame was in evidence in the way he treated his employees and how he conducted his business in general. At first, he was very demanding, but once he trusted them, he empowered them and did not intrude on their work.

Rockefeller inspired his subordinates with his strong work ethic. He never did anything without careful preparation. He wrote hundreds of business letters that were models of concise phrasing. He never seemed to waste a word. Dictating letters to his secretary, he went through five or six drafts before he was satisfied. Then he signed them with his meticulous penmanship. Rockefeller's structural tendencies led him to become the forbearer of Frederick Taylor's idea of scientific management. Like Taylor, Rockefeller would study an operation, break it down into its component parts, and devise ways to improve it. He was greatly attentive to detail. For example, after watching a machine operator solder caps onto cans, he asked the machine operator, "How many drops of solder do you use on each can?" "Forty," the man replied. "Have you ever tried thirty-eight?" Rockefeller asked. "No? Would you mind having some sealed with thirty-eight and let me know?" (Chernow, 1998, 180).

Strategic thinking and planning were other structural qualities that Rockefeller often practiced. For example, he knew that if he got too greedy, other products could easily be substituted for kerosene. Thus he limited his profits to keep kerosene easily affordable.

Oil was just one of many fossil fuels and kerosene one of many potential illuminants. So when Thomas Edison reported that he had invented a practical electric light bulb, in true structural leadership style, Rockefeller knew it was time to diversify. So, in 1893, Rockefeller bought Carnegie Steel and consolidated it into U.S. Steel to form a trust even larger than Standard Oil.

THE HUMAN RESOURCE FRAME

Human resource leaders believe in people and communicate that belief. They are passionate about productivity through people. Although clearly not one of Rockefeller's strongest frames, there is evidence that he operated out of the human resource frame quite often.

Rockefeller revealed the human resource side of this leadership behavior during the Civil War. Although the war was certainly an opportunity to accumulate riches, Rockefeller had intense sympathy for the Union cause and fervently advocated abolishing slavery. He also displayed the human side of his personality at home with his wife and children. When they played blind man's bluff, he thrilled them with daring feints and sudden thrusts, followed by his childlike whoops of delight when he won. At home, he created a make-believe market economy, calling his wife, Cettie, the "general manager" and requiring the children to do the bookkeeping.

Rockefeller also utilized human resource behavior at work. In the early days, Rockefeller knew the name and face of each employee and occasionally ambled about the office to greet them. The people who worked for him usually found him a model of propriety and paternalistic concern. "John could always get along so easily with everyone," one of his managers declared. "Indeed, had he not possessed some charm, or at least cordiality, he could never have accomplished so much in the business world" (Chernow, 1998, 177).

So highly did Rockefeller value human resources that during the first years of Standard Oil he personally attended to routine hiring matters. After his business grew astronomically and the payroll ballooned to three thousand people and beyond, this personal touch became more difficult. Still, he continued to show the value that he placed on human resources by hiring talented people when found, not necessarily when needed. "The ability to deal with people is as purchasable a commodity as sugar or coffee," he once said. "And, I pay more for that ability than for any other under the sun" (Chernow, 1998, 177).

Employees were invited to send complaints or suggestions directly to him, and he always responded and took an interest in their affairs. His correspondence is dotted with inquiries about sick or retired employees. Rather generous in wages, salaries, and working conditions, he paid somewhat above the industry average. Forty years later, a former subordinate wrote of the firm, with some exaggeration, "It has never had a strike or a dissatisfied workman; and today no business organization cares for its veterans in their old age as does the Standard Oil Company" (Chernow, 1998, 177).

When it came to old friends, his generosity was remarkable. When he received word from Pittsburgh that a trust company he directed was verging on bankruptcy, Rockefeller telegraphed promptly, "How much do you want?" "One million dollars," came the response, to which Rockefeller replied, "Check for one million is on the way" (Chernow, 1998, 338).

Rockefeller's magnanimous philanthropy also grew out of his human resource tendencies. As the sheer magnitude of his wealth rendered his accustomed deliberate approach to philanthropy outmoded, he became frustrated when he could not give money away quickly enough to keep pace with his ever-increasing income. It took several years before he learned to donate money in a systematic, scientific fashion that worked. In effect, he had to employ some structural leadership behavior to enable himself to activate his human resource behavior.

THE SYMBOLIC FRAME

In the symbolic frame, the organization is seen as a stage, a theater in which every actor plays certain roles, and the symbolic leader attempts to communicate the right impressions to the right audiences. One could convincingly argue that John D. Rockefeller's frequent use of the symbolic leadership frame differentiated him from many of the industrialists of his era.

Rockefeller consciously worked at cultivating an image of an industrious, self-made, God-fearing man. The opening quotation to this chapter alludes to Rockefeller's belief that he owed his riches to God. Early in life, he learned that God wanted his flock to earn money and then donate the money to worthy causes in a cyclical process. "I was trained from the beginning to work and to save," Rockefeller declared (Chernow, 1998, 20). He made a public display of being grateful to God that kerosene, his major product, was so helpful to society.

Like Ford and Edison, Rockefeller fashioned his image after that of the common man. He was often seen at his plants as early as 6:30 a.m., going into the shop to roll out barrels and sweep the floor, reflecting his puritanical religious upbringing.

Rockefeller's decision to get into the rather speculative and inconsistent oil business was also symbolic in nature. He believed in divine providence and had faith that "God would provide."

Rockefeller also projected the image of a creative and innovative businessman, sometimes with questionable ethical practices. One of his innovative business practices was to extract cash rebates from the railroad companies, giving him a huge competitive advantage. Not until the Interstate Commerce Act of 1887 did it become illegal for railroads to give rebates, and not until the 1903 Elkins Act did the practice end entirely. Both laws were aimed directly at his excesses.

Rockefeller moderated his sometimes negative business image by being a model husband and father. He and his family reflected the commonly accepted Victorian values of civility, kindness, and religiosity. As we have seen, Rockefeller perceived virtually everything in religious terms. Even when he monopolized the oil-refining industry, sometimes using questionable means, he would rationalize that he was doing God's will by providing employment and useful products for millions of people.

So, where Rockefeller differed from most of his fellow industrialists was in wanting to be both rich and virtuous. He projected the image of a man that God had blessed with the talent of making money, just as He had blessed artists and musicians with the talent to paint and compose music.

Rockefeller often explained and defended the rationale for the monopolistic practices of Standard Oil by resorting to religious imagery. "Standard Oil was an angel of mercy, reaching down from the sky, and saying, 'Get into the ark. Put in your old junk. We'll take all the risks!'" (Chernow, 1998, 153). Rockefeller's somewhat-convoluted argument was that without Standard Oil, there would have been the survival of only the fittest and only Standard Oil would have survived. Thus, in his mind, the Standard Oil Trust saved all the other oil refiners from bankruptcy by including them in the Standard Oil conglomerate.

Rockefeller also worked hard to project an image of excellence. And he was determined to sustain it. "More than once I have gone to luncheon with a number of our heads of departments and have seen the sweat start out on the foreheads of some of them when that little red notebook was pulled out," Rockefeller declared (Chernow, 1998, 180).

Faithful to his image as the common man, Rockefeller shunned big-city society and stuck with his old Cleveland pastimes like constructing a large ice-skating rink every winter in a space adjoining his house. Of course, this was the inspiration for one of the present-day symbols of his dynasty, the ice-skating rink at New York's Rockefeller Plaza.

Another image that Rockefeller cultivated was that of the great philanthropist. Partly to offset his image as a callous businessman, Rockefeller concerned himself with poverty in the cities, often connected to industrialization, and the duties of noblesse oblige.

But the most important contribution Rockefeller made to philanthropy was the systemized, scientific approach that he developed for wholesale gift giving. It revolutionized the institutional development process and many of his procedures are still used today.

Despite his best efforts at image building, by 1914, after the monopolization of the oil- refining industry and the Ludlow Massacre, where iron ore miners were forced to return to work after eight months because their strike fund was depleted, Rockefeller suffered a long-lasting blow to his reputation. But he underwent a metamorphosis in his later years, and his positive image was restored.

In addition to his philanthropy, one of his better symbolic brainstorms was undoubtedly his decision to dispense shiny souvenir dimes to adults and nickels to children as he moved about. He delivered brief sermons along with the coins, exhorting small children to work hard and be frugal if they wanted to succeed. "I think it is easier to remember a lesson when we have some token to recall it by, something we can look at which reminds us of the idea," he remarked (Chernow, 1998, 613).

THE POLITICAL FRAME

Leaders operating out of the political frame clarify what they want and what they can get. Political leaders are realists above all. They never let what they want cloud their judgment about what is possible. They assess the distribution of power and interests. It is fair to say that John D. Rockefeller was extraordinarily active in the political frame.

As proponents of political frame leadership behavior are apt to do, Rockefeller compared navigating the oil business with finding one's way through a dense jungle. As his operation grew, Rockefeller became fixated with secrecy to the point of paranoia. As a result, he demanded circumspection of both himself and his staff.

Rockefeller was particularly astute in applying political leadership behavior when negotiating the deals that established the Standard Oil Corporation as a monopoly in the oil-refining business. As mentioned earlier, his initial decision to specialize in oil refining rather than oil exploration was a politically calculated one. The oil-refining business was far less speculative and much more reliable than the oil-drilling business.

Again, as mentioned earlier, Rockefeller also used political behavior in extracting rebates from the railroads, thus giving Standard Oil a competitive advantage over the other oil refineries. When the other refiners got wind of the rebates, they of course demanded equal treatment. Rockefeller, however, still demanded special treatment. He considered the railroads' refusal to continue giving rebates to be disloyal.

When the railroads persisted in denying him rebates, Rockefeller idled his Pittsburgh refineries and ordered increases in production at his Cleveland refineries, where the railroads were still granting the rebates. Eventually, Rockefeller's use of political behavior prevailed and the railroads restored the rebates.

Despite his political maneuverings, Standard Oil generally did an excellent job of providing kerosene at affordable prices. It offered significantly lower unit costs than its competitors and constantly reduced costs, routinely passing the savings on to customers. Still, in spite of its efficiencies, Rockefeller never sought a perfect monopoly because he realized that it was politically prudent to allow some competition, albeit weak. As he admitted, "We realized that public sentiment would be against us if we actually refined all the oil" (Chernow, 1998, 259).

With all the hostile publicity that was directed at Standard Oil during the debate over railroad rebates, Rockefeller engaged in an astute application of political behavior by using it as an opportunity to launch his philanthropic efforts. He was America's richest man, and it was a perfect time for him to give back. He began his charitable works with the funding of a new university, the world-renowned University of Chicago.

Even when Theodore Roosevelt, the great trust buster and Rockefeller's archenemy, won reelection, Rockefeller exhibited political frame leadership behavior. Swallowing hard, he sent Roosevelt a telegram saying, "I congratulate you most heartily on the grand result of yesterday's election" (Chernow, 1998, 520).

THE MORAL FRAME

The moral frame is my own contribution to situational leadership theory. In my view, the moral frame completes situational leadership theory. Without it, leaders could just as easily use their leadership skills for promoting evil as for promoting good. Leaders operating out of the moral frame are concerned about their obligations and responsibilities to their followers. Moral frame leaders use some type of moral compass to direct their behavior. They practice what has been described as servant leadership and are concerned with those individuals and groups that are marginalized in their organizations and in society. In short, they are concerned about equality, fairness, and social justice.

When one considers the robber baron reputation that dominated the businessmen of the U.S. industrial age, Rockefeller was known to have operated out of the moral frame more frequently than most, if not all, of his counterparts. Early in life, he became convinced that God wanted his disciples to earn money and then share it with those less fortunate.

Rockefeller was raised to believe that nobody was ever irretrievably lost and through the exercise of free will could redeem themselves. From his early religious and moral experiences, Rockefeller came away with a deep, abiding respect for those in need. His attitude was very much unlike other moguls of his era who believed in the biblical adage, "The poor, we will always have with us."

Rockefeller possessed the Protestant work ethic in its purest form and led his life accordingly. He was a proponent of the idea of steward leadership long before it became popular. He believed that he and others like him were instruments of God and only temporarily in charge of their riches and expected by God to redistribute their bounty to those more needy.

Rockefeller operationalized his moral beliefs by being a stickler for the truth and by promptly repaying loans. He also remained faithful to his wife for their many years of marriage. However, he sometimes came off as self-righteous and paternalistic to the point where he imposed penalties on any executive who divorced or was implicated in an adulterous affair.

As at Standard Oil, Rockefeller was a fatherly figure and imposed his moral standards at home. Among the three hundred, mostly black and Italian, workmen who took care of his home and the grounds around it, he outlawed profanity and even tried to purchase and close down the local tavern they frequented. Though he was exacting in his demands, he never raised his voice to his employees. He dealt with them in a patient, considerate manner, and he was known for sitting down with them for "fireside chats."

Again, with an eye on his moral compass, Rockefeller and his wife, Cettie, never administered corporal punishment at home, and they inculcated moral principles by instruction and example. Each child was taught to listen to his or her conscience as an infallible guide to acceptable behavior. Rockefeller modeled his moral principles further by serving as superintendent of the local Sunday school, while Cettie ran the infant school.

As we have seen in examining Rockefeller's symbolic leadership behavior, he contributed huge sums to education and medical research, because education and medicine better prepared people for the evolutionary struggle and equipped them to compete. He was careful never to use his wealth to try to alleviate poverty directly. He believed in teaching the poor how to fish rather than giving them fish.

Lest the reader be left with the impression that Rockefeller was some kind of saint, it is fair to say that many of his detractors believed otherwise. He was said to be unscrupulous when dealing with adversaries, but he always following the letter, if not the spirit, of the law. And, although he was often accused of illegal conduct, he was never convicted of it. Albeit with mixed results, Rockefeller made every attempt to act out of the moral frame in virtually everything that he did in both his personal and professional life.

CONCLUSION

John D. Rockefeller was definitely a leader in the situational mold. We saw how he used structural leadership behavior to build an empire that surpassed those of most other industrialists of his era. In the process, he taught the American public an important but paradoxical lesson that unfortunately has had to be reinforced recently: free markets, if left completely to their own devices, can wind up extremely unfree. We also saw that Rockefeller had a human side and generously utilized human resource behavior in both his personal and professional life.

Rockefeller practiced symbolic behavior through his altruistic and magnanimous philanthropy. He believed that a rich man should give away his money during his lifetime, lest idle heirs fritter it away. He used his fellow industrialist Andrew Carnegie's famous quote as his inspiration: "The man who dies thus rich dies disgraced" (Chernow, 1998, 308). We also saw how Rockefeller used symbolic leadership behavior later in life by distributing nickels and dimes to people he met.

His use of political leadership behavior was also extensive, especially in establishing a monopoly in the oil-refining business and virtually eliminating all competition. The so-called Cleveland Massacre, in which he bought up all the refineries in the refining capital of the world to begin his domination of the oil-refining business, was a political move. Finally, we saw that he operated out of the moral frame with great enthusiasm. In his mind, the business of business was truly God's work, and he saw himself as a mere instrument in that divine plan. There is much to learn from examining the leadership behavior of this great businessman and philanthropist. The leadership principles he espoused were those for the ages and are just as applicable today as they were in his era.

Rockefeller, at the age of eighty-six, penned the following words, which best sum up his life:

> I was early taught to work as well as play.
> My life has been one long, happy holiday.
> Full of work and full of play,
> I dropped the worry on the way,
> And God was good to me every day. (Chernow, 1998)

Chapter 14

To Lead as Jesus Did

> A new commandment I give to you, that you love one another; as I have
> loved you, that you also love one another.
>
> —John 13:34

BACKGROUND

According to the Gospel writers Matthew and Luke, Jesus Christ was
born in Bethlehem to Mary, a virgin, by a miracle of the Holy Spirit. In
the Gospel of Luke, the angel Gabriel tells Mary that she was chosen to
bear the Son of God. An order of Caesar Augustus mandated that Mary
and Joseph, Christ's foster father, leave their homes in Nazareth and come
to the home of Joseph's ancestors for a census. After Christ's birth, the
couple had to use a manger in a stable for a crib because there was no
room for them in the town's inn.

According to the New Testament, an angel spread the word of Christ's
birth to shepherds who came to see the newborn child and subsequently
spread the word throughout the area about what they had witnessed.
Some accounts tell of the Wise Men, or Magi, who brought gifts to the
infant Jesus after following a star that they believed was a sign that the
Messiah had been born.

Christ's childhood home was the town of Nazareth in Galilee, where
he worked with his father, Joseph, as a carpenter. Luke's "Finding in the
Temple" (Luke 2:41–52) is the only event between Christ's infancy and his
adult life mentioned in any of the canonical Gospels.

Jesus was baptized by John the Baptist, which biblical scholars describe
as the beginning of Christ's public ministry. Christ came to the Jordan
River where John the Baptist had been preaching and baptizing people in
the crowd. After Christ had been baptized and rose from the water, Mark
states that Christ "saw the heavens torn apart and the Spirit descending
like a dove on him. And a voice came from heaven, 'You are my Son, the
Beloved; with you I am well pleased'" (Mark 1:10–11).

Following his baptism, according to Matthew, Christ was led into the
desert by God, where he fasted for forty days and forty nights. During
this time, the devil appeared to him three times and tempted Christ to
demonstrate his supernatural powers as proof of his identity, with each
temptation being refused by Christ.

The Gospels describe three different Passover feasts over the course
of Christ's ministry, implying that Christ preached for a period of three
years. The focus of his ministry was toward the twelve apostles, though
his less intimate followers were called disciples. At the height of his ministry, Christ attracted huge crowds numbering in the thousands, primarily in the area of Galilee (modern-day northern Israel).

Some of Christ's most famous teachings came from the Sermon on the Mount, which contains the beatitudes and the Lord's Prayer. During his sermons, he preached against anger, lust, divorce, false oaths, and revenge. He also expounded the Mosaic Law and taught what he called a new commandment, to love your neighbor as yourself. Christ advocated, among other things, turning the other cheek, love for one's enemies as well as friends, and the need to follow the spirit of the law in addition to the letter.

Christ used parables, such as those of the prodigal son, the sower, and the good shepherd to make his points. His teachings centered on unconditional, self-sacrificing love for God and for all people (Matthew 22:34–40). He also preached about service and humility, the forgiveness of sin, pacifism, faith, and attaining everlasting life in heaven.

Christ also debated with other religious leaders of his time. He disagreed with the Sadducees because they did not believe in the resurrection of the dead (Matthew 22:23–32). The relationship between Christ and the Pharisees is more complex. Although Christ condemned the Pharisees for their hypocrisy, he also dined with them, taught in their synagogues, articulated their teachings to his followers, and counted Pharisees such as Nicodemus among his disciples.

All four Gospels record Christ's triumphal entry into Jerusalem at the end of his ministry. The famous narrative of Christ and the money changers occurred when Christ arrived in Jerusalem. In this episode, Christ is stated to have visited the temple in Jerusalem at which the courtyard is described as being filled with livestock, which were sold for use in the temple, and the tables of the money changers, who changed other currencies into the Jewish half shekel, which was the only coinage allowed in temple ceremonies. According to the Gospels, Christ took offense at this and drove out the livestock, scattered the coins of the money changers, and turned over their tables. After overturning the money tables, Christ chastised the money changers by saying, "My house will be called a house of prayer, but you are making it a den of robbers" (Matthew 21:13; Mark 11:17; Luke 19:46).

Sometime after casting the money changers out of the temple, Christ ate a meal, called the Last Supper, with his disciples before going to pray in the Garden of Gethsemane. In the course of the Last Supper, Christ broke bread, said grace, and handed the pieces of bread to his disciples, saying, "This is My body." He then took a cup of wine and handed it the them, saying, "This is My blood of the covenant, which is poured for many." Finally, he told the disciples, "Do this in remembrance of me" (Mark 14:22–26).

While praying in the Garden of Gethsemane, Christ was arrested by Roman soldiers on the orders of the Sanhedrin and the high priest, Caiaphas. The religious authorities had decided to arrest Christ since some of them had come to consider him a threat to their power because of his growing popularity, his new interpretations of scripture, and his revelations of their hypocrisy. According to the Gospels, Judas Iscariot, one of his apostles, betrayed Christ by identifying him to the guards with a kiss.

The high priests accused Christ of blasphemy because he claimed to be the Son of God, and they turned Christ over to the Roman prefect Pontius Pilate for punishment. Pilate personally felt that Christ was not guilty of any crime against the Romans, and since there was a custom during Passover for the Roman governor to free a prisoner, Pilate offered the crowd a choice between Christ and an insurrectionist named Barabbas. The crowd chose to have Barabbas freed and Christ crucified.

According to all four Gospels, Christ died before late afternoon, and the wealthy Judean Joseph of Arimathea received Pilate's permission to take possession of Christ's body and place it in a tomb. According to the Gospels, God raised Christ from the dead on the third day. The Acts of the Apostles tells that Christ appeared to various people in various places over the next forty days before he ascended into heaven. According to the Gospel of John, during one of these visits, Christ's disciple Thomas initially doubted the resurrection, but after being invited to place his finger in Christ's pierced side, he said to him, "My Lord and my God!"

Regardless of whether one considers him to be divine, judging from the over two billion followers who currently refer to themselves as Christians, one could legitimately argue that Jesus Christ was the most successful and transformational leader in recorded history. Nevertheless, from the standpoint of leadership theory, the question remains whether he was a situational leader.

SITUATIONAL LEADERSHIP ANALYSIS

Situational models of leadership differ from earlier trait and behavioral models in asserting that no single way of leading works in all situations. Rather, appropriate behavior depends on the circumstances at a given time. Effective managers diagnose the situation, identify the leadership style or behavior that will be most effective, and then determine whether they can implement the required style.

The Gospels of Matthew, Mark, Luke, and John leave little doubt that Jesus Christ was a situational leader. A review of Christ's leadership behavior is replete with instances of the use of structural, human resource, symbolic, and even political behavior. Being the consummate teacher, Christ was quite adept at varying his teaching style to the learning style of his "students." He used parables, lectures, stories, and even miracles, depending on the readiness level of his audience.

Perhaps the most notable instance in which Christ modeled situational leadership behavior was in speaking to the Pharisees regarding whether the Jewish law would allow them to pay taxes to the Roman emperor. The Pharisees expected a yes-or-no answer, planning to criticize Christ whichever way he answered. However, in a most situational manner, he asked them to identify the head on the coin, and when they identified it as Caesar's, he said, "Then pay Caesar what is due to Caesar, and pay God what is due God" (Matthew 22:21–22).

Another instance among the many in which Christ was situational in his application of leadership behavior was at the Sermon on the Mount, when Christ preached the beatitudes. He knew that there were at least two "situations" among the crowd—those who would immediately understand his message, and those who would need help in doing so. So, in addition to using structural leadership behavior in enumerating the eight beatitudes, Christ used symbolic behavior by cloaking the beatitudes in language that even the most illiterate in the assemblage could understand. Instead of merely telling them to be kind, merciful, and just, he taught them, saying,

> Blessed are the poor in spirit, for theirs is the kingdom of heaven.
> Blessed are those who mourn, for they shall be comforted.
> Blessed are the meek, for they shall inherit the earth.
> Blessed are those who hunger and thirst for righteousness, for they shall be filled.
> Blessed are the merciful, for they shall obtain mercy.
> Blessed are the pure in heart, for they shall see God.
> Blessed are the peacemakers, for they shall be called sons of God.
> Blessed are those who are persecuted for righteousness' sake, for theirs is the kingdom of heaven. (Matthew 5:2–10)

Lastly, early in his ministry, Christ used situational leadership behavior in refusing the devil's invitation to perform a miracle, while readily agreeing to do so for his mother, Mary. One of the first Gospel stories is the temptation of Christ. The devil tempts Christ three times in the desert. On one occasion, the devil urges the fasting Christ to turn stones into bread to feed himself. Christ refuses to display his power in such a self-serving way. However, he did at the marriage feast of Cana what he would not do in the desert. He did in public what he would not do in private. The devil asked him to change stones into bread to save himself, which he refused to do; his mother asked him to change water into wine to help others, which he immediately did—two different situations calling for two very different leadership behaviors (John 2:10).

THE STRUCTURAL FRAME

Structural frame leaders seek to develop a new model of the relationship of structure, strategy, and environment for their organizations. Strategic planning, extensive preparation, and effecting change are priorities for them. Jesus Christ took thirty years to develop a plan to transform the spiritual and personal lives of humankind. By the time he began his public ministry, he had in mind what amounted to a strategic plan for changing the way people would behave and how they would relate to one another.

He had developed a moral code to guide his followers' behavior. As mentioned above, Christ was essentially a teacher. To be effective, he had to make abundant use of structural frame leadership behavior. He used structural leadership behavior in the form of preaching, storytelling, parables, and miracles to make his points and attain his goals. As we shall see, there are myriad examples of Christ effectively utilizing the structural frame.

Even before his public life began, he used structural leadership behavior. In the Gospel story of the "Finding in the Temple," Christ used structural leadership behavior in the form of teaching the temple elders when he was merely twelve years old. In this Gospel episode, Christ accompanies Mary and Joseph to Jerusalem on a pilgrimage. On the day of their return, Christ lingered in the temple, but Mary and Joseph thought he had gone ahead of them. Mary and Joseph headed back home and after a day of travel realized Christ was missing, so they returned to Jerusalem and found Christ three days later. He was found in the temple in discussion with the elders who were amazed at his learning, especially given his young age. When admonished by Mary, Christ replied, "Why did you seek me? Did you not know that I must be about My Father's business?" (Luke 2:42–51).

Jesus Christ used structural leadership behavior very early in his public ministry when he recruited his apostles, most of whom were fishermen, and said very directly to them, "Follow me and I will make you fishers of men" (Matthew 5:19). In those few words, he instructed them to become his followers and revealed to them their primary goal of "saving" humankind. He also indicated that they would have to make sacrifices along the journey. "If anyone desires to come after me, let him deny himself, and take up his cross, and follow me" (Matthew 16:24).

Later, in reciting the beatitudes, he revealed to his disciples exactly who would be their audience and eligible for salvation. "Blessed are the poor in spirit," he said, "for theirs is the kingdom of heaven." He continued, "Blessed are those who mourn, for they shall be comforted. Blessed are the meek, for they shall inherit the earth. Blessed are those who hunger and thirst for righteousness, for they shall be filled. Blessed are the merciful, for they shall obtain mercy. Blessed are the pure in heart, for they shall see God. Blessed are the peacemakers, for they shall be called sons of God." And, finally, "Blessed are those who are persecuted for righteousness' sake, for theirs is the kingdom of heaven" (Matthew 5:3–10).

In typical structural frame form, Christ further instructed his disciples to "take heed that you do not do your charitable deeds before men, to be seen by them." Unless they practiced their service in humility, he declared, they would not be rewarded either on earth or in heaven. In effect, he was instructing them that virtue is its own reward, a message that he frequently reiterated.

When his disciples asked him to teach them how to communicate with their God, Christ again used structural behavior and taught them to pray. "In this manner," he said, "pray: Our Father who art in heaven, hallowed be thy name. Thy kingdom come. Thy will be done on earth as it is in heaven" (Matthew 6:9–10). Continuing in his teaching and structural frame mode, Christ instructed his disciples to seek good and avoid evil. "No one can serve two masters; for either he will hate the one and love the other, or else he will be loyal to the one and despise the other. You cannot serve God and mammon," he declared (Matthew 7:1–5).

Another lesson that he taught his followers was to be nonjudgmental. "Judge not," he instructed, "that you be not judged. For with what judgment you judge, you will be judged; and with the same measure you use, it will be measured back to you." In true structural frame form, Christ went on to clarify and reinforce his point. "And why do you look at the speck in your brother's eye, but do not consider the plank in your own eye? Or how can you say to your brother, 'Let me remove the speck out of your eye'; and look, a plank is in your own eye? Hypocrite! First remove the plank from your own eye, and then you will see clearly to remove the speck out of your brother's eye" (Matthew 7:2–6).

Then, since every well-structured organization has its unique set of duties and responsibilities, Christ gave his apostles what amounted to their job descriptions, that is, ministering to the marginalized in society. "Do not go into the way of the Gentiles and do not enter a city of the Samaritans," he told them. "But go rather to the lost sheep of the house of Israel. And as you go, preach, saying, 'The kingdom of heaven is at hand.' Heal the sick, cleanse the lepers, raise the dead, cast out demons. Freely you have received, freely give" (Matthew 10:5–9).

Christ taught his disciples the virtue of justice through the parable of the wheat and the tares (weeds). He said, "The kingdom of heaven is like a man who sowed good seed in his field. But while men slept, his enemy came and sowed tares among the wheat and went his way. But when the grain had sprouted and produced a crop, then the tares also appeared." The servants then asked the owner what they should do. The owner replied, "Let both grow together until the harvest, and at the time of harvest I will say to the reapers, 'First gather together the tares and bind them in bundles to burn them, but gather the wheat into my barn'" (Matthew 13:24–30). Christ explained further that the wheat represented those who do good in their lives, and the tares are those who do evil. Those who do good are rewarded, and those who do evil are punished.

Christ further elucidated on the finality of justice in the parable of the dragnet. He said, "Again, the kingdom of heaven is like a dragnet that was cast into the sea and gathered some of every kind, which when it was full, they drew to shore; and they sat down and gathered the good into vessels, but threw the bad away. So it will be at the end of the age. The angels will come forth, separate the wicked from among the just, and cast them into the furnace of fire. There will be wailing and gnashing of teeth" (Matthew 13:47–50).

And Christ constantly warned of the necessity to always be ready for Judgment Day. He used the parable of the wise and foolish virgins to get his point across: "Then the kingdom of heaven shall be likened to ten virgins who took their lamps and went out to meet the bridegroom. Now five of them were wise, and five were foolish. Those who were foolish took their lamps and took no oil with them. But the wise took oil in their vessels with their lamps. But while the bridegroom was delayed, they all slumbered and slept. And at midnight a cry was heard, 'Behold, the bridegroom is coming; go up to meet him!' Then all those virgins arose and trimmed their lamps. And the foolish said to the wise 'Give us some of your oil for our lamps are going out. But the wise answered, saying 'No, lest there should not be enough for us and you; but go rather to those who sell and buy for yourselves.' And while they went to buy, the bridegroom came, and those who were ready went in with him to the wedding; and the door was shut. Afterward the other virgins came also, saying, Lord, Lord, open to us!' But he answered and said, 'Assuredly, I say to you, I do not know you'; Watch therefore, for you know neither the day nor the hour in which the Son of Man is coming" (Matthew 25:1–13).

Christ used structural behavior to set out the rules and regulations regarding marriage and divorce to his disciples. In responding to the Pharisees' question regarding whether it is lawful for a man to divorce his wife for just any reason, Christ replied, "Have you not read that He who made them at the beginning made them male and female, and said, 'For this reason a man shall leave his father and mother and be joined to this wife, and the two shall become one flesh'? So then, they are no longer two but one flesh. Therefore what God has joined together, let no man put asunder. And I say to you, whoever divorces his wife, except for sexual immorality, and marries another, commits adultery; and whoever marries her who is divorced commits adultery" (Matthew 19:4–9).

Christ also used the structural frame to enumerate the requirements for meriting eternal life in heaven, namely, keeping the commandments. "If you want to enter into life, keep the commandments," he said. "You shall not murder. You shall not commit adultery. You shall not steal. You shall not bear false witness. Honor your father and your mother. And, you shall love your neighbor as yourself. If you want to be perfect, go, sell what you have and give to the poor, and you will have treasure in heaven" (Matthew 19:17–21).

Perhaps the most famous example of Christ using structural frame leadership behavior is in the Gospel story depicting his cleansing of the temple. The evangelist Matthew writes an account of Christ's visit to the Jewish temple in Jerusalem: "Then Jesus went into the temple of God and drove out all those who bought and sold in the temple, and overturned the tables of the money changers and the seats of those who sold doves. And He said to them, 'It is written, My house shall be called a house of prayer; but you have made it a den of thieves'" (Matthew 21:12–13).

When the scribes tested Christ by asking him which was the greatest commandment, he responded in a very direct, structural way: "You shall love the Lord your God with all your heart, with all your soul, and with all your mind. This is the first and great commandment. And the second is like it: You shall love your neighbor as yourself" (Matthew 22:37–40).

Christ sometimes had to use structural leadership behavior in chastising his apostles for some of their transgressions. For example, when he was in the Garden of Gethsemane preparing to face his crucifixion, he asked his apostles, "sit here while I go and pray over there." Then he came to the disciples and found them asleep, and he said to Peter, "What, could you not watch with Me one hour? Watch and pray, lest you enter into temptation. The spirit indeed is willing, but the flesh is weak" (Matthew 26:36–41). And later that same evening, when the Roman soldiers came to arrest Christ, one of his apostles drew his sword and cut off the ear of one of them. Ever the teacher, Christ said to his apostle, "Put your sword in its place, for all who live by the sword will die by the sword" (Matthew 26:52).

In true structural leadership form, Christ used the parable of the light under the basket to teach a lesson on the importance of fully utilizing the gifts and talents that have been inherited. He started by posing a rhetorical question: "Is a lamp bought to put under a basket or under a bed? Is it not to be set on a lampstand? For there is nothing hidden which will not be revealed, nor has anything been kept secret but that it would come to light. If anyone has ears to hear, let him ear. Take heed what you hear. With the same measure you use, it will be measured to you; and to you who hear, more will be given. For whoever has, to him more will be given; but whoever does not have, even what he has will be taken away from him" (Mark 4:21–25).

Likewise, Christ called on his followers to practice mercy and forgiveness. He said to his disciples, "It is impossible that no offenses should come, but woe to him through whom they do come! It would be better for him if a millstone were hung around his neck, and he were thrown into the sea, than that he should offend one of these little ones. Take heed to yourselves. If your brother sins against you, rebuke him; and if he repents, forgive him. And if he sins against you seven times a day, and seven times a day returns to you saying, 'I repent,' you shall forgive him seventy times seventy" (Mark 17:1–4).

And in teaching the importance of gratitude, he again used structural frame behavior in the form of the parable of the ten lepers. The ten lepers asked Christ to have mercy on them and cure them of their affliction. He said to them, "Go show yourselves to the priests." And so they went and were cleansed. But only one of them, a Samaritan, came back to thank Christ. Christ asked the leper, "Were there not ten cleansed? But where are the nine? Were there not any found who returned to give glory to God except this foreigner? Arise, go on your way. Your faith has made thee whole" (Mark 17:14–19).

THE HUMAN RESOURCE FRAME

Human resource leaders believe in people and communicate that belief. They are passionate about productivity through people. One could easily argue that human resource leadership behavior was Christ's primary frame of reference. His primary mission was the salvation of mankind. Thus his life story is replete with instances of his concern for humanity. He was the source of the age-old adage, "Greater love has no one than this, than to lay down one's life for his friends" (John 15:13). And, of course, Christ did just that.

Christ not only had concern for humanity himself but also commanded his followers to manifest the same concern. In preaching concern for humanity to his disciples, he said, "You have heard that it was said, 'An eye for an eye and tooth for a tooth.' But I tell you not to resist an evil person. But whoever slaps you on your right cheek, turn the other to him also" (Matthew 5:38–40). The same theme was reiterated by Christ in these words: "You have heard that it was said, 'You shall love your neighbor and hate your enemy.' But I say to you, love your enemies, bless those who curse you, do good to those who hate you, and pray for those who spitefully use you and persecute you" (Matthew 6:43–44). Christ had such a profound concern for people that he instructed them to "ask, and it will be given to you; seek, and you will find; knock, and it will be opened to you" (Matthew 7:7–8).

Virtually all of Christ's miracles were performed out of love and concern for others. This display of human resource leadership behavior began early in his public life and continued throughout his ministry. One of the first recorded miracles was the cleansing of the leper. "When Christ had come down from the mountain, great multitudes followed Him. And behold, a leper came and worshiped Him, saying, 'Lord, if You are willing, You can make me clean.' Then Jesus put out His hand and touched him saying, 'I am willing; be cleansed,' and immediately his leprosy was cleansed" (Matthew, 8:1–3).

Another of his early miracles that demonstrated his concern for others was the familiar story of the water turned to wine at the marriage feast at Cana. "And when they ran out of wine, the mother of Jesus said to Him, 'They have no wine.' His mother said to the servants, 'Whatever He says to do, do it.' Jesus said to them, 'Fill the waterpots with water.' And they filled them up to the brim. And He said to them, 'Draw some out now, and take to the master of the feast.' When the master of the feast had tasted the water that was made wine, and did not know where it came from, the master of the feast called the bridegroom. And he said to him, 'Every man at the beginning sets out the good wine, and when the guests have well drunk, then that which is inferior; but you have kept the good wine until now'" (John 2:1–10).

Still another miracle that demonstrated Christ's concern for his fellow human beings was the healing of the centurion's servant. "Now when Jesus had entered Capernaum, a centurion came to Him, pleading with Him, saying, 'Lord, my servant is lying at home paralyzed, dreadfully tormented.' And Jesus said to him, 'I will come and heal him.' The centurion answered and said, 'Lord, I am not worthy that You should come under my roof. But only speak a word, and my servant will be healed'" (Matthew 8:5–8). And then there was the healing of the apostle Peter's mother-in-law. "Now when Jesus had come into Peter's house, He saw his wife's mother lying sick with a fever. And He touched her hand, and the fever left her. Then she arose and served them" (Matthew 8:14–15).

A little later in the Gospels, we learn of Christ saving his apostles while they were out at sea. "Now when He got into a boat, His disciples followed Him. And suddenly a great tempest arose on the sea, so that the boat was covered with the waves. But He was asleep. Then His disciples came to Him and awoke Him, saying, 'Lord, save us! We are perishing!' But He said to them, 'Why are you fearful, O you of little faith?' Then he arose and rebuked the winds and the sea. And there was a great calm" (Matthew 8:23–26). Matthew records further the miracles of the healing of the two demon-possessed men, the healing of the paralytic, and the girl restored to life. These accounts are followed by the healing of the two blind men and the healing of the mute man (Matthew 9:28–38).

All of these miracles manifested Christ's compassion and love for humanity. "And Jesus went about all the cities and villages, teaching in their synagogues, preaching the gospel of the kingdom, and healing every sickness and every disease among the people. But when He saw the multitudes, He was moved with compassion for them, because they were weary and scattered, like sheep having no shepherd" (Matthew 9:35–36). Later, Christ said to the people, "Come to Me, all you who labor and are heavy laden, and I will give you rest. Take My yoke upon you and learn from Me, for I am gentle and lowly in heart, and you will find rest for your souls. For My yoke is easy and My burden is light" (Matthew 11:28–30).

One of the more famous Gospel stories that demonstrated Christ's use of human resource behavior is the miracle of the loaves and the fishes. "And they said to Him, 'We have here only five loaves and two fish.' He said, 'Bring them to Me.' Then He commanded the multitudes to sit down on the grass. And He took the five loaves and the two fish, and looking up to heaven, He blessed and broke and gave the loaves to the disciples; and the disciples gave to the multitudes. So they all ate and were filled, and they took up twelve baskets full of fragments that remained. Now those who had eaten were about five thousand men, besides women and children" (Matthew 14:26–21).

Another beloved Gospel story that is demonstrative of Christ's propensity for human resource behavior is the parable of the good shepherd. "What do you think? If a man has a hundred sheep, and one of them goes astray, does he not leave the ninety-nine and go to the mountains to seek the one that is straying? And if he should find it, assuredly, I say to you, he rejoices more over that sheep than over the ninety-nine that did not go astray" (Matthew 18:10–13). And then there was the parable of the unforgiving servant. "Peter came to Him and said, 'Lord, how often shall my brother sin against me, and I forgive him? Up to seven times?' Jesus said to him, 'I do not say to you, up to seven times, but up to seventy times seven'" (Matthew 18:21–22).

The Gospel writer Mark reinforced Christ's frequent use of human resource leadership behavior by recording such miracles as the healing of the demon-possessed man, the girl restored to health and a woman healed, a blind, paralytic man healed at Bethsaida, the healing of Bartimaeus, and the raising of Lazarus. The evangelist Luke told of Christ's concern for others through the familiar parable of the Good Samaritan.

In this story, Christ once again admonished his disciples to "love your neighbor as yourself" and told of a certain man who went down from Jerusalem to Jericho and fell among thieves who stripped him of his clothing, wounded him, and departed, leaving him half dead. "Now by chance a certain priest came down that road. And when he saw him, he passed by on the other side. Likewise a Levite, when he arrived at the place, came and looked, and passed by on the other side. But a certain Samaritan, as he journeyed, came where he was. And when he saw him, he had compassion on him, and went to him and bandaged his wounds, pouring on oil and wine; and he set him on his own animal, brought him to an inn, and took care of him. So which of these three do you think was neighbor to him who fell among the thieves?" And they said, "He who showed mercy on him." Then Christ said to them, "Go and do likewise" (Luke 10:30–37).

In yet another instance of Christ's penchant for modeling human resource behavior, he told the story of the lost coin. "Or what woman, having ten silver coins, if she loses one coin, does not light a lamp, sweep the house, and seek diligently until she finds it? And when she has found it, she calls her friends and neighbors together, saying, 'Rejoice with me, for I have found the piece which I lost!' Likewise, I say to you, there is joy in the presence of the angels of God over one sinner who repents" (Luke 15:8–10).

The parable of the prodigal son is another example of how Christ was concerned about all humanity, but especially those who are marginalized and otherwise underserved. Christ said, "A certain man had two sons. And the younger of them said to his father, 'Father, give me the portion of goods that falls to me.' So he divided to them his livelihood. And many days later, the younger son gathered all together, journeyed to a far country, and there wasted his possessions with prodigal living."

After his fortune was gone, the prodigal son decided to return home and ask his father's forgiveness. "And he arose and came to his father. But when he was still a great way off, his father saw him and had compassion, and ran and fell on his knees and kissed him. And the son said to him, 'Father, I have sinned against heaven and in your sight, and am no longer worthy to be called your son.' . . . Now his older son was in the field. And as he came and drew near to the house, he heard music and dancing. . . . When he saw his father he said, 'Lo, these many years I have been serving you; I never transgressed your commandment at any time; and yet you never gave me a young goat that I might make merry with my friends.' . . . The father said, 'Son, you are always with me and all I have is yours. It is right that we should make merry and be glad, for your brother was dead and is alive again, and was lost and is found'" (Luke 15:11–32).

Another familiar Gospel story reflecting Christ's sensitivity to others is the story of the good thief. "Now one of the criminals hanging there reviled Jesus, saying, 'Are you not the Messiah? Save yourself and us.' The other, however, rebuking him, said in reply, 'Have you no fear of God, for you are subject to the same condemnation? And indeed, we have been condemned justly, for the sentence we received corresponds to our crimes, but this man has done nothing criminal.' Then he said, 'Jesus, remember me when you come into your kingdom.' Jesus replied to him, 'Amen, I say to you, today you will be with me in Paradise'" (Luke 23:39–43).

Lastly, John the Evangelist tells of perhaps Christ's most poignant and compelling words regarding the nature and importance of human resource behavior. "As the Father loved Me, I also love you. If you keep My commandments, you will abide in My love, just as I have kept My Father's commandments and abide in His love. These things I have spoken to you, that My joy may remain in you, and that your joy may be full. This is My commandment, that you love one another as I have loved you. Greater love has no one than this, than to lay down one's life for his friend. You are My friends if you do whatever I command you. No longer do I call you servants, for a servant does not know what his master is doing; but I have called you friends, for all things that I heard from My Father, I have made known to you" (John 15:9–15).

THE SYMBOLIC FRAME

In the symbolic frame, the organization is seen as a stage, a theater in which every actor plays certain roles, and the symbolic leader attempts to communicate the right impressions to the right audiences. This is another frame in which Jesus Christ excelled. His use of stories in the form of parables is a prime example of his prolific use of symbolic frame leadership behavior. The various miracles that he performed were also symbolic in nature.

There are myriad examples of Christ's use of symbolic leadership behavior in the Gospel accounts of his life. Early in his public life, the Gospels tell us that he was tempted by the devil while he was fasting for forty days and forty nights in preparation for his ministry. Knowing that Christ would be hungry by the end of his fasting, the devil said, "If you are the Son of God, command that these stones become bread." Christ's symbolic response was, "It is written, 'Man shall not live by bread alone but by every word that proceeds from the mouth of God'" (Matthew 4:3–4)—the point being that the spiritual or supernatural is oftentimes more important than the material things in life.

Another symbolic gesture on the part of Christ was the parable of the salt and light. In speaking to the multitudes, he said, "You are the salt of the earth, but if the salt loses its flavor, how shall it be seasoned? It is then good for nothing but to be thrown out and trampled under foot by men. You are the light of the world. A city that is set on the hill cannot be hidden. Nor do they light a lamp and put it under a basket, but on a lampstand, and it gives light to all who are in the house. Let your light so shine before men, that they may see your good works, and glorify your Father in heaven" (Matthew 5:13–16).

Using a parable, Christ made the point that immoral thoughts were as evil as immoral deeds. "You have heard that it was said to those of old, 'You shall not commit adultery.' But I say to you that whoever looks at a woman to lust for her has already committed adultery with her in his heart. And if your right eye causes you to sin, pluck it out and cast it from you; for it is more profitable for you that one of your members perish, than for your whole body to be cast into hell" (Matthew 5:27–29).

Christ used a parable to warn his followers to beware of duplicitous individuals. "Beware of false prophets who come to you in sheep's clothing, but inwardly they are ravenous wolves," he said. "You will know them by their fruits. Do men gather grapes from thornbushes or figs from thistles? Even so, every good tree bears good fruit, but a bad tree bears bad fruit. . . . Therefore by their fruits you will know them" (Matthew 6:1–3).

Long before the three little pigs found the importance of building one's house on a strong foundation, Christ urged his disciples to build their spiritual lives on a foundation of good works. "Therefore whoever hears these sayings of Mine, and does them, I will liken him to a wise man who built his house on the rock; and the rain descended, the floods came, and the winds blew and beat on that house; and it did not fall, for it was founded on the rock. Now everyone who hears these sayings of Mine, and does not do them, will be like a foolish man who built his house on the sand: and the rain descended, the floods came, and winds blew and beat on that house; and it fell" (Matthew 7:24–28).

The Gospel story of Matthew is another example of Christ using symbolic behavior to indicate that all, no matter their role in society or their class, are welcome to join his ministry. After asking Matthew, a tax collector, to join him, the Pharisees asked Jesus why he "ate with tax collectors and sinners." Christ responded by saying, "Those who are well have no need of a physician, but those who are sick? But go and learn what this means: 'I desire mercy and not sacrifice.' For I did not come to call the righteous, but sinners, to repentance" (Matthew 9:12–13).

Oftentimes, instead of directly answering the question of whether he was the Son of God, Christ responded in symbolic terms. On one occasion, John the Baptist's disciples asked him, "Are you the Coming One, or do we look for another?" Christ said to them, "Go and tell John the things which you hear and see: The blind receive their sight and the lame walk; the lepers are cleansed and the deaf hear; the dead are raised up and the poor have the gospel preached to them" (Matthew 11:3–5).

Christ taught the value of loyalty and teamwork through the parable of a house divided against itself. Despite both Christ and the Pharisees being Jewish preachers, the Pharisees oftentimes challenged Christ. In one instance in the Gospels, they accused him of performing miracles in the name of Beelzebub, or the devil. But Christ knew their real thoughts and said to them, "Every kingdom divided against itself will not stand. And if Satan casts out Satan, he is divided against himself. How then will his kingdom stand? . . . He who is not with Me is against Me, and he who does not gather with Me scatters abroad" (Matthew 12:25–26, 30).

Even though Christ intended his message for all humankind, he warned his followers in symbolic terms that many would not heed his word. In the parable of the sower, Christ said to the multitude, "Behold, a sower went out to sow. And as he sowed, some seed fell by the wayside; and the birds came and devoured them. Some fell on stony places, where they did not have much earth; and they immediately sprang up because they had no depth of earth. But when the sun was up they were scorched, and because they had no root they withered away. And some fell among thorns, and the thorns sprang up and choked them. But others fell on good ground and yielded a crop: some a hundredfold, some sixty, some thirty. He who has ears to hear, let him hear!" (Matthew 13:1–9).

Christ preached that everyone, even the most lowly, is born with gifts and talents. In the familiar parable of the mustard seed, Christ once again makes his point in a symbolic way. "The kingdom of heaven is like a mustard seed, which a man took and sowed in his field, which indeed is the least of all the seeds; but when it is grown it is greater than the herbs and becomes a tree, so that the birds of the air come and nest in its branches" (Matthew 13:31–32).

In yet another symbolic gesture, Christ observes that prophets and other leaders are rarely appreciated immediately. It is usually left to history to determine their effectiveness. He said, "A prophet is not without honor except in his own country and in his own house" (Matthew 13:57). The obvious message to leaders is not to expect credit for their achievements in the short term; better to be intrinsically motivated and let history be the judge.

Instead of simply asserting his claim to be the Son of God, Christ performed many miracles to indicate symbolically that he was a special leader and, in his followers' view, their Savior. One such miracle was the familiar Gospel story of Christ walking on water. "Immediately Jesus made His disciples get into the boat and go before Him to the other side, while He sent the multitudes away. . . . But the boat was now in the middle of the seas, tossed by the waves, for the wind was contrary. . . . And they cried out in fear. Now . . . Jesus went to them, walking on the seas. And when the disciples saw Him walking on the sea, they were troubled, saying, 'It is a ghost!' But immediately Jesus spoke to them, saying, 'Be of good cheer! It is I: don't be afraid.'" Christ asked Peter to come to him in the water, and Peter walked on the water to go to Jesus. "But when he saw that the wind was boisterous, he was afraid: and beginning to sink he cried out, saying, 'Lord, save me!' And immediately Jesus stretched out

His hand and caught him, and said to him, 'O you of little faith, why did you doubt?'" (Matthew 14:22–31).

Christ warned his followers in symbolic terms that they should beware of "false prophets," or those who stretch and manipulate the facts in symbolic terms. He likened these individuals to blind persons. "They are blind leaders of the blind. And if the blind leads the blind, both will fall into a ditch" (Matthew 15:14).

Christ even established his church and named its earthly leader by using symbolic leadership behavior. He said to the apostle Simon Peter, whose name meant "rock" in Hebrew, "Blessed are you, Simon Bar-Jonah, for flesh and blood has not revealed this to you, but My Father who is in heaven. And I also say to you that you are Peter, and on this rock I will build My church, and the gates of Hades shall not prevail against it. And I will give you the keys of the kingdom of heaven, and whatever you bind on earth will be bound in heaven and whatever you loose on earth will be loosed in heaven" (Matthew 16:17–19).

The miracle of the transfiguration is another instance of Christ using symbolic behavior to demonstrate his divine nature to his disciples. "Now after six days Jesus took Peter, James, and John his brother, brought them up on a high mountain by themselves, and was transfigured before them. His face shone like the sun, and His clothes became as white as the light. Now as they came down from the mountain, Jesus commanded them, saying, 'Tell the vision to no one until the Son of Man is risen from the dead'" (Matthew 19:9).

For those of his followers who were fortunate enough to be materially successful, Christ had the following symbolic advice for them: "Assuredly, I say to you that it is hard for a rich man to enter the kingdom of heaven. And again I say to you, it is easier for a camel to go through the eye of a needle than for a rich man to enter the kingdom of God" (Matthew 19:23). He also reminded us that "many who are first will be last and the last first. For many are called and few are chosen" (Matthew 19:23–30).

Christ beseeched his followers to seek good and avoid evil and to do so constantly, in that one never knows when life will come to an end. His disciples, of course, believed that a good life will be rewarded, if not in this life, then in the next. But Christ warned, "But of that day and hour no one knows, no, not even the angels of heaven, but My Father only. . . . Therefore you also be ready, for the Son of Man is coming at an hour when you do not expect Him" (Matthew 24:36–44). Christ further espoused doing good over evil when he said, "And if your hand makes you sin, cut it off. It is better for you to enter into life maimed, than having two hands to go to hell, into the fire that shall never be quenched" (Mark 9:43).

Christ also preached social justice and urged his followers to treat everyone with human dignity. He once again used symbolism to get this point across to his disciples. "Then the King will say to those on His right hand, 'Come, you blessed of My Father, inherit the kingdom prepared for you from the foundation of the world: for I was hungry and you gave Me food; I was thirsty and you gave Me drink; I was a stranger and you took Me in. I was naked and you clothed Me; I was sick and you visited Me; I was in prison and you came to Me.' And the righteous will answer Him, saying, 'Lord, when did we see You hungry and feed You, or thirsty and give You drink? When did we see You a stranger and take You in, or naked and clothe You? Or when did we see You sick, or in prison, and come to You?' And the King will answer and say to them, 'Assuredly, I say to you, in as much as you did it to one of the least of these My brethren, you did it to Me'" (Matthew 25:34–40).

In perhaps Christ's most memorable symbolic leadership gesture, he left his followers with a symbol to remember him by after he had gone. In the Gospel story of the Last Supper, Christ took bread, blessed it and broke it, and gave it to the disciples and said, "Take, eat; this is My body." Then he took the cup, gave thanks, and gave it to them, saying, "Drink from it, all of you. For this is My blood of the new covenant, which is shed for many for the remission of sins. Do this in remembrance of Me" (Matthew 26:26–29). These words are repeated even today at every Roman Catholic Mass and similar services in other Christian rites.

Another value that Christ promoted symbolically was that of generosity or philanthropy. However, he also cautioned against being boastful about one's own generosity as opposed to another's in the parable of the widow's two mites. "Now Jesus sat opposite the treasury and saw how the people put money into the treasury. And many who were rich put in much. Then one poor widow came and threw in two mites, which make a quadrans. So He called His disciples to Him and said to them, 'Assuredly, I say to you that this poor widow has put in more than all those who have given to the treasury; for they all put in out of their abundance, but she out of her poverty put in all that she had, her whole livelihood'" (Mark 12:41–44).

Christ also taught the value of sacrifice in a symbolic way. "Then He said to them all, 'If anyone desire to come after Me, let him deny himself, and take up his cross daily, and follow Me. For whoever desires to save his life will lose it, but whoever loses his life for My sake will save it. For what advantage is it to a man if he gains the whole world, and is himself destroyed or lost?'" (Luke 9:23–25).

In the parable of the Pharisee and the tax collector, Christ taught his followers the virtue of humility. "Also He spoke this parable to some who trusted in themselves that they were righteous, and despised others: 'Two men went up to the temple to pray, one a Pharisee and other a tax collector. The Pharisee stood and prayed thus with himself, 'God, I thank You that I am not like other men—extortioners, unjust, adulterers, or even as this tax collector. I fast twice a week; I give tithes of all that I possess.' And the tax collector, standing afar off, would not so much as raise his eyes to heaven, but beat his breast, saying, 'God be merciful to me a sinner!' I tell you, this man went down to his house justified rather than the other; for everyone who exalts himself will be abased, and he who humbles himself will be exalted'" (Luke 18:9–14).

Lastly, Christ used symbolic language to foretell his resurrection and death. "Jesus answered and said to them, 'Destroy this temple, and in three days I will raise it up'" (John 3:19). Later Christ likened himself to bread in saying, "I am the bread of life. He who comes to Me shall never hunger, and he who believes in Me shall never thirst" (John 6:35). Next, Christ made a point of the need to seek the truth by saying, "And you shall know the truth, and the truth shall set you free" (John 8:33), a quote often used by Martin Luther King Jr. As these many examples indicate, Jesus Christ made frequent use of symbolic frame leadership behavior.

THE POLITICAL FRAME

Leaders operating out of the political frame clarify what they want and what they can get. Political leaders are realists above all. They never let what they want cloud their judgment about what is possible. They assess the distribution of power and interests.

Although Jesus Christ did not utilize the political frame as often as others portrayed in this book, there is ample evidence in the Gospels that he used this type of leadership behavior when the situation demanded it. He warned his disciples that he was sending them out into a political world and suggested ways in which they could survive it. "Behold, I send you out as sheep in the midst of wolves. Therefore be wise as serpents and harmless as doves," he counseled them (Matthew 10:16). Then he identified for them the traits of the "serpents" that they would encounter. He said, "Either make the tree good and its fruit good, or else make the tree bad and its fruit bad; for a tree is known by its fruit. Brood of vipers! How can you, being evil, speak good things? For out of the abundance of the heart the mouth speaks. But I say to you that for every idle word men may speak, they will give account of it in the day of judgment. For by your words you will be justified, and by your words you will be condemned" (Matthew 12:33–37).

Much of Christ's political frame behavior was aimed at the Pharisees and other religious leaders who were continually testing him. "Then some of the scribes and Pharisees answered, saying, 'Teacher, we want to see a sign from You.' But He answered and said to them, 'An evil and adulterous generation seeks after a sign, and no sign will be given to it except the sign of the prophet Jonah. For as Jonah was three days and three nights in the belly of the great fish, so will the Son of Man be three days and three nights in the heart of the earth" (Matthew 12:38–40). In other words, the Pharisees would have to wait for their "sign" until Christ rose from the dead.

Christ utilized the political frame once again in dealing with these religious officials. "Now when He came into the temple, the chief priests and the elders of the people confronted Him as He was teaching, and said, 'By what authority are You doing these things? And who gave You this authority?' But Jesus answered and said to them, 'I also will ask you one thing, which if you tell Me, I likewise will tell you by what authority I do these things. The baptism of John, where was it from? From heaven or from men?' And they reasoned among themselves, saying, 'If we say, "From heaven," He will say to us, "Why then did you not believe him?" But if we say, "From men," we fear the multitude, for all count John as a prophet.' So they answered Jesus and said, 'we do not know.' And He said to them, 'Neither will I tell you by what authority I do these things'" (Matthew 21:23–27). Thus, those setting the trap found themselves trapped by Christ.

In perhaps Christ's most famous use of political frame leadership behavior, the Pharisees were once again trying to trap him. "Then the Pharisees went and plotted how they might entangle Him in His talk. And they sent to Him their disciples with the Herodians, saying 'Teacher, we know that You are true, and teach the way of God in truth; nor do you care about anyone, for You do not regard the person of men. Tell us, therefore, what do You think? Is it lawful to pay taxes to Caesar, or not?' But Jesus perceived their wickedness, and said, 'Why do you test Me, you hypocrites? Show Me the tax money.' So they brought Him a denarius. And He said to them, 'Whose image and inscription is this?' They said to Him, 'Caesar's.' And He said to them, 'Render therefore to Caesar the things that are Caesar's, and to God the things that are God's.' When they had heard these words, they marveled, and left Him and went on their way" (Matthew 22:15–22). Game, set, match, Jesus Christ!

Christ then showed his disciples how to engage in political frame behavior when appropriate. "Then Jesus spoke to the multitudes and to His disciples, saying: 'The scribes and the Pharisees sit in Moses' seat. Therefore whatever they tell you to observe, that observe and do, but do not do according to their works; for they say, and do not do'" (Matthew 23:1–3). Christ, in effect, advised his disciples to obey the law, but not to behave like the scribes and Pharisees—the age-old adage of doing what I say, not what I do.

Christ also warned his disciples about the misuse of political behavior in the form of hypocrisy and lies. He said to the multitude, "Beware of the leaven of the Pharisees, which is hypocrisy. For there is nothing covered that will not be revealed, nor hidden that will not be known. Therefore whatever you have spoken in the dark will be heard in the light, and what you have spoken in the ear in inner rooms will be proclaimed on the housetops" (Luke 12:1–3).

In a typical political frame gesture, Christ advised his followers to make peace with their adversaries whenever possible. "Yes, and why, even of yourselves, do you not judge what is right? When you go with your adversary to the magistrate, make every effort along the way to settle with him, lest he drag you to the judge, the judge deliver you to the officer, and the officer throw you into prison" (Luke 12:57–58).

Christ found a need to engage in political behavior on the last days of his earthly life. After he had been arrested in the Garden of Gethsemane, the Jewish Sanhedrin questioned him about whether he was really the Son of God, hoping to convict him of blasphemy if he said he was. However, in true political frame form, Christ deflected the question right back at them and induced them into making the claim rather than himself having to do so. "As soon as it was day, the elders of the people, both chief priests and scribes came together and led Him into their council, saying, 'If You are the Christ, tell us.' But He said to them, 'If I tell you, you will by no means believe. And if I also ask you, you will by no means answer Me or let Me go. Hereafter the Son of Man will sit on the right hand of the power of God.' Then they all said, 'Are You then the Son of God?' And He said to them, '*You* rightly say that I am'" (Luke 22:66–70). Of course, even though Christ outwitted them, they crucified him anyway.

THE MORAL FRAME

As mentioned earlier, the moral frame is my own contribution to situational leadership theory. In my view, the moral frame completes situational leadership theory. Without it, leaders could just as easily use their leadership skills for promoting evil as for promoting good. Leaders operating out of the moral frame are concerned about their obligations and responsibilities to their followers. Moral frame leaders use some type of moral compass to direct their behavior. They practice what has been described as servant leadership and are concerned with those individuals and groups that are marginalized in their organizations and in society. In short, they are concerned about social justice.

In effect, Jesus Christ may be said to have created the moral frame of leadership behavior. Certainly, the prophets and moral men and women who preceded him were practitioners of moral frame leadership behavior, but it could be argued that such behavior was codified by Jesus Christ and perpetuated by his followers, who called themselves Christians. At any rate, it is abundantly clear from the Gospel stories cited here that Jesus Christ viewed his leadership behavior through a moral lens and was vitally concerned with social justice. His most fundamental message was to "do unto others what you would have them do unto you."

CONCLUSION

Jesus Christ was a prototypical situational leader. As perhaps the most effective leader in history, he operated out of all five of the leadership frames suggested here. He engaged in structural leadership behavior by clearly stating what he expected of his followers—that they would love him, keep his commandments, and love their neighbors as they loved themselves. Basic to his mission was his love for humankind, a human resource leadership trait. He proved his love for humankind by making the ultimate sacrifice and giving up his life for them.

Christ promulgated his message in the form of parables and stories, a distinctly symbolic frame leadership behavior. He also performed miracles to verify his message, which is another indication of his use of symbolic behavior. He even engaged in political leadership behavior when appropriate. His classic advice to give God what is God's and Caesar what is Caesar's is the epitome of an effective use of the political leadership frame. Finally, his entire public life was dedicated to establishing a moral code by which his followers could live. So it could be accurately asserted that he made prolific use of moral frame leadership behavior. In fact, it could be argued that the moral frame was Christ's foundational frame. Suffice it to say, Christians and non-Christians alike would do well to model their leadership behavior after that of Jesus Christ and truly reflect the title of this chapter, "To Lead as Jesus Did."

Chapter 15

Leadership Lessons Learned

The greatest discovery of my generation is that man can alter his life simply by altering his attitude of mind.

—William James

INTRODUCTION

What do we learn about leadership from these eleven great leaders? First, we learn that situational leadership theory makes eminent sense. Virtually all of these leaders were effective as leaders because they were able to adapt their leadership behavior to changing situations. None of them was stuck in one paradigm. Some might be criticized for using one or another leadership frame too exclusively, but the reality is that, by and large, they were successful because, to a person, they were able to balance their use of the four leadership frames enunciated by Lee Bolman and Terrence Deal (1991) very effectively.

More specifically, we have learned that there are four requisites for effective leadership:

1. Knowledge of, and passion for, one's field (competency).
2. An ability to engender mutual trust and respect with one's followers.
3. Knowledge of the organizational culture (readiness level) of one's followers.
4. An ability to apply situational leadership theory to one's practice.

215

LEADING WITH MIND

Knowledge of one's field is a sine qua non for effective leadership. This quality usually manifests itself in one's structural frame leadership behavior. In sports terms, the leader must have a good command of the fundamentals of the game. In business terms, the effective leader must have thorough knowledge of the technical aspects of how a business operates and a sense of how to develop a viable business plan. In education, the leader needs to know how schools and school systems operate and what the best practices in the field are in curriculum and instruction. In a family situation, the leader (parent or guardian) needs to have at least a modicum of knowledge regarding the principles of child psychology to be effective. In short, leaders in any field need to know the field and be able to apply that knowledge through the theory and practice of organizational development, which would include the following:

1. Organizational Structure: how an institution is organized.
2. Organizational Culture: the values and beliefs of an institution.
3. Motivation: the system of rewards and incentives provided.
4. Communication: the clarity and accuracy of the communication process.
5. Decision Making: how and by whom decisions are made.
6. Conflict Management: how dysfunctional conflict is handled.
7. Power Distribution: how the power in an institution is distributed.
8. Strategic Planning: how the mission, vision, and strategic plan are developed.
9. Change: how change is effectively implemented in an institution.

I will not go into detail about these processes here. If the reader is interested in a comprehensive look at these processes, I would recommend an earlier publication of mine, *Educational Administration: Leading with Mind and Heart*, second edition. However, included in the appendix is a survey entitled "The Heart Smart Survey," which I developed to help leaders assess the organizational health of their institutions and to identify which of the factors listed above are in need of improvement.

LEADING WITH HEART

To recap, then, the effective leader needs to be *technically* competent. However, being technically competent is not enough. To be truly effective, leaders need to master the *art* of leadership and learn to lead with *heart*. In effect, leaders need to operate out of both the structural and political frames (science) and the human resource, symbolic, and moral frames (art) to maximize their effectiveness. This means that they must be concerned about the person (*cura personalis*). They must abide by the golden rule and treat others as they wish to be treated. As noted in chapter 2, truly effective leaders treat their employees like volunteers and empower them to actualize their true potential, thus engendering mutual trust and respect among virtually all of their colleagues.

In their new book entitled *Leading with Kindness*, William Baker and Michael O'Malley reiterate my views. They explore how one of the most unheralded features of leadership, basic human kindness, drives successful organizations. And while most scholars generally recognize that a leader's emotional intelligence factors into that person's leadership behavior, most are reticent to consider it as important as analytical ability, decision-making skills, or implementation skills. Such emotions as compassion, empathy, and kindness are often dismissed as unquantifiable and are often seen as weaknesses. Yet research in neuroscience and the social sciences clearly reveals that one's physiological and emotional states have measurable effects on both individual and group performance.

In the jargon of the day, individuals who lead with heart or kindness are said to have a high degree of emotional intelligence. Most of us are familiar with the current notion of multiple intelligences; that is, individuals have a number of intelligences in addition to cognitive intelligence. Among these intelligences is emotional intelligence. Several theories within the emotional intelligence paradigm seek to understand how individuals perceive, understand, utilize, and manage emotions in an effort to predict and foster personal effectiveness.

Most of these models define emotional intelligence as an array of traits and abilities related to emotional and social knowledge that influence our overall ability to effectively cope with environmental demands; as such, it can be viewed as a model of psychological well-being and adaptation. This includes the ability to be aware of, to understand, and to relate to others; the ability to deal with strong emotions and to control one's impulses; and the ability to adapt to change and to solve problems of a personal and social nature. The five main domains of these models are intrapersonal skills, interpersonal skills, adaptability, stress management, and general mood. If the reader sees a similarity between emotional intelligence and what I term *leading with heart*, and what Baker and O'Malley call *leading with kindness*, it is not coincidental.

LEADING WITH MIND AND HEART

So, truly effective leaders lead with both mind (science) and heart (art)—with both cognitive intelligence and emotional intelligence. One or the other will not suffice. Only by mastering both will the leader succeed. For example, former president Bill Clinton was rendered ineffective as a leader because of the Monica Lewinsky affair and was nearly impeached. Why? Because he suddenly lost the *knowledge* (science) of how government works? No! He lost his ability to lead because he lost the *trust and respect* (art) of much of the American public. He could still lead with his mind, but he had lost the ability to lead with his heart.

On the contrary, one could argue that former president Jimmie Carter lost his ability to lead because of a perceived lack of competency. The majority of the voting public did not believe that he had the knowledge necessary to manage government operations and effectively lead with mind. However, virtually no one questioned his concern for people and his ability to lead with heart. Absent the perceived ability to do *both*, however, he lost the 1980 election to Ronald Reagan.

I conclude, then, that effective leaders are situational; that is, they are capable of adapting their leadership behavior to the situation. They utilize structural, human resource, symbolic, political, and moral leadership behavior when appropriate. They lead with both mind (structural and political behavior) and with heart (human resource, symbolic, and moral behavior). They master both the science (mind) and art (heart) of leadership, and in doing so, they are transformational, leading their organizations to new heights. As Chris Lowney writes in *Heroic Leadership*, such leaders are truly, in a word, heroic.

ORGANIZATIONAL CULTURE

Effectively balancing the use of the five frames of leadership behavior assumes that the leader has a thorough knowledge and understanding of the leader's organizational culture. In the words of Harold Hill in *The Music Man*, the leader needs to "know the territory." Knowing the territory, or knowing the organizational culture, means that the leader must know the beliefs, expectations, and shared values of the organization, as well as the personality of the individuals and the organization as a whole. Without such knowledge, the leader cannot appropriately apply the correct leadership frame to the situation.

As mentioned in chapter 1, Paul Hersey and Ken Blanchard (1988) contribute to our understanding of what it means to know the culture of an organization with their concept of *readiness level*. They define readiness level as the follower's ability and willingness to accomplish a specific task; this is the major contingency that influences which leadership frame behavior should be applied. Follower readiness incorporates the follower's level of achievement motivation, ability, and willingness to assume responsibility for his or her own behavior in accomplishing specific tasks, as well as his or her education and experience relevant to the task. So, a person with a low readiness level should be dealt with by using structural frame behavior (telling behavior), while a person with a very high readiness level should be dealt with using human resource and symbolic frame behavior (delegating behavior).

At this point, the reader may be thinking that using leadership theory to determine one's leadership behavior is an exercise in futility. How can one be realistically expected to assess accurately and immediately the individual's or group's readiness level before acting? It seems like a complex and utterly overwhelming task. When confronted with this reaction, I relate using leadership theory for determining one's leadership behavior to riding a bike. When we first learn to ride a bike, we have to concern ourselves with keeping our balance, steering, pedaling, and being ready to brake at a moment's notice. However, once we learn and have had experience riding the bike, we seldom think of these details. We have learned to ride the bike by instinct or habit.

Having used situational leadership theory to determine my own leadership behavior, I can attest to the fact that its use becomes as instinctive as riding a bike after a while. At this point, I can almost always instantly assess the readiness level of an individual or group and apply the appropriate leadership frame behavior—and believe me when I tell you that if I can do it, so can you.

TRANSFORMATIONAL LEADERSHIP

We all aspire to be transformational leaders—leaders who inspire positive change in their followers. As we saw in chapter 1, charismatic or transformational leaders use charisma to inspire their followers. They talk to followers about how essential their performance is and how they expect the group's performance to exceed expectations. Such leaders use dominance, self-confidence, a need for influence, and conviction of moral righteousness to increase their charisma and consequently their leadership effectiveness. A transformational leader changes an organization by recognizing an opportunity and developing a vision, communicating that vision to organizational members, building trust in the vision, and achieving the vision by motivating organizational members.

Virtually all of the leaders profiled in this book could be considered transformational leaders. In almost every case, they moved their organizations from being ineffective to being extremely effective. Most of them inherited inferior situations only to transform them into supremely effective ones. They achieved this success by displaying the characteristics of a transformational leader. They all had a vision, personal charisma, and the ability to convince others to join them in achieving their vision.

However, they did so in different ways by applying the appropriate leadership behavior to their differing situations. They were able to gauge the readiness level of their followers accurately and apply the appropriate leadership behavior, whether it was structural, human resource, symbolic, political, or moral frame behavior, or some combination thereof. Although this is easier said than done, studying these historical leaders' leadership behavior as depicted in this book should be helpful to anyone aspiring to become a transformational leader.

LEADERSHIP AS A MORAL SCIENCE

Left on its own, situational leadership theory is secular and amoral. As such, it is just as likely to produce a leader like Adolph Hitler or, in the modern era, Bernie Madoff as it is to produce a leader like Martin Luther King Jr. or the rock singer Bono. So, to further ensure that leaders lead with heart as well as mind, I would suggest the use of the Ignatian vision as the lens through which one views his or her leadership behavior.

As recommended in chapter 2, asking ourselves whether our leadership behavior conforms to Ignatius' principles of the *magis, cura personalis*, discernment, service to others, and social justice will bring to completion our understanding and use of situational leadership theory and transform leadership into a moral science. In my view, using the Ignatian vision, or a similar model, as a moral compass will help ensure that history will witness more leaders like Martin Luther King Jr. and fewer like Adolf Hitler.

CONCLUSION

Recently, a plethora of research studies have been conducted on leadership and leadership styles. The overwhelming evidence indicates that there is not one leadership style that is most effective in all situations. Rather, it has been found that a leader's leadership behavior should be adapted to the situation so that at various times, structural, human resource, symbolic, political, or moral frame leadership behavior may be most effective.

The emergence of transformational leadership has seen leadership theory come full circle. Transformational leadership theory combines aspects of early trait theory with more current situational models. The personal charisma of the leader, along with his or her ability to formulate an organizational vision and communicate it to others, determines the transformational leader's effectiveness.

Since the effective leader is expected to adapt his or her leadership style to an ever-changing environment, leadership becomes an even more complex and challenging task. However, thorough knowledge of one's organizational culture and of leadership theory can make some sense out of the apparent chaos that a leader faces on a daily basis. It is my hope that this book will shed some light on the *situation*—pun intended.

Appendix

The Heart Smart
Organizational Diagnosis Model

Just as there are vital signs in measuring individual health, I believe that there are vital signs in measuring the health of organizations. This survey will help identify those vital signs in your school system. The purpose of the Heart Smart Organizational Diagnosis Questionnaire, therefore, is to provide feedback data for intensive diagnostic efforts. Use of the questionnaire, either by itself or in conjunction with other information-collecting techniques such as systematic observation or interviewing, will provide the data needed for identifying strengths and weaknesses in the functioning of an educational institution and help determine whether the leaders are leading with both mind and heart.

A meaningful diagnostic effort must be based on a theory or model of organizational development. This makes action research possible, as it facilitates problem identification, which is essential to determining the proper functioning of an organization. The model suggested here establishes a systematic approach for analyzing relationships among the variables that influence how an organization is managed. It provides information for assessment of ten areas of formal and informal activity: structure, identity and culture, leadership, motivation, communication, decision making, conflict resolution, goal setting and planning, power distribution, and attitude toward change. The outer circle in Figure A.1 is an organizational boundary for diagnosis. This boundary demarcates the functioning of the internal and external environments. Since the underlying organizational theory upon which this survey is based is an open systems model, it is essential that influences from both the internal and external environment be considered for the analysis to be complete.

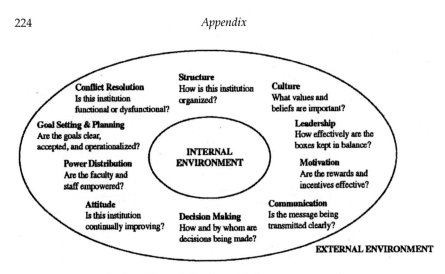

Figure A.1   Organizational boundaries for analysis

Please think of your *present personal or professional environment* and indicate the degree to which you agree or disagree with each of the following statements. A "1" is *disagree strongly* and a "7" is *agree strongly*.

Disagree Strongly	Disagree	Neither Disagree Slightly	Neither Agree nor Disagree	Agree Slightly	Agree	Agree Strongly
1	2	3	4	5	6	7

1. The manner in which the tasks in this institution are divided is logical.
2. The relationships among co-workers are harmonious.
3. This institution's leadership efforts result in the fulfillment of its purposes.
4. My work at this institution offers me an opportunity to grow as a person.
5. I can always talk to someone at work, if I have a work-related problem.
6. The faculty actively participates in decisions.
7. There is little evidence of unresolved conflict in this institution.
8. There is a strong fit between this institution's mission and my own values.
9. The faculty and staff are represented on most committees and task forces.
10. Staff development routinely accompanies any significant changes that occur in this institution.
11. The manner in which the tasks in this institution are distributed is fair.

12. Older faculty's opinions are valued.
13. The administrators display the behaviors required for effective leadership.
14. The rewards and incentives here are both internal and external.
15. There is open and direct communication among all levels of this institution.
16. Participative decision making is fostered at this institution.
17. What little conflict exists at this institution is not dysfunctional.
18. Representatives of all segments of the school community participate in the strategic planning process.
19. The faculty and staff have an appropriate voice in the operation of this institution.
20. This institution is not resistant to constructive change.
21. The division of labor in this organization helps its efforts to reach its goals.
22. I feel valued by this institution.
23. The administration encourages an appropriate amount of participation in decision making.
24. Faculty and staff members are often recognized for special achievements.
25. There are no significant barriers to effective communication at this institution.
26. When the acceptance of a decision is important, a group decision-making model is used.
27. Mechanisms at this institution effectively manage conflict and stress.
28. Most of the employees understand the mission and goals of this institution.
29. The faculty and staff feel empowered to make their own decisions regarding their daily work.
30. Tolerance toward change is modeled by the administration of this institution.
31. The various grade-level teachers and departments work well together.
32. Differences among people are accepted.
33. The leadership is able to generate continuous improvement in the institution.
34. My ideas are encouraged, recognized, and used.
35. Communication is carried out in a non-aggressive style.
36. In general, the decision-making process is effective.
37. Conflicts are usually resolved before they become dysfunctional.
38. For the most part, the employees of this institution feel an "ownership" of its goals.
39. The faculty and staff are encouraged to be creative in their work.
40. When changes are made, they do so within a rational process.

41. This institution's organizational design responds well to changes in the internal and external environment.
42. The teaching and the non-teaching staffs get along with one another.
43. The leadership of this institution espouses a clear educational vision.
44. The goals and objectives for the year are mutually developed by the faculty and the administration.
45. I believe that my opinions and ideas are listened to.
46. Usually, a collaborative style of decision making is utilized at this institution.
47. A collaborative approach to conflict resolution is ordinarily used.
48. This institution has a clear educational vision.
49. The faculty and staff can express their opinions without fear of retribution.
50. I feel confident that I will have an opportunity for input if a significant change were to take place in this institution.
51. This institution is "people-oriented."
52. Administrators and faculty have mutual respect for one another.
53. Administrators give people the freedom to do their job.
54. The rewards and incentives in this institution are designed to satisfy a variety of individual needs.
55. The opportunity for feedback is always available in the communications process.
56. Group decision-making techniques, like brainstorming and group surveys, are sometimes used in the decision-making process.
57. Conflicts are often prevented by early intervention.
58. This institution has a strategic plan for the future.
59. Most administrators here use the power of persuasion rather than the power of coercion.
60. This institution is committed to continually improving through the process of change.
61. This institution does not adhere to a strict chain of command.
62. This institution exhibits grace, style, and civility.
63. The administrators model desired behavior.
64. At this institution, employees are not normally coerced into doing things.
65. I have the information that I need to do a good job.
66. I can constructively challenge the decisions in this institution.
67. A process to resolve work-related grievances is available.
68. This institution has an ongoing planning process.
69. The faculty and staff have input into the operation of this institution through a collective bargaining unit or through a faculty governance body.
70. The policies, procedures, and programs of this institution are periodically reviewed.

HEART SMART SCORING SHEET

Instructions: Transfer the numbers you circled on the questionnaire to the blanks below. Add each column and divide each sum by seven. This will give you comparable scores for each of the ten areas.

Structure	Identity and Culture	Leadership	Motivation
1 _____	2 _____	3 _____	4 _____
11 _____	12 _____	13 _____	14 _____
21 _____	22 _____	23 _____	24 _____
31 _____	32 _____	33 _____	34 _____
41 _____	42 _____	43 _____	44 _____
51 _____	52 _____	53 _____	54 _____
61 _____	62 _____	63 _____	64 _____
Total			
_____	_____	_____	_____
Average			
_____	_____	_____	_____

Communication	Decision Making	Conflict Resolution	Goal Setting/ Planning
5 _____	6 _____	7 _____	8 _____
15 _____	16 _____	17 _____	18 _____
25 _____	26 _____	27 _____	28 _____
35 _____	36 _____	37 _____	38 _____
45 _____	46 _____	47 _____	48 _____
55 _____	56 _____	57 _____	58 _____
65 _____	66 _____	67 _____	68 _____
Total			
_____	_____	_____	_____
Average			
_____	_____	_____	_____

Power Distribution	Attitude toward Change
9 _____	10 _____
19 _____	20 _____
29 _____	30 _____
39 _____	40 _____
49 _____	50 _____
59 _____	60 _____
69 _____	70 _____
Total	
_____	_____
Average	
_____	_____

INTERPRETATION SHEET

Instructions: Study the background information and interpretation suggestions that follow.

Background

The Heart Smart Organizational Diagnosis Questionnaire is a survey feedback instrument designed to collect data on organizational functioning. It measures the perceptions of persons in an organization to determine areas of activity that would benefit from an organizational development effort. It can be used as the sole data-collection technique or in conjunction with other techniques (interview, observation, etc.). The instrument and the model reflect a systematic approach for analyzing relationships among variables that influence how an organization is managed. Using the Heart Smart Organizational Diagnosis Questionnaire is the first step in determining appropriate interventions for organizational change efforts.

INTERPRETATION AND DIAGNOSIS

A crucial consideration is the diagnosis based on data interpretation. The simplest diagnosis would be to assess the amount of variance for each of the ten variables in relation to a score of 4, which is the neutral point. Scores below 4 would indicate a problem with organizational functioning. The closer the score is to 1, the more severe the problem would be. Scores above 4 indicate the lack of a problem, with a score of 7 indicating optimum functioning.

Another diagnostic approach follows the same guidelines of assessment in relation to the neutral point (score) of 4. The score of each of the 70 items on the questionnaire can be reviewed to produce more exacting information on problematic areas. Thus, diagnosis would be more precise. For example, let us suppose that the average score on item number 8 is 1.4. This would indicate not only a problem in organizational purpose or goal setting, but also a more specific problem in that there is a gap between organizational and individual goals. This more precise diagnostic effort is likely to lead to a more appropriate intervention in the organization than the generalized diagnostic approach described in the preceding paragraph.

Appropriate diagnosis must address the relationships between the boxes to determine the interconnectedness of problems. For example, if there is a problem with *communication*, it could be that the organizational *structure* does not foster effective communication. This might be the case if the average score on item 25 was well below 4 (2.5 or lower) and all the items on organizational *structure* (1, 11, 21, 31, 41, 51, 61) averaged below 4.

References

Baker, W., and M. O'Malley. 2008. *Leading with Kindness*. New York: AMACOM.

Baldwin, N. 1995. *Edison: Inventing the Century*. New York: Hyperion.

Bass, B. M. 1990. *Bass & Stogdill's Handbook of Leadership*. New York: Free Press.

Bernstein, C. 1996. *His Holiness*. New York: Doubleday.

Biggart, N. W., and G. G. Hamilton. 1987. "An Institutional Theory of Leadership." *Journal of Applied Behavioral Sciences* 234:429–41.

Bolman, L. B., and Terrence E. Deal. 1991. *Reframing Organizations: Artistry, Choice, and Leadership*. San Francisco: Jossey-Bass.

Bullock, A. 1952. *The Hitler of History*. New York: Knopf.

Chapple, C. 1993. *The Jesuit Tradition in Education and Missions*. Scranton, PA: University of Scranton Press.

Chernow, R. 1998. *Titan: The Life of John D. Rockefeller, Sr*. New York: Random House.

Conger, A., and R. N. Kanungo. 1987. "Toward a Behavioral Theory of Charismatic Leadership in Organizational Settings." *Academy of Management Review* 12:637–47.

Davis, A. F. 1973. *American Heroine: The Life and Legend of Jane Addams*. New York: Oxford University Press.

DePree, M. 1989. *Leadership Is an Art*. New York: Dell.

Diliberto, G. 1999. *A Useful Woman: The Early Life of Jane Addams*. New York: Scribner.

D'Souza, D. 1997. *Ronald Reagan: How an Ordinary Man Became an Extraordinary Leader*. New York: Simon & Schuster.

Erickson, F. 1984. "School Literacy, Reasoning and Civility: An Anthropologist's Perspective." *Review of Educational Research* 54:525–46.

Fiedler, F. E., and M. M. Chemers. 1984. *Improving Leadership Effectiveness: The Leader Match Concept*. 2nd ed. New York: Wiley.

Fiedler, F. E., and J. E. Garcia. 1987. *New Approaches to Effective Leadership*. New York: Wiley.

Field, R. H. G. 1982. "A Test of the Vroom-Yetton Normative Model of Leadership." *Journal of Applied Psychology* 67:523–32.

Fleishman, E., and E. F. Harris. 1959. "Patterns of Leadership Behavior Related to Employee Grievances and Turnover." *Personnel Psychology* 1:45–53.

Fleishman, E., E. F. Harris, and R. D. Buret. 1955. *Leadership and Supervision in Industry*. Columbus: Ohio State University Press.

Foster, W. 1986. *Paradigms and Promises: New Approaches to Educational Administration*. New York: Prometheus Books.

Gabler, N. 2006. *Walt Disney: The Triumph of the American Imagination*. New York: Knopf.

Glasser, W. 1984. *Control Theory: A New Explanation of How We Control Our Lives*. New York: Harper & Row.

Gordon, J. 1993. *A Diagnostic Approach to Organizational Behavior*. Boston: Allyn & Bacon.

Greenleaf, R. 1977. *Servant Leadership: A Journey into the Nature of Legitimate Power and Greatness*. New York: Paulist Press. Quoted in DePree 1989, 12.

Griffiths, D., and P. Ribbins. 1995. "Leadership Matters in Education: Regarding Secondary Headship." Inaugural lecture, University of Birmingham, Edgbaston.

Halliday, J. 2005. *The Unknown Mao*. New York: Knopf.

Hersey, P., and K. H. Blanchard. 1988. *Management of Organizational Behavior*. 5th ed. Englewood Cliffs, NJ: Prentice-Hall.

House, R. J. 1971. "A Path-Goal Theory of Leader Effectiveness." *Administrative Science Quarterly* 16:321–38.

———. 1977. "A 1976 Theory of Charismatic Leadership." In *Leadership: The Cutting Edge*, ed. J. G. Hunt and L. L. Larson, 355–400. Carbondale: Southern Illinois University Press.

House, R. J., and T. R. Mitchell. 1974. "Path-Goal Theory of Leadership." *Journal of Contemporary Business* (Autumn): 81–97.

Jardim, A. 1970. *The First Henry Ford*. Boston: MIT Press.

Kirkpatrick, S. A., and E. A. Locke. 1991. "Leadership: Do Traits Matter?" *Academy of Management Executive* 5 (2): 49.

Lacey, R. 1986. *Ford: The Man and the Machine*. Boston: Little, Brown.

Lowney, C. 2003. *Heroic Leadership*. Chicago: Loyola Press.

Machtan, L. 2001. *The Hidden Hitler*. New York: Basic.

Marcello, P. C. 2006. *Mohandas K. Gandhi*. Westport, CT: Greenwood.

McGregor, D. 1961. *The Human Side of Enterprise*. New York: McGraw-Hill.

Mintzberg, H. 1979. *The Nature of Managerial Work*. 2nd ed. Englewood Cliffs, NJ: Prentice-Hall.

Oates, S. 1982. *Let the Trumpets Sound. The Life of Martin Luther King, Jr*. New York: Harper & Row.

Pasten, A. 2006. *Biography: Gandhi—A Photographic Story of a Life*. New York: DK Publishing.

Ravier, A., SJ. 1987. *Ignatius of Loyola and the Founding of the Society of Jesus*. San Francisco: Ignatius Press.

Redlich, F. 1998. *Hitler: Diagnosis of a Destructive Prophet*. New York: Oxford Press.

Schein, E. H. 1974. "The Hawthorne Studies Revisited: A Defense of Theory Y." Sloan School of Management Working Paper #756-74. Cambridge: Massachusetts Institute of Technology.

Senge, P. M. 1990. *The Fifth Discipline: The Art and Practice of the Learning Organization*. New York: Doubleday.

Service, R. 2000. *Lenin*. Cambridge, MA: Harvard University Press.

Society of Jesus. 1995. *Documents of the 34th General Congregation of the Society of Jesus*. St. Louis: Institute of Jesuit Sources.

Solzhenitsyn, A. 1978. *A World Split Apart*. New York: Harper & Row.

Spink, K. 1997. *Mother Teresa*. San Francisco: Harper & Row.

Stogdill, R. M., and A. E. Coons, eds. 1957. *Leader Behavior: Its Description and Measurement*. Columbus: Ohio State University Bureau of Business Research.

Toner, J. J., SJ. 1991. *Discerning God's Will: Ignatius of Loyola's Teaching on Christian Decision Making*. St. Louis: Institute of Jesuit Sources.

Tripole, M. R., SJ. 2004. *Faith beyond Justice*. St. Louis: Institute of Jesuit Sources.

Vroom, V. H., and G. Jago. 1988. *The New Leadership: Managing Participation in Organizations*. Englewood Cliffs, NJ: Prentice-Hall.

Vroom, V. H., and P. W. Yetton. 1973. *Leadership and Decision Making*. Pittsburgh: University of Pittsburgh Press.

Willner, A. R. 1984. *The Spellbinders: Charismatic Political Leadership*. New Haven, CT: Yale University Press.